THE WORLD'S
20 WORST
CRIMES

THE WORLD'S
20 WORST
CRIMES

TRUE STORIES OF 20 KILLERS
AND THEIR 1000 VICTIMS

KATE KRAY

JOHN BLAKE

This book is dedicated to all the victims and their families,
whose loved ones can never be replaced.

Published by John Blake Publishing Ltd,
3 Bramber Court, 2 Bramber Road,
London W14 9PB, England

www.johnblakepublishing.co.uk

First published in paperback in 2007

ISBN: 978 1 84454 424 0

British Library Cataloguing-in-Publication Data:

A catalogue record for this book is available from the British Library.

Design by www.envydesign.co.uk

Printed and bound by CPI Group (UK) Ltd, Croydon, CR0 4YY

7 9 10 8

Papers used by John Blake Publishing are natural, recyclable products made from wood
grown in sustainable forests. The manufacturing processes conform to the environmental
regulations of the country of origin.

Every attempt has been made to contact the relevant copyright-holders, but some were
unobtainable. We would be grateful if the appropriate people could contact us.

CONTENTS

FOREWORD

What makes a man skin the head of a woman and hang her lipstick-smeared face above his festering rag-strewn bed? What makes a man saw a person's skull in half and use it as a crude soup bowl? What makes a man wear a vest created from the skin of a woman's body? What makes a serial killer?

The term 'serial killer' was created in the mid-1970s following the well-publicised crimes of Americans Ted Bundy, Kenneth Bianchi and Angelo Buono, all brutal murderers. Bundy killed at least 28 people and Bianchi and Buono 12. From then on, anyone who committed three or more murders over an extended period of time was known as a serial murderer. And there were many who qualified.

Most serial killers come from the United States. As many as 85 per cent of the world's serial killers are American, and according to the FBI serial killing in the USA has today reached almost epidemic proportions. At any one time, there are between 20 and 50 serial killers on the loose. They are almost always male and almost always white.

But what motivates these monsters to carry out their horrific crimes? These aren't just random outbursts of intense anger or fury. They are frequently fuelled by a desire for power or a need to fulfil a sexual compulsion, driving the killer on and on and on. Extreme sadistic urges cause them to mutilate for sexual pleasure and kill their victims slowly over a prolonged period of time. These killers have no compassion or understanding for the suffering they are inflicting on others. The truth is – they just don't care.

Serial killers often keep mementoes of their victims as souvenirs, personal items that allow them to relive the memory of their crimes and savour the moment over and over again. They also, on occasion, keep body parts of their victims like some trophy. Jeffrey Dahmer, the Milwaukee Cannibal, who killed at least 17 men, kept the skulls of his victims in the closets, refrigerator and freezer of his home. He also preserved their genitalia in formaldehyde. Eddie Gein, a Wisconsin farmer, made soup bowls out of his victims' skulls and a chair and clothes from their skin. Yet, inside, many of these crazy maniacs suffer from feelings of inadequacy and worthlessness, often caused by humiliating experiences, peer rejection and abuse in their childhood, or because of pressures of poverty and lack of respect in adulthood. John Wayne Gacy, one of the most prolific murderers in American history (he killed at least 34 young boys), grew up in a violent household and was branded a 'sissy' and a 'faggot' by his father. In his adulthood, Gacy went on to rape and torture boys, who he in turn called sissies and faggots.

Of course, not everyone who is abused as a child goes on to become a serial murderer. Many circumstances in childhood can contribute to a serial killer's horrific behaviour in later life. For some serial murderers, adoption or rejection as a child undermines their sense of identity. They might fantasise as to who their real parents actually were. Were their parents good or bad? Was their mother a prostitute? Was their father a gangster? And why were they given up for adoption? If they then meet their biological parents and are again rejected, this rejection deepens the wound and can have a profound effect on an already unstable psyche.

According to Ted Bundy, his emotional growth stopped in its tracks at the age of 13 when he learned he was illegitimate.

'It was like I was hit by a brick wall,' Bundy said.

Of course, it is difficult to take his word (or the word of any mass murderer) as to when his family life became screwed-up.

Witnessing violence as a child can also be a contributing factor on the path to killing. Eddie Gein said that seeing farm animals slaughtered gave him perverted ideas. Albert Fish (Thomas Harris's real-life model for Hannibal Lecter), who mutilated and murdered sixteen people, witnessed brutal acts of abuse and violence during his four years in an orphanage. Andrei Chikatilo, the Ukrainian cannibal who got his sexual kicks from torturing, mutilating and murdering more than fifty victims, blamed his sadistic bloodlust on being read frightening stories as a child.

But are all these whys and wherefores just reasons and excuses?

No one event is the sole trigger for creating a serial murderer. The events simply act as pieces of a jigsaw that go to make the bigger picture. So predicting who will go on to kill and who will not is an almost impossible task.

However, there are three classic 'red-light' warning signs that are often associated with future serial killers: cruelty to animals, fire starting and bedwetting well beyond the age at which children usually grow out of such behaviour. If these symptoms aren't identified and addressed early enough, there is a strong possibility that they will eventually escalate and the person may go on to commit crimes against fellow human beings.

Ed Kemper, the Californian killer who decapitated ten people, began his gruesome killing by practising on the family cat. He buried it alive, dug it up and cut off its head. Jeffrey Dahmer also cut off dogs' heads and placed them on sticks behind his house.

These violent acts against animals helped the killers express their rage without the fear of any comeback for their actions. Once confident, they could go in search of greater satisfaction by using their well-practised technique on human beings.

Peter Kurten, the 'Düsseldorf Vampire', who often drank the blood of his victims, got his adolescent kicks by watching houses burn. Because serial killers do not see their victims as anything more than objects, the leap between setting fires to buildings and killing people is an easy one to make.

Bedwetting is probably the most difficult symptom of the three to identify, as it is often kept secret, but by some estimates about 60 per cent of serial murderers wet their beds past adolescence.

Whatever the events that go into the making of a serial killer, the motives behind their killings can often be separated into four different categories:

Power/control: This is the most common type of serial killer. They kill to get the feeling of power over their victim. Often, such killers were abused as children leaving them feeling powerless and inadequate. It is common for them to practise the same form of abuse on their victims as they suffered themselves, in some way purging themselves of their feelings of humiliation.

Visionary: These serial killers have hallucinations or believe they hear voices telling them to commit murder. Although many claim this is the reason they killed (usually as a way of trying to get acquitted by reason of insanity), there are few genuine serial killers who truly experience such delusions.

Mission-orientated: These killers feel they are doing society a favour by eliminating certain types of people, such as prostitutes.

Hedonistic: These serial killers murder for the sheer pleasure of it, although the aspect of killing that gives them the pleasure varies. Some get their kicks from the chase – hunting down their victim – while others enjoy torturing their prey once they're caught, and others still enjoy indulging themselves once their victim is dead – having sex with them or actually eating them.

Serial killers might fall into one or, sometimes, more than one of these categories. The British serial killer Peter Sutcliffe, for instance, appeared to be both a visionary and a mission-orientated killer. He claimed to have heard voices telling him to clean the streets of prostitutes.

As much as we try to analyse and categorise serial murderers, however, one fact remains. They are all people. Often ones, who hold down jobs, have wives and families and operate in our community. How often have we heard neighbours say on hearing that the bloke next door has been arrested for horrific crimes of murder, 'But he seemed such a nice bloke. He was just an ordinary guy'? In some way, you expect serial killers to look different. To have the world 'KILLER' stamped on their forehead. But the fact is, they don't. They look like you or me, which is quite frightening. I'd heard one story about Peter Sutcliffe, the Yorkshire Ripper, who, when he was on the loose, was asked by a female work colleague if he would give her a lift home – because she was scared of being out on her own with the Ripper at large. She had no idea that the colleague she had asked for a lift was the man the police were desperately searching for.

Being a crime writer, I've met many murderers. In fact, I was married to a gangster serving 30 years in prison for murder. His brother was also a gangster serving life for murder and many of their friends were murderers. I got to know these people as people, and because of that I suppose, in some way, I am guilty of glossing over the severity of their crimes. I've spent hours researching backgrounds for my numerous books, talking to murderers in different prisons and hospitals for the criminally insane and I thought I knew what made a murderer tick. The reality, however, is that I don't. There were times when I met serial killers without ever realising who they were or what crimes they had committed. I remember one time, when I was visiting Broadmoor Hospital for the Criminally Insane, I was served tea by a young black inmate – or trustee as they call them. 'He's a nice boy, isn't he lovely?' I said. I didn't know what crime he had committed or who he was.

'That's the Stockwell Strangler', a nurse said.

I didn't really know until I read up on it, what the Stockwell Strangler was all about. He was a man who strangled eleven elderly people and sexually abused them. But the words 'sexually abused' do not hit home the severity of his crimes. In fact, the Stockwell Strangler sodomised one 94-year-old woman at the same time as throttling her so violently that he snapped her neck – and this was the bloke serving me Jaffa cakes and tea!

That's the point – you just can't tell who these people really are. They could be your husband, brother, uncle, grandfather, next-door neighbour. Or maybe the bloke sitting next to you on the train or walking past you in the street. You just can't tell.

I suppose that everyone could be capable of murder through anger, retribution, honour, money, greed, love or hate – any one of these emotions could stir up enough feeling to make someone kill. I can understand how someone could kill through anger, because with anger you have a reason, but the killers in this book – don't have any reason. Most of the time, they killed for sexual or self-gratification, and all the excuses they put up during their trials of being rejected or not loved, or they are schizophrenic or paranoid are just that – excuses. Nobody can choose when they are mad. I've seen real insanity, and if you're truly mad you can't function in the normal world or hold down a job like many of these killers did.

Dennis Nilsen, the Muswell Hill Murderer, who flushed the remains of his victims down the toilet, worked in the local job centre in Kentish Town, London. He'd spend all day liaising and talking with people, and then at night he would go home and cut up the bodies of his murder victims. That takes some self-control and planning. If you're insane, you couldn't do this. No way. It's just not possible.

Of all the murderers that I have interviewed (and I've interviewed hundreds), I'd say that 99 per cent of them are sorry for what they have done. They're not sorry for the murder they committed they're sorry that they've been caught and are now paying the price for it. Most murderers look for any excuse to explain why they killed, rather than take responsibility for their own actions. I'll give you an example. Late one afternoon, I had a telephone call from a man that I had only met briefly five years before in a prison visiting hall. He said that he had been given my number by my brother-in-law and that he really needed to see me. He told me that I was the only person he could trust. I was intrigued, and decided to go and see him, even though he was several hours' drive away.

When I arrived, I hardly recognised the man who came out to see me. In the five years, he had turned grey and sallow-looking – a shadow of his former self. I offered to get him a cup of tea or piece of cake, but he wasn't interested in pleasantries. He dumped a large folder of legal papers on the table in front of me and said, 'The gun was faulty.'

I didn't have a clue what he was talking about. What did he mean, 'The gun was faulty?' With a bit of probing I managed to establish that the gun he had been pointing at the woman he had killed had been faulty, in which case, he believed that he should not have been given a life sentence. I just looked at the man and said, 'You shouldn't have been bleedin' pointing it at her!'

With that, the visit was over. He picked up his bundle of papers and left. I don't know what happened to him. The gun was faulty… whatever!

Until now, I didn't believe in the death penalty. My husband had been put away for murder, and I could never see how executing someone made up for the murder they had committed. Two wrongs didn't make a right. Being inside was punishment enough. My husband did 30 years in prison and had often told me that it would have been kinder to hang him. Harry Roberts, who has served 40 years inside for murdering three policemen, told me the same thing, as did John Straffen, Britain's longest-serving prisoner.

John's been inside since 1951 for the killing of three young children. He told me that it would have been better to hang him because being in prison is simply a long drawn-out death.

In 2005, while I was doing the research for this book, I decided to watch *Fox News*, which was covering the execution of LA gang member Stanley 'Tookie' Williams. Although not a serial murderer in the true sense of the term, Williams had been a member of the notorious South central Los Angeles 'Crips' Gang and was on Death Row for the brutal slaying of four people. At the time Williams was hoping for a stay of execution from the Governor of California, Arnold Schwarzenegger. The television was showing reports from the family and friends of the murder victims, and I wanted to watch the proceedings to see how I felt.

Time was running out for Tookie – he was due to be executed that day. As it turned out, there was no stay of execution and at 12.01 Californian time Stanley Williams walked into the execution room unaided.

He sat down on something similar to a dentist's chair and was strapped tight shoulder to ankle. Drips were placed into both arms.

As the spectators in the room watched the proceedings, Williams showed no sign of remorse, nor did he have any final words to say. Little by little, the lethal fluid that would take his life away seeped slowly into his veins. Tookie Williams raised his head up as if trying to hold back the effects of the drug. At 12.36 he gave up the fight. Over a loud speaker came the words, 'It's flat lined'. Tookie Williams was dead.

At that point, I had a feeling of emptiness. I suppose part of me wanted them to stop the execution, but the other part felt that having committed these terrible crimes, this man should be executed. I felt that nobody won.

It took Tookie Williams 35 minutes to die. I cannot even begin to imagine how he felt knowing that his last few minutes of life were ticking away. But these murderers never thought about what they were doing to their victims; certainly, many of their victims took an awful lot longer to die.

I've spent many hours trying to understand how the monsters in this book could do the terrible things they've done. They weren't done for money, or for anger, or for love. Lust. Yes. Sexual gratification. Yes. Power. Yes. Serial killers can't be human beings; they have no thoughts, feelings, guilt. Love, compassion or understanding. If they had one ounce of decency, they could not commit these heinous crimes.

So, no, I don't think the murderers contained in this book are human beings. They are the Devil's disciples depicted as human figures, sent to Earth to try and corrupt and do atrocities in the name of the Devil.

But, unlike Lucifer, they haven't got horns sticking out the top of their head or cloven hooves and a tail – but they are the chief spirits of pure evil and the enemy of God and I strongly believe that after the hideous crimes they have committed and the untold suffering they have caused these men should be shown any humanity themselves. They should be executed.

I never thought that I would believe in the death penalty. I never thought that I could find it within myself to say another person deserved to have their life taken from them. But knowing the details of the brutal murders that these serial killers committed again and again, I can see no option other than to execute these monsters. They are pure evil through and through and I strongly believe they will burn in the pit of hell.

Kate Kray

THE HILLSIDE
STRANGLERS

Names: Kenneth Bianchi and Angelo Buono
Dates of birth: 5/12/1951 and 5/10/1934
Location: Los Angeles, USA
Type of Murderers: Sex maniacs
Body count: 12
Sentence: Life, without parole
Outcome: Angelo Buono died from unknown causes in Calipatria State Prison on 21 September 2002 at the age of sixty-seven, while Bianchi remains behind bars

'I'm asking for forgiveness. I know I'll go to hell.'
KENNETH BIANCHI

The small town of Bellingham, in Washington State, looks out on one of the prettiest views in the American Northwest: the pine-covered slopes of San Juan and Vancouver Island, and the Strait of Juan de Fuca.

With a population of only 40,000, violent crime there is pretty rare. So, when the town's chief of police, Terry Managan, was told one Friday morning that two girls were missing, his first thought was that they had left for a long weekend. Their names were Karen Mandic and Diane Wilder, students at Western Washington University. Karen's boyfriend always insisted that she would not go away without telling him and when the police discovered that Karen had left her beloved cat unfed, he began to fear the worst.

On the night before, 11 January 1979, Karen had told her boyfriend that she and Diane were going on a 'house-sitting' job. It was at the home of a couple who were travelling in Europe. The plush house was in the Bayside area and apparently, its security alarm system had broken and Karen only had to wait in the house for two hours while the alarm was taken away and repaired.

The man who had offered her this job was a security supervisor called Kenneth Bianchi.

Police checked with Bianchi's boss, Mark Lawrence, who owned the Coastal Security agency, Mr Lawrence said that Bianchi was a smashing bloke, a conscientious worker and squeaky clean. He lived with a local girl called Kelli Boyd. They had a baby son and Bianchi was known to be a devoted father. But he had no authority to offer Karen a house-sitting job.

This was soon confirmed by Bianchi himself. He told his boss that he had never heard of Karen Mandic, nor offered anyone a house-sitting job. Detectives were sent to the empty house, in the expensive area. A locksmith opened the front door and the detectives entered cautiously. Everything seemed to be in order. The house was neat and there was no sign of a struggle. But on the kitchen floor, the searchers found a man's single wet footprint. Since it was still wet, they reckoned that it must have been made within the last 12 hours or so.

At noon that day, the local radio station broadcast the first descriptions of Karen's car – a green Mercury Bobcat. At 4.30pm, that description was heard by a woman who had seen such a car that morning, parked in a nearby cul-de-sac. She rang the police and officers were sent to investigate.

Detectives approached the car and glanced through the rear window. They saw the corpses of the two missing girls huddled together, as if thrown into the vehicle. They had been strangled and then sexually assaulted.

Bianchi was the chief suspect for the murder. A warrant was drawn up for his arrest, but by the time it was issued he was out on the road, driving his security truck.

Mark Lawrence, Bianchi's boss, agreed to help the police set a trap. Contacting Bianchi by radio, he asked him to go to a guard hut on the south side of town, where he would receive further instructions.

Half an hour later, the police arrived. But the good-looking young man merely looked surprised and surrendered without protest. Bianchi wasn't bothered at all, so much so, that detectives began to suspect that this was all a mistake. Either Ken Bianchi was innocent, or he was a bloody good actor.

Back at the police station, Bianchi denied knowing Karen Mandic. He said there must have been an impostor using his name. The interrogators were inclined to believe him. They were even more convinced when Kelli Boyd, his common-law wife, arrived at the station. She was horrified at the idea that Ken Bianchi might be a murderer. To her, he was a gentle lover and adoring father, incapable of violence. When the police asked permission to search their home, both gave it without hesitation.

The search revealed that, whether Bianchi was a murderer or not, he was certainly a thief. Hidden in the basement, there were several expensive telephones and a brand-new chainsaw. These items had been reported as stolen from the place where Bianchi had worked as a security guard. Bianchi was charged with grand theft and taken to the county jail.

A search of Bianchi's security truck produced more evidence – the keys of the Bayside house, and a woman's scarf. Diane Wilder was known to have a passion for scarves. But the most convincing evidence came from examination of the bodies. Both girls had been strangled by some kind of ligature applied from behind and its angle showed that the murderer had been standing above them, as if walking downstairs.

On the stairs leading to the basement of the Bayside home, detectives found a single pubic hair. Semen stains were found on the underwear of both girls. Carpet fibres found on their clothing and on the soles of their shoes matched the fibres in the empty house.

Detectives were able to reconstruct the crime piece by piece. Ken Bianchi had telephoned Karen Mandic and offered her the house-sitting job. He had met her when he was a security guard in the department store where she worked, which proved he was lying in saying he had never heard of her. Bianchi had sworn her to silence about the job but Karen had told her boyfriend and he had been slightly suspicious about the size of the payment for a couple of hours 'house-sitting'.

At seven o'clock that evening, in the police theory, Karen and Diane had driven to the Bayside house. Bianchi was waiting for them in his security truck – local residents had noticed it. Karen parked her car in the drive, outside the front door. Bianchi had asked her to go with him inside to turn on the lights, while Diane waited in the car.

When he reappeared a few minutes later, Diane had no idea that her friend was now lying dead in the basement. Like Karen, she was strangled on the stairs. He had carried both bodies out to Karen's car and driven to the cul-de-sac, sexually assaulted both girls, wiped the car clean of finger-prints and walked back to the Bayside house where his own truck was parked, disposing of the ligature on the way. The baffling thing about the crime was that it seemed pointless.

The case against Bianchi looked conclusive, even though he continued to insist that he had no memory of the murders. While he was held in jail, the police began checking on his background. He had been living in Glendale, a suburb eight miles north of downtown Los Angeles, before his move to Bellingham the previous May.

A detective rang the Los Angeles County Sheriff's Department. The call was taken by Detective Sergeant Frank Salerno of the Homicide Division. When Frank was told that a former Glendale resident called Kenneth Bianchi had been booked on suspicion of a double sex murder, his ears pricked up.

For the past 14 months, he had been looking for a sex killer who had committed up to 12 similar murders in Los Angeles. The newspapers had dubbed him the 'Hillside Strangler'. The last murder had taken place shortly before Bianchi left Los Angeles for Bellingham.

It was early morning on the 17 October 1977. The corpse lay sprawled on a hillside near Forest Lawn Cemetery, south of Ventura freeway. The girl was tall and black and had been stripped naked. The girl's body temperature indicated that she had died the previous night. Identifying her was easy. Her fingerprints were on police files. She was a prostitute called Yolanda Washington, who worked around Hollywood Boulevard. The autopsy showed that sexual intercourse had taken place and had involved two men. One of these was a 'non secretor', a man whose blood group cannot be determined from his bodily fluids. But the men could simply have been clients, and had nothing to do with her murder. She had been strangled with a piece of cord while she was lying down, with the murderer above her. Her body had been tossed from a car.

The crime aroused little interest in the news media. Nor did the death of a second woman, found on the morning of 1 November 1977. She lay close to the kerb in Alta Terrace Drive in La Crescenta, a town near Glendale and it looked again as if the victim had been dumped from a car.

As in the case of Yolanda Washington, the body was naked and death was due to strangulation with a ligature. The victim was little more than a child – 15 years-old at most.

The autopsy showed a possible link with the murder of Yolanda Washington. The girl had been subjected to sexual intercourse by two men, one of them a non-secretor. The position of the body also showed that she had been carried by two men, one holding her under the armpits and the other by the knees. Now police were sure they were looking for two killers.

This time the victim's fingerprints were not on file. Police displayed an artist's sketch of the dead girl to the area's down-

and-outs, drug addicts and prostitutes. Several 'street people' said that she resembled a girl called Judy Miller, who had not been seen recently.

It took police another week to track down her parents. They lived in a cheap motel room and one of their two remaining children slept in a cardboard box. At the morgue, they identified their daughter. Judy had run away from home a month before. Police already knew that she had made a living from prostitution – but in a half hearted, amateurish way.

By the time police located Judy's parents, there had already been another murder. On 6 November, a jogger near the Chevy Chase Country Club in Glendale discovered the body of 20 year-old Lissa Kastin lying near the golf course.

She had been strangled with a ligature and subjected to a vicious sexual assault. Glendale was outside Frank Salerno's jurisdiction, but he went to view the body. The ligature marks around the neck, and red lines around the wrists and ankles, suggested that the stranglers had been at work again. As Frank Salerno looked down on the body, the third in three weeks, he thought that this might be the work of serial killers.

Even Salerno, was unprepared for what happened in the last three weeks of November 1977. Seven more strangled corpses were found, all of them naked. One, 18-year-old Jill Barcomb, discovered on 10 November, was a prostitute. Kathleen Robinson, 17, was found on 17 November. But the day that shocked the news media into taking notice of the 'Hillside Strangler' was Sunday, 20 November, when three naked bodies were found, two of them schoolgirls. These were Dolly Cepeda, 12 and Sonja

Johnson, 14, who had been missing for a week. The girls had been raped and sodomised.

Earlier that day, another nude body had been found in the hills. A missing person report identified her as Kristina Weckler, a 20-year-old art student.

The next victim was found on 23 November, in some bushes. She was Jane King, a 28-year-old Scientology student.

The last victim of this month's killing spree was found in some bushes on 29 November. Her parents identified her as Lauren Wagner, an 18-year-old student who had failed to return home the previous night.

Ten sex murders in six weeks was a grisly toll even by Los Angeles standards, where there are several murders a day. The 'Hillside Strangler' featured in television reports all over the world. But the police took care not to publicise that they were looking for two men. Women were afraid to go out alone at night and Los Angeles was on panic meltdown.

Undeterred, the Hillside Stranglers found another victim two weeks later, and on 14 December the naked body of a 17-year-old prostitute, Kimberly Martin, was found sprawled in a vacant parking lot. This time there were more clues. It was discovered that the call-girl agency that she worked for had received a call from a man asking for a blonde in black underwear, for which he would pay $150 in cash. The girl was sent to the Tamarind apartment building and disappeared. Police interviewed everyone in the apartment building and one tenant – a personable young man called Kenneth Bianchi – said that he had heard screams.

During the remainder of 1977, there were no more murders and the Los Angeles Police hoped that the killers had stopped.

On 17 February 1978, that hope was dashed when

someone reported seeing an orange Datsun halfway down a cliff below a lay-by on the Angeles Crest Highway, north of Glendale.

In the boot of the vehicle was another woman's naked body. She was later identified as Cindy Hudspeth, 20, a part-time waitress at the Robin Hood Inn. Medical evidence showed that she'd been raped by two men.

At last, after the death of Cindy Hudspeth, the murders ceased in the Los Angeles area. But, when Salerno heard that Bianchi had been arrested for a double sex killing in Washington State, he lost no time in travelling to Bellingham. Within hours of arriving, he was certain that one of the Hillside Stranglers had been found. Jewellery found in Bianchi's apartment matched items taken from victims in Los Angeles.

In custody, Bianchi continued to behave like an innocent man. He was highly co-operative, informing police that his only close friend in Los Angeles was his cousin Angelo Buono.

As the detectives delved into Buono's background, it became clear that he was a nasty piece of work. He'd fathered eight children and had had four wives, all of whom had left him because of his brutality. His preference was for girls in their early teens, and he was proud of his sexual stamina and deviant ways. He had bushy hair, and was 45 years-old – Ken's senior by 17 years.

Information about Buono came in thick and fast one call came from a wealthy Hollywood lawyer. In August 1976, he telephoned a call-girl agency and asked for a woman to be sent over to his Bel-Air home. The 15-year-old girl, Becky Spears, looked so miserable that the lawyer asked her how she became a prostitute when she obviously hated it.

Her answer was that she had been lured from her home in Phoenix Arizona, to work for a man called Angelo Buono.

Buono and his cousin Bianchi had offered the girl work as a 'model' and then forced her to work as a prostitute beating her and threatening to kill her.

Police had little doubt that Buono and Bianchi were the Hillside Stranglers. Buono had by now been interviewed a number of times and his arrogant attitude needled the detectives. He seemed to enjoy the thought that the police had no real evidence against him. . Buono was the dominant one, Bianchi, for all his charm, was something of a weakling. Bianchi looked certain to be convicted of the Bellingham murders. In Washington State, that would probably mean the death penalty. Faced with that prospect, Bianchi would prefer a trial in Los Angeles, where he could expect a life sentence. It would be in his best interest to confess to the 'Hillside murders and to implicate his cousin. At that stage, the evidence against Buono was slim but, with Bianchi's co-operation, it could be made watertight. The case appeared to be virtually tied up.

Then, suddenly, the case threatened to collapse when doubts were raised about Bianchi's sanity.

Ever since his arrest, Bianchi had been insisting that he remembered absolutely nothing about the murders. Police called in a psychiatric social worker, John Johnston, who was swayed by Bianchi's charm, gentleness and intelligence. If his claims of amnesia were genuine, then there was only one possible conclusion: Bianchi had a multiple personality disorder.

On 21 March 1979, a specialist in multiple personalities and hypnosis from the University of Montana was brought in to investigate. Bianchi was eager to co-operate. Within a few minutes of being placed in a trance, Bianchi was speaking in a strange, low voice, introducing himself as 'Steve'.

'Steve' came over as an evil bastard with a sneering laugh. He told the specialist that he hated 'Ken' and that he had done his best to fix him. Then, with a little more prompting, he described how 'Ken' had walked in one evening when his cousin Angelo Buono was murdering a girl. At that point, 'Steve' admitted he had taken over 'Ken's' personality and turned him into his cousin's willing accomplice. Ken's sinister alter-ego 'Steve' told stories of Buono's insatiable sexual appetite and his habit of killing girls after he had raped them. These stories tended to swerve certain bits – almost as if 'Steve' wished to minimise his own part in the murders. But his confessions were crystal clear and horrifying beyond belief: The first victim was the prostitute Yolanda Washington, raped and killed by both men.

They had found the experience so pleasurable that two weeks later they'd picked up 15-year-old part-time prostitute Judy Miller. Pretending to be policemen and that she was under arrest, they'd taken her back to Buono's house and raped her, even though she would have had sex with them willingly for just a few dollars. But, with Bianchi kneeling on her legs, they had strangled and suffocated her at the same time.

According to Bianchi's 'Steve', the next victim was the out-of-work dancer Lissa Kastin. They stopped her in her car and identified themselves by showing a police badge. They said they were taking her back to the station for questioning. Back in Buono's house, she was handcuffed raped and strangled. They dumped Lissa Kastin's body near the Chevy Chase golf course, in Glendale.

Four days later, Bianchi had seen an attractive girl waiting at a bus stop and had begun chatting to her. She'd told him that she was a Scientology student. During their conversation, Buono had driven up, pretending he hadn't seen Bianchi for months, and offered him a lift. Jane King made the mistake of accepting a lift home with them. She, too, died in Buono's house.

Four days after Jane King's murder, according to Steve, Bianchi and Buono saw schoolgirls Dolly Cepeda and Sonja Johnson boarding a bus in Eagle Rock Plaza. They followed the bus and, when the girls got off near their home, beckoned them over to their car. Bianchi again posed as a policeman, and told the girls that a dangerous burglar was in the neighbourhood. At Buono's home, they were both violated and murdered. Their bodies were dumped on a rubbish tip.

The next victim was an art student Bianchi had known when he lived in Hollywood, Kristina Weckler, had once spurned Bianchi's advances. Now they knocked on her door and Bianchi said, 'Hi, remember me?'

Bianchi said that he had joined the police reserve and that someone had crashed into Kristina's car. Outside she was bundled into Buono's car, taken to his house and killed.

Once again, 'Steve' described horrific details of the Thanksgiving killing spree on Monday, 28 November 1977, they followed a redheaded girl in her car. When Lauren Wagner pulled up in front of her parents' home, Bianchi flashed his police badge and said they were arresting her. While she protested – as a dog barked loudly in a nearby house – they bundled her into their car and drove away. She was raped and strangled.

Three week later, they summoned Kimberly Martin, a call girl to the Tamarind apartment building and took her back to

Buono's house. After raping her, they dumped her body in a vacant lot.

The final Killing was almost unplanned. Bianchi arrived at Buono's house to find an orange Datsun parked outside. A girl named Cindy Hudspeth had called to enquire about some new mats for her car.

The two men spread eagled the naked girl on the bed, tied her wrists and ankles and raped her. After that, they strangled her. They pushed her Datsun off a cliff with her body in the boot. The entire series of killings had been recounted by 'Steve' during the sessions with hypnotists.

Kenneth Bianchi pleaded guilty to the two Bellingham murders and to five murders in Los Angeles. In the dock, he sobbed and professed deep remorse. The judge sentenced him to life imprisonment. But there remained five more murder charges to answer in Los Angeles. Bianchi agreed to plead guilty and testify against his cousin in return for life with the possibility of parole.

In interviews with police, he described every murder with a precision of detail that left no doubt that 'Ken', not 'Steve' was guilty.

On 31 October, a jury convicted Angelo Buono of the murder of Lauren Wagner. During the next two weeks, they also found him guilty of murdering Judy Miller, Dolores Cepeda, Sonja Johnson, Kristina Weckler, Kimberly Martin, Jane King, Lissa Kastin and Cindy Hudspeth.

But possibly influenced by the fact that Bianchi had avoided execution, the judge decided that Buono should not receive the death sentence, then sentenced Angelo Buono to life imprisonment.

THE FREEWAY KILLER

Name: William George Bonin
Date of birth: 1 August 1947
Location: Los Angeles, USA
Type of murderer: Psychopathic sexual predator
Body count: 41
Sentence: Death
Outcome: Executed in San Quentin on 23 February 1996 via lethal injection

'I couldn't stop killing. It got easier and easier with each one.'
WILLIAM BONIN

By the time the curtains were drawn back, William Bonin was already strapped in place and lying on his back with his eyes closed. Needles had already been inserted into his arms to deliver the fatal mix of chemicals. He may well have been lying in state. He already looked dead. There was an eight minute delay with the first lethal injection because technicians had trouble inserting the needles. 12.08am, the curtains were pulled back. Bonin was not moving or noticeably breathing. His eyes were closed as if sleeping. Within seconds, the first of three injections were administered by someone out of sight. Thirty seconds later, his chest heaved. Twenty seconds after that, his cheeks began to bulge and his face began to turn purple.

William Bonin never opened his small primeval eyes. He never spoke or looked at any of the mothers of his victims or showed any signs of remorse, indifference or hate. He never gave those poor mothers any chance to search his eyes and his soul one last time for any shred of humanity that might be buried somewhere inside. He offered no rebuttal to those who called him a remorseless animal. He didn't offer one word of regret, explanation or apology for taking the lives of so many young men, and the hopes in the hearts of the loved ones of those boys, left behind. That left no reason for anyone to doubt that mainlining poison in the death chamber at San Quentin was exactly what the mass murderer deserved. Yet, there wasn't much joy in the cramped room, early on that Friday afternoon – yes, retribution and closure, but no joy.

As the lethal chemicals coursed into William Bonin's arms, one of the mothers stared blankly at the motionless fiend. She held the picture of her son, and another boy killed by Bonin.

David McVicar who was once kidnapped and assaulted by Bonin wept softly. He had his comforting arms around Sandra Miller, a woman whose son was murdered. She pumped her fist and whispered 'yes', as Bonin was pronounced dead. There was no look of pity, or sadness, as everyone stared at the motionless man no more than 2ft away.

At 12.14pm, there was a knock from inside the chamber and a peephole slid open. Two fingers pushed through a piece of paper which was taken by a guard. At 12.15pm, William Bonin was clinically pronounced dead.

William George Bonin was born on 8 January 1947 to a household run by his mother Alice, and two brothers. Bonin's father was a veteran of the armed forces and was living in a veterans' hospital, while his wife and sons continued to lived on the quiet road of Angel Street in Downey, California. William lived with his mother till he was eight years old, when he ran away from home. He was eventually picked up by Connecticut State Police 3,000 miles away from California and was placed in a detention centre.

Several years passed before Bonin was sent home to Downey, California, to live with his brothers and his mother. She loved William very much he was the light of her life and she doted on her son. But from the moment he returned from the detention centre he was different.

Immediately she started to see a lot of changes in her son – he became withdrawn, secretive and deviant. He started drinking alcohol and taking drugs and becoming abusive and unruly.

When Bill was old enough he was sent to fight in Vietnam. He was assigned to the 205th Assault Support Helicopter Unit in the jungle and logged more than 700 hours manning a machine gun. Wind whipped his trouser legs as they hung from the helicopter. In the distance, he could see orange flames against the blood-red palette of the setting sun. The jungle grew larger and larger as the helicopter sank – around and around, spiralling down, noise and vibration from the aircraft was deafening as it descended through the turbulence towards the jungle. Bonin hesitated momentarily, downed another beer from a can as he aimed his machine gun.

The Vietnam War was the longest military conflict in US history. The hostilities in Vietnam, Laos, and Cambodia claimed the lives of more than 58,000 Americans. Another 304,000 were wounded during the conflict, approximately 3 to 4 million Vietnamese were killed. Later, Bonin claimed to have witnessed and committed atrocities in Vietnam, which shaped his future demise.

Soon after his return from his tour of duty, Bonin was arrested and convicted of sexually assaulting five young men. In each of these cases, he would drive the freeway looking for young men and boys to get into his van of death and torture them as they screamed for their lives, which made this killer even more crazy and ready to kill again. Bonin had become a serial killer -In his eyes, each murder would get easier each time he killed.

By the late 1970s, Bonin's neighbours began to suspect that something was horribly wrong. James Hunter, a man who lived on the next street, remembered Bonin going after his boy. A woman who lived just behind the Bonin home remembers one night when sounds came from the house. It was frightful to her and it reminded her of watching a horror movie. There was bloodcurdling screams coming from that house which the neighbours will never forget.

As Bonin continued his killing spree, he had to find a job in the day time to throw the police of his trails of killings that by now, sent panic on the streets of California. Parents escorted their kids to school and then picked them up again when the day was over, so that the killer wouldn't get their sons.

Announcements were placed on television by the police stating that all kids under the age of 18 must be in their homes no later than 6pm every night until the killer was caught. Businesses were losing customers, stores were being closed and the Olympics that was scheduled for Los Angeles was cancelled and moved to another state all because of the killer.

On 2 June 1980, William Bonin was at work with his roommate James Munroe, the day was ending and they were on their way home when Bonin saw a hitchhiker on the side of the street trying to thumb a ride. Bonin pulled over, Munroe opened the side door of the rusting old van and Stephen Wells got in and closed the door. Bonin asked him where he was going and Stephen replied, 'I'm on my way home just down the street'.

Bonin, Munroe and the boy went on their way. While they were driving down the road, Bonin in a matter-of-fact voice, asked the young boy, 'Hey, what do you think of gays?'

The young lad shrugged. 'They're OK. I'm bisexual myself.'

Bonin's face lit up. 'Oh, really?' He pulled the van over to the side of the road, told Munroe to drive the rest of the way home, and then got into the back of the van and started to have oral sex with the boy. Munroe kept his eyes firmly on the road ahead and drove to Bonin's home in Downey.

When they arrived at the scruffy house, all three men got out of the van and went inside. Munroe opened a tin of beer and sat watching TV while Bonin was having sex with Wells in the bedroom. Munroe found it difficult to concentrate on the black-and-white movie, while listening to the grunts and groans coming from the bedroom. He opened another beer and listened at the bedroom door. He felt aroused by the urge to gratify his sexual needs. Gingerly he tapped on the bedroom door: 'Bill can I join in…?' Bill laughed. 'Sure. Come and have some fun…'

Munroe went into the bedroom. The young boy was tied up. Munroe was excited but scared. Bonin was wide-eyed and rampant.

'Here, you have a go…' he drooled then went into the kitchen, before returning with a knife and some more rope. He picked up his T-shirt and started to twist it around Stephen Wells's neck. Stephen started to thrash about, trying to get free.

'Hold his feet!' yelled Bonin.

Munroe obediently held Wells's feet while Bonin strangled him.

When Wells had stopped moving, Bonin turned him over and his face was blue. Bonin and Munroe then went back into the front room, sat down and opened a couple of beers. Later that evening, they threw a tarpaulin over the body, bundled it into the back of the van and waited until it was dark enough to transport the body.

That evening, Bonin told Munroe that he was the man that the police had dubbed the 'Freeway Killer', that he had another partner who'd helped him to kill on previous occasions and that he'd killed a total of 45 people.

Munroe was shaking – he couldn't believe what he was hearing he was scared and started to cry. Bonin laughed at him and told him to stop whimpering like a sissy, he couldn't go to the police because he was now an accomplice. Bonin shouted at Munroe, 'You're a fucking killer now and there ain't nothing you can do about it'

Both men got into the van with the body in the back and drove to the home of Vernon Butts, the other partner in crime.

Vernon Butts was six foot tall, white, and a complete loon. He was a lowlife, a drifter with a long criminal record of petty offences who was doing what's referred to as life in prison on the instalment plan. He had been in and out of penal institutions and was excited by sadistic homosexual activities, undoubtedly something he had picked up during one of his stays behind bars. As they knocked on the door, Butts came out in a Darth Vader uniform like the *Star Wars* movie. Bonin shook his head and laughed: 'This is our new partner meet Jim Munroe.'

Butts wave his hand in the air: 'May the force be with you…'

The three men sat down and opened a six-pack. As they started to relax, Butts began to show off and produced 21 identity cards, belonging to the people he'd killed.

Later, the three men climbed into Bonin's van, drove to a Mobil gas station, dumped the body behind it and took off. As they were driving home, they stopped at a McDonalds and bought burgers and fries.

Wells was the latest victim in an extended spree of violence that had begun the previous year. Bonin and Butts had previously preyed on a seventeen-year-old exchange student from Germany named Marcus Grabbs, who had been on a backpacking tour of the United States. He was last seen alive hitchhiking on the scenic Pacific Coast highway in Newport Beach on 5 August 1979. His last mistake in his life was to accept a lift from William Bonin and his friend Vernon Butts, picked up Marcus Grabs, sodomised and beat to death the German, leaving his nude body in Malibu Canyon. Marcus had been stabbed more than 70 times was found with a yellow nylon rope around his neck. An electrical cord was wrapped around one ankle. The violent killings escalated at this point Bonin, Butts and Monroe was committing no less than murder a month.

On 27 August 1979, Bonin and Butts picked up Donald Hyden at a community service centre in Los Angeles. His nude body was found near a freeway ramp on the Ventura freeway. Donald had been strangled by a ligature and stabbed. He had been sodomised and an attempt had been made to cut off his testicles, and his throat had been slashed.

On 9 September 1979, in the early hours of the morning, David Murillo, who was 17, was cycling to the movies in Los Angeles. Bonin and Butts abducted him. David's nude body was found three days later on a highway off-ramp, his head had been bashed in with a tyre iron and he had been sodomised and strangled with a ligature.

On 3 February 1980, the two men were at it again. They drove to West Hollywood, where they picked up a young boy called Charlie. They drove several blocks away, parked, and Bonin sodomised the young boy. Butts also tried to sodomise him but was unable to sustain an erection. They then robbed Charles and the two men then decided to tie his hands and feet together. Both men wrapped a T-shirt round Charlie's neck and using a jack handle they twisted the T-shirt like a tourniquet until Charlie was nearly dead. But before he died they took a large object and inserted it into his anus. Ripping and tearing at the boy until he was dead. Both men then drove back to Los Angeles and dumped Charlie's nude body, and then continued on Huntington Beach to seek another victim.

A little while later, they noticed a small boy walking along the street. They stopped the van and began talking to James McCabe, aged 12, who said he was on his way to Disneyland.

Bonin said that they would give him a lift, and James jumped into the van. While Bonin had sex with him, his friend drove, later, James was beaten and strangled with his shirt, and they crushed his neck with a jack handle. They stole his money from his wallet and left his body next to a dumpster in the city of Warner.

Bonin and Butts had become sadistic killers each murder becoming more depraved than the last. The more the victims screamed and suffered – the more they loved it.

The next 21 victims were killed by Bonin and Butts.

Thomas Lundgren, aged 14, 28 May 1979
Mark Sheldon, aged 17, 4 August 1979
Marcus Grabbs, aged 17, 6 August 1979
Donald Hyden, aged 15, 27 August 1979
David Murillo, aged 17, 7 September 1979
Robert Wirostek, aged 18, 27 September 1979
John Done, aged 14, 30 November 1979
Frank Fox, aged 18, 13 December 1979
Michael McDonald, aged 16, 1 January 1980
Charles Maranda, aged 14, 3 February 1980
James Michael McCabe, aged 12, 5 February 1980
Ronald Gatley, aged 18, 14 March 1980
Russell Pugh, aged 15, 21 March 1980
Glen Baker, aged 15, 21 March 1980
Henry Todd Turner, aged 15, 5 April 1980
Stephen Wood, aged 16, 19 April 1980
Larry Sharp, aged 18, 11 April 1980
Darren Kendrick, aged 19, 10 May 1980
Shaun King, aged 14, 19 May 1980
Stephen Wells, aged 18, June 1980

The police finally got their break on 10 June 1980 when an 18-year-old man called William Ray Pugh confessed to inside knowledge of the freeway killers. Pugh, identified the killer as William George Bonin. Officers established round the clock surveillance on Bonin.

On the night of 11 June 1980, the suspect was arrested while sodomising a young man in his van. He was booked on suspicion of murder and various sex charges. On 29 October 1980, Bonin was finally charged on 17 felony counts including conspiracy, kidnapping, robbery, sodomy, oral copulation and sexual perversion.

In December 1980, Bonin's friend, Vernon pleaded guilty on various felony charges and received a life sentence in return for his promise to testify against Bonin. He spelled out details of the torture suffered by assorted freeway victims and the glee with which Bonin inflicted pain. He remarked on how Bill, loved the sound of the screams.

Then, on 11 January 1981, after telling police of Bonin's hypnotic control over him, Butts hanged himself in his cell, finally succeeding in his fifth attempt at suicide since his arrest.

William Bonin's trial opened on 4 November 1981. He admitted 21 murders: 'I couldn't stop killing,' he said, 'it got easier with each one.'

On 5 January 1982, after eight days of deliberation, the jurors convicted Bonin on ten counts of murder and ten counts to be held on file. Two weeks later, he was formally sentenced to death.

THE LADY KILLER

Name: Theodore Robert Bundy
Date of birth: 24 November 1946
Location: Burlington, Vermont, USA
Type of murderer: Homicidal maniac
Body count: 28
Sentence: Death
Outcome: Electrocuted on 24 January 1989

'We serial killers are your sons. We are your husbands.
We are everywhere.'
TED BUNDY

Ted Bundy was a handsome, self-assured, charming, politically ambitious homicidal maniac. Who had no difficulty attracting a wide variety of beautiful woman. Inside however, his private demons drove him to extremes of violence that made the most gruesome of horror films seem tame. His chameleon-like ability to blend effortlessly into society posed the biggest danger to the pretty dark-haired women he selected as his victims.

Linda Ann Healy, a 21-year-old psychology student, was Bundy's first kill. On the night of 31 January 1974, she vanished from her rented room in a house in Seattle, Washington. Her four other housemates never heard a sound. A small bloodstain was found on Linda's bottom sheet but her top sheet and a pillowcase were missing. Her nightgown, which also had blood on it, had been carefully hung up in the closet. Because the authorities believed that foul play had not been involved, her bedroom was never dusted for fingerprints, and a semen stain on her bed was never tested.

Just four weeks earlier, 18-year-old Joni Lenz had been brutally attacked by Bundy in her basement room of the house she shared with her housemates in Seattle. She had been severely beaten about the head and face with a bedframe rod and had had a speculum, a medical vaginal probe, jammed inside her body. Joni was alive, but had suffered brain damage and terrible internal injuries. Bundy had apparently entered and exited via an unlocked basement window.

At this point the police had no idea that the attack on Joni Lenz and the disappearance of Linda Healy were in any way connected, but that would not be long in coming.

On 12 March, Donna Failmanson disappeared en route to a concert in Olympia, Washington. On 17 April, Susan Rancourt vanished on her way to see a German-language film in Ellensburg. The following month, Roberta Clark failed to return from a late-night stroll in her Corvallis neighbourhood, and the month after that Brenda Ball left Seattle's Flame Tavern with an unknown man and vanished, as if into thin air. Just days later, 18-year-old University of

Washington student, Georgann Hawks joined the list of missing women. She had been walking from her boyfriend's apartment to her own sorority house no more than 90ft away when she vanished.

A clear pattern was emerging. All the missing women had been young and attractive with dark shoulder-length or longer hair which was parted in middle. In their photos, which the police had laid out side by side, they could have passed for sisters, some for twins. As yet, the police had found no corpses, but as much as they hoped they would find the women alive, too many had gone missing. In their hearts, they did not believe these cases would have a happy ending.

On 14 July, the shores of Lake Sammamish, twelve miles from downtown Seattle, were packed with people enjoying the weekend sun and water sports. Several people remembered seeing a man with his arm in a cast asking women for help in securing his sailboat to his car. He said his name was Ted. One woman, Doris Grayling had followed Ted to where his small Volkswagen Beetle was parked, but became suspicious when she saw no sign of a sail boat and withdrew her offer of help and left. Without realising it, she had just saved her own life.

Twenty-three-year-old Janice Ott and 19-year-old Denise Naslund were not so lucky. Both disappeared that afternoon and were never seen alive again.

But detectives now had a lead. Doris was able to give them a clear description of the man and his Volkswagen car, and they had a name – Ted. The media leaped on the story and as television and radio reports went out with a description of the suspect, calls to the police came flooding in. One of the callers suggested the police check out a man by the name of

'Theodore Robert Bundy', who had been a psychology student at the University of Washington.

The police followed every lead they could, but when they talked to Bundy they found him squeaky clean. Bundy was studying law and was a young Republican who actively campaigned on behalf of the party. He also did charity work and had once chased a mugger several blocks to make a citizen's arrest. Bundy's name was filed away with countless others and – for the time being, at least – forgotten.

Then, on 7 September 1974, ramblers found a makeshift graveyard on a wooded hillside of Washington's Lake Sammamish State Park. In the graves were the remains of some of the missing girls. The police found strands of various colours of hair, thighbones, two skulls and a jaw bone. Dental records revealed that two of the bodies had belonged to Janice Ott and Denise Naslund, but the others could not be identified. Five weeks later, on 12 October, another rambler found the bones of two more women in Clarke County. One victim was identified as Carol Valenzuela, who had disappeared two months earlier from Vancouver, Washington, on the Oregon border. The second victim was again, impossible to identify.

The police were hopeful that the discovery of these victims would help lead them to the killer, but they had no way of knowing that their man had already given them the slip. He had moved on in search of safer hunting grounds and fresh prey.

On 18 October 1974, in Midvale, Utah, 17-year-old Melissa Smith went missing. She was the daughter of local police chief Louis Smith. When Melissa's naked body turned up nine days later, it was found that, she had been strangled with her own stockings, raped and sodomised. Dirt and twigs had also been stuffed into her vagina, and it seemed as if her killer had touched up her make-up before dumping her body. Thirteen days later, 17-year-old Laura Aime also disappeared. Her body was found a few weeks later. She had been beaten about the head and face with a crowbar, raped and sodomised.

Until now, Bundy had been smart at covering his tracks, but he was about to make his first big mistake. On 8 November 1974, he approached Carol DaRonch outside a shopping centre in Salt Lake City, posing as a police officer. He claimed that a man had been arrested for trying to break into her car and asked her if she would accompany him to the police headquarters to file a report. He was so convincing in his story, even showing her his badge, that Carol agreed to go with him. When she saw his car – an old Volkswagen Beetle – she became suspicious and asked the man to tell her his name. He told her he was Officer Roseland of the Murray Police Department, and again he was so convincing that Carol got into the car.

As they drove off, Carol realised they were going in the wrong direction and knew she had made a terrible mistake. She reached for the door handle and tried to get out, but Bundy snapped a handcuff on to her wrist. He pulled a handgun out and threatened to shoot her. Carol's instincts took over. She pushed at the door again, broke away and leaped out before Bundy could secure the other end of the handcuffs to her wrist. Carol ran for her life, flagging down a passing motorist who took her to the real police. Unfortunately for the police, no prints could be lifted from the handcuffs that still clung to Carol's wrist.

Even though Carol DaRonch had managed to get away

from Bundy and he knew he could now be identified, he was still hungry to kill. Later that night he abducted 17-year-old Debbie Kent after she left a school play in Bountiful, Utah. Debbie had left early to go and pick up her brother, but never made it to her car. Local residents had heard screams coming from the parking lot, and a key that fitted the handcuffs that had been on Carol DaRonch's wrist was later found on the ground near by. Debbie was never seen again.

Bundy had taken a huge risk in abducting Debbie Kent. He had been clearly seen lurking in the back of the auditorium where the play was held and had boldly gone backstage to talk to the drama teacher Raelynn Shepherd. Raelynn told police that a strange man had approached her several times during the play, trying to convince her to come out to the parking lot to allegedly identify a vehicle. It was the same ruse he had used with Carol DaRonch. Knowing his cover was blown Bundy moved on yet again, this time to Aspen, Colorado.

On 12 January 1975, Caryn Campbell was enjoying a short vacation to the mountains with her fiancé and his two children. They were staying at Aspen's Wild Wood Inn and Caryn had briefly returned to her room to get a magazine. She was seen walking down the second-floor hallway towards the room but never returned to the lobby. On 18 February, Caryn's naked body was found a short distance from the roadside, a couple of miles from the hotel. She had suffered severe head injuries that would have been fatal.

From then on, the murders kept coming. On 15 March, Julie Cunningham disappeared while walking to a nearby tavern in Vail, Colorado. Her body was never found.

Denise Oliverson disappeared three weeks later after leaving her home to visit her parents in Grand Junction. Her bike and sandals were found under a nearby viaduct. Eighteen-year-old Melanie Clooney was last seen in Nederland, Colorado, on 15 April. She was found eight days later twenty miles away, dead from head injuries. Her hands were bound and a pillow case was tied around her neck.

By May, Bundy was back in Idaho and on 6 May snatched Lynette Culver, who was only 13 years old, from her school playground in Pocatello. Her body was never found. In June, it was Washington's turn again with 15-year-old Susan Curtis. She was abducted from the campus of Brigham Young University where she was attending a youth conference. Susan had left her friends to walk back to her dorm and was never seen again. Tragically, Susan was from Bountiful, Utah, the same town as Melissa Smith, who had been abducted the previous year. Shelly Robertson was next. She was last seen on 1 June 1975, talking to a man in a pickup truck at a gas station in Golden, Colorado. The 24-year-old's nude and decomposing body was found near Vale Colorado, 500ft inside an old mining entrance.

By now, Washington State Police knew that they had a serial killer on their hands and Utah authorities had a strong suspicion that they did too, but at this point the two States had failed to link the killings. After nine confirmed murders and several unsolved disappearances, the Washington taskforce was making slow headway in finding the killer, but they had developed a computer program to determine a list of the most likely suspects based on the incredible amount of tip-offs and information they had compiled. Cumbersome and laborious as it was, the computer had narrowed down the suspects to just 25, one of whom was Ted Bundy. Before they had found and interviewed him however, good fortune intervened.

On 16 August 1975, a Utah highway patrol officer, Bob Hayward, noticed a light-coloured Volkswagen Beetle in his neighbourhood of Granger, a suburb of Salt Lake City. It was an unfamiliar vehicle to him so he turned his lights onto the vehicle to get a better look at the licence plate. Immediately, the driver of the Beetle turned off his lights and sped away. He jumped two stop signs before finally pulling over. Officer Hayward asked for identification and the driver produced his car registration details and licence. They were both in the name of Ted Bundy.

As Officer Hayward questioned Bundy, he noticed that there was no front passenger seat in Bundy's car. On closer inspection, he discovered a balaclava, a stocking mask, iron bar, ice pick and a pair of handcuffs on the floor of the vehicle. Bundy was immediately arrested on suspicion of burglary. As ever, Bundy remained self-confident and cool under questioning and explained that the balaclava and mask he used for skiing. The handcuffs, he said, he had found in a rubbish bin. Bundy's apartment was searched and maps of Colorado and Aspen were discovered. A check on the handcuffs showed that they were the same model as those used to handcuff Carol DaRonch. There were too many co-incidences for the police to ignore, but they had no concrete evidence to charge Bundy with any crime.

Carol DaRonch. however, was their key. On 2 October 1975, Carol along with the director of the Viewmont High School play and a friend of Debbie Kent were asked to attend an identity parade of seven men. Carol picked out Bundy as the man who had abducted her and the play director picked out Bundy as the man who had been loitering backstage at the play the night Debbie Kent had vanished. Despite Bundy's insistence of his innocence, the police were confident they had their man and launched an all-out investigation. Bundy was arrested and charged with the Carol DaRonch assault.

Bundy's pretty girlfriend, Liz Kendal, was interviewed by Utah detectives. She told them he would often sleep during the day and go out at night and that in the last year he had pressured her to partake in his sexual fantasies of bondage. She also told them that he had a supply of plaster of Paris to make plaster casts and remembered that in July Ted had gone to Lake Sammamish supposedly to water-ski. It was a week after this that Janice Ott and Denise Naslund were reported missing. Other eyewitnesses also recognised Bundy as being the man they had seen at Lake Sammamish, and checks on Bundy's credit cards revealed purchases for gas in the towns where some of his victims had disappeared. It was becoming obvious that Bundy had had something to do with the murders and disappearances in Washington, Utah and Colorado.

Bundy was charged with the aggravated kidnapping of Carol DaRonch in what was to be an open-and-shut trial. On 30 June 1975, he was sentenced to between one and fifteen years in prison.

The Utah conviction served its main purpose of holding Bundy until he could be put on trial for murder. The State of Colorado was first up to bat and Ted was transferred to the Pitkin County Jail to await trial for the murder of Caryn Campbell, who had disappeared from the Wild Wood Inn in Aspen. One of Caryn's hairs had been found by the forensics team during a search of Bundy's Volkswagen. Further examination of Caryn's skull showed that she had been struck by a blunt instrument, the impressions of which matched the crowbar found in Bundy's car.

The preliminary trial began poorly when a witness from the Wild Wood Inn pointed to the wrong man having been asked to identify Bundy in the courtroom. However, the case did continue and Bundy fired his attorney and defended himself. In order to prepare his case Bundy was allowed access to the Court House law library in Aspen and it was during a visit there on 7 June 1977 that Bundy, who was loosely supervised, leaped from a second-storey window and escaped.

Bundy knew better than to try to flee the town. Roadblocks had been quickly set up around it. As Police launched a massive search which included bringing in the tracker dogs, Bundy hid out in the woods, stole food from log cabins and nearby campers and eluded them for days. Finally, he stole a car in the hope that he could pass through the police barriers unnoticed, but he was spotted and arrested six days after his escape.

Back in jail, Bundy was ordered to wear leg irons and handcuffs on all future visits to the Court House Library.

Almost seven months later, Bundy attempted to escape again. This time he was more successful. On 30 December 1977, he hacked his way through an old welded light fixture in the ceiling of his cell and crawled through to a deputy's living quarters, put on some civilian clothes and literally walked out of the prison. He made his way to the bus station, took a bus to Denver and from there boarded a plane to Chicago. By the time the authorities discovered him missing the next day, Bundy had a 17-hour head start.

In Chicago, Bundy stole a car, drove to Atlanta, Georgia, and then took a bus to Tallahassee, Florida. Here he took a one-room apartment near the campus of Florida's State University under the alias of Chris Hagen.

Bundy lived by shop lifting, stealing credit cards and purse-snatching, but it was only a matter of time before he killed again.

On 14 January 1978, Lisa Levy and Margaret Bowman were found dead in their beds in the Chi Omega Sorority House. In the early hours of the morning a housemate had arrived back after a night out to find the back door wide open. She heard footsteps coming towards her and as she hid in the shadows saw a man, with a club in his hand, run down the stairs and out of the front door. Thinking that they had been burgled, the girl ran up the stairs only to see one of her room mates staggering down the hall. Her head was soaked with blood. They immediately called the police, who searched the house and found Lisa Levy and Margaret Bowman dead in their rooms. Lisa had been bludgeoned about the head, raped and strangled a Clairol hairspray bottle had been inserted into her Virginia. Bite marks were on her buttocks and her right nipple had been almost completely bitten off. Margaret had been strangled with a stocking which was still tied around her neck and her skull had been shattered.

The same night and just a few blocks away, Cheryl Thomas was attacked while she lay sleeping in her bed. Her skull was fractured in five places, her jaw broken and her shoulder dislocated, but miraculously Cheryl survived the brutal beating, although she would suffer permanent loss of hearing and equilibrium problems. At the foot of her bed, police found a stocking mask similar to the one found by detectives in Bundy's car in Utah five months earlier. They were able to obtain hair samples of the assailant from the mask and teeth impressions from the bite marks on Cheryl's body. The great tragedy was that they had no knowledge of the monster Ted Bundy or of the havoc that he'd already wreaked in Washington, Utah and Colorado.

Ted Bundy remained holed up in Tallahassee, but his reign of terror was coming to an end.

On 6 February 1978, Bundy stole a van from Florida State University's media centre and left Tallahassee. Two days later, he attempted to abduct a 14-year-old girl in Jacksonville, Florida, but, when the girl's brother drove up, Bundy ran off. On 9 February, Bundy struck for what would be the last time. He abducted 12-year-old Kimberly Ann Leach from her school in Lake City, Florida. She had left one building to go to another and collect her purse during the first period. Kimberly made it safely to the other building, but never returned to class. She was last seen by a passer by being led away by an angry-looking man to a white van. The witnesses assumed the pair were father and daughter. Kimberly Ann's body was found on 12 April about 30 miles away in the Suwanee River State Park. She was partially clothed and hidden under an old hog shed. The rest of her clothing was piled up next to her body. Marks were visible on her neck but the exact cause of death could not be determined because of the advanced state of decomposition of her body. In fact, she had been there long enough to be partly mummified.

After the murder of Kimberly Ann Leach, Bundy dumped the stolen van. He then stole another vehicle, one that he was more comfortable driving – a Volkswagen Beetle – and fled to Pensacola, Florida.

Late at night on 15 February, a patrol officer spotted the car in the neighbourhood. Not recognising it as being a local vehicle, he ran a check on it, only to find that the car was stolen. The officer pulled Bundy over and ordered him to get out. As he started to handcuff him, Bundy broke free and ran off. The officer fired his gun and Bundy dropped to the ground, pretending to be hit.

As the officer approached him, Bundy leaped up and attacked the policeman, but after a brief struggle was overpowered. Ted Bundy's reign of terror had ended.

True to character, Bundy played the innocent to the last. He told Pensacola police his name was Chris Hagen, but since Bundy was on the FBI's ten-most-wanted list it was only a matter of time before his true identity was revealed. Bundy was transferred to Tallahassee and was indicted on 27 July 1978, for the Chi Omega killings and for the Leach murder four days later.

It was the Chi Omega killings which would nail Bundy once and for all. When his trial began on 25 June 1979, it was to a media circus. Bundy was suspected of killing at least 36 women in four different states and his name was now infamous across America. He was a monster, the Devil, evil reincarnate and his trial was the most publicised trial of the decade.

As before, Bundy conducted his own defence, but he was on to a losing battle. The sorority housemate's testimony of what she had witnessed that night and her identification of Bundy as the man she had seen running down the stairs was damning. But most damning of all was the evidence of the teeth marks on Lisa Levy's buttocks. They were a perfect match of Bundy's. In a single bite, Bundy had signed his own death sentence.

Bundy was found guilty on 23 July 1979, and on 31 July the

jury recommended that Ted Bundy should die. The judge affirmed their recommendation and imposed the death penalty twice for the murders of Lisa Levy and Margaret Bowman. Ted Bundy would meet his end in the electric chair.

Even now, Bundy still proclaimed his innocence, claiming that the prejudice of the media had given him an unfair trial.

He spent months dragging the system out, methodically exhausting his appeals. Of the many stays of execution he managed to acquire, one was given a mere 15 minutes before he was scheduled to die on 2 July 1986. Another on 18 November was just seven hours before his termination.

But Bundy could not buy time indefinitely. On 17 January 1989, the State of Florida lost its patience and Bundy's final death warrant was issued. It was to be carried out a week later. In a sickening last-ditch effort Bundy asked for a stay of execution of an additional three years in order to confess to all of his killings. He tried to coerce his victims' families to plead with the court to allow him time to properly confess to the murders and to tell where he had hidden the bodies. Despite not knowing the fate of many of their loved ones, all of the families refused.

Bundy never did hold his confessions. It was obvious he was not ready to admit everything, especially the murders involving some of the younger victims. On the day of his death Bundy called his mother, refused the last meal, and was electrocuted as scheduled on 24 January 1989. He was pronounced dead at 7.16am. The baying crowd outside the prison chanted: 'Burn, Bundy, Burn…'

THE ROSTOV RIPPER

Name: Andrei Romanovich Chikatilo
Date of birth: 16 October 1936
Location: Ukraine
Type of murderer: Cannibal
Body count: 53 plus
Sentence: Death
Outcome: Executed on 16 February 1994

*'What I did was not for sexual pleasure. Rather,
it brought me some peace of mind.'*
ANDREI CHIKATILO

Throughout his trial Andrei Chikatilo was transported to and
from court in a large metal cage. This was to keep both the
public out and more importantly Chikatilo in. He was kept
locked inside the cage during the court sessions and lived up
to his image as a raving lunatic with an enormous blood lust.
Baring his teeth menacingly Andrei Chikatilo emitted a
blood-curdling growl and lunged at the iron bars with all the

ferocity he could muster. As he beat himself against the cage, blood splattered the surrounding walls of the courtroom. He rattled the bars, screaming insults and obscenities and raving like a madman!

Andrei Chikatilo was born during the great Ukrainian famine of the early 1930s, a time when cannibalism was rife. Millions perished in the dreadful conditions throughout Russia and the Ukraine, and Andrei and his sisters were repeatedly told how an older brother, Stepan, had died of starvation and neighbours had eaten him to save themselves from the same fate. Andrei was convinced that the story was true. In actual fact, no record exists of Stepan Chikatilo's birth or death, but Chikatilo's mother told the story so convincingly, in near hysterics, that her children grew up believing it was true.

The young Andrei was further traumatised when the German Army invaded the Ukraine during the Second World War. Hiding in a cupboard, he watched helplessly as a group of Nazi soldiers held down his mother and took turns to rape her. Afterwards Andrei became sullen, morose and withdrawn. In fact, Andrei's youth was filled with misery, hate and anger. He was a gangly ugly bug with very poor eyesight and children at school regularly ridiculed him about his appearance, circling him to laugh, taunt and jeer. They spat at him and beat him.

To a child, the future is the next five seconds and a day seems like a lifetime. Throughout his school years, there were times when Andrei wished he had never been born. Life was hell, but it was about to get worse – much worse.

In 1955, at the age of 19, Andrei was called up to join the army. From the outset, he was ridiculed and taunted by his comrades calling him a 'freak and a weirdo' – eventually he was cornered by soldiers in the barracks, held down and repeatedly raped. From then on Andrei pulled up the shutters, battened down the hatches and cocooned himself in his own world of hostility and hatred.

After leaving the army in 1960, Andrei dated a girl, but that relationship failed miserably, mainly because of his inability to gain an erection. The girl laughed in Andrei's face and told her friends in the village about his problem. They began to mock and taunt Andrei. Everyone, it seemed, made fun of him. He felt vulnerable and exposed, and for Andrei this was the final straw and the trigger for his deep-rooted anger. He started to hate everyone, especially girls.

At the age of 24, Andrei took a job as a telephone repair man in Rostov – but his sexual urges were becoming obsessive and he spent most of his time masturbating. In fact, Andrei masturbated any time and anywhere he felt the urge. It didn't matter if he was repairing a telephone in someone's house or office – if the compulsion came so did he. Andrei was happily masturbating in a storeroom when an unsuspecting work colleague walked in. More ridicule, taunts and jeers.

When Andre turned 27, he was introduced by his sister to a 24-year-old girl named Feodosia. This developed into a whirlwind romance and the pair married. But the honeymoon, as he feared, turned into a disaster. Unable to rise to the occasion, Feodosia persuaded him to try again and again. Andrei persevered, and two years later Feodosia give birth to a daughter.

Andrei then began studying for a degree, taking up a correspondence course through a university. In 1970, he graduated enabling him to become a teacher. With a university degree, a wife, and by now two children, he presented the appearance of a meek, family man, but dark urges were brooding behind that façade.

On 22 December 1978, nine-year-old Yelena Zakonova was chatting to a friend much longer than she had planned. It was getting late and knowing her parents would worry Yelena pulled her collar up, put her head down against the chill wind and started to walk home through the town of Shakhty, near the Russia–Ukraine border. It was bone-chillingly cold. In the shadows, Andrei Chikatilo was also shivering against the night chill. As he peered through the icy fog he saw little Yelena hurrying towards him. Andrei didn't move a muscle. He held his breath and waited like a coiled spring. As her footsteps grew closer, the only sound was the beating of his heart. Andrei wiped the saliva from the corner of his mouth, barely able to contain his excitement.

In a flash, he pounced, scooping the unsuspecting youngster into his arms and disappearing into the icy darkness. Clutching the terrified girl against his chest Andrei ran to the edge of the town and into the woods, not stopping until he reached a clearing. There he forced the terror-stricken Yelena on to the frosted wintry ground and ripped off her clothes. Grunting and panting and unable to gain an erection he straddled the petrified girl and proceeded to rub himself up against her. This didn't satisfy him, so he penetrated her with a serrated knife – the sight of her blood excited him and made him want more. He slashed and stabbed with unbridled ferocity until he climaxed, then Andrei placed his huge hands around the little girl's delicate throat and squeezed the last gasp out of her dying body.

Andrei had now discovered what gave him sexual ecstasy – domination, mutilation, and his victim's agony and terror as his knife did the work.

Two days later, Yelena Zakonova's mutilated body was found near a riverbank. Police were called and a manhunt began. During a door-to-door inquiry, residents said that they had seen Chikatilo in the area, but Andrei's wife told detectives that he had been at home all night. Believing her, detectives switched their attention to another suspect, 25-year-old Alexandra Kravchenko. Kravchenko was a suspect because he had committed a similar crime in his youth. The police beat a confession out of him for the murder of Yelena Zakonova and Kravchenko was executed by firing squad.

Andrei's second victim was on 3 September 1981. She was 17-year-old Larisa Tkachenko, who was playing truant from school. Andrei spotted her in Rostov city and started talking to her. He suggested that they go and get some refreshments at a place which was on the fringe of a wood. As they chatted and walked through the woods, the smell of her perspiration started to turn Andrei on. It turned him on so much that he pushed her to the ground and began tearing her clothes off. He pushed earth into her mouth to muffle her screams and then began to throttle her. The sensation of her life ebbing away beneath him only intensified his lust. He mutilated her body until she died.

It was nine months before Andrei found his third victim, a 13-year-old girl, and he orgasmed as she bled and screamed as he killed her. A 14-year-old girl was next, followed a month later by a nine-year-old boy. Three days later, he mutilated and murdered a girl of sixteen, and two weeks after that he killed an 18-year-old girl.

Victim by victim, Andrei refined his technique, managing to keep each successive victim alive longer than the last in order to fulfil his cravings as much as he could. He would lightly slash his victims with his knife in order to make them struggle and scream more. Then he would cut off their genitals and eat them while they were still warm. He preferred each to be still breathing when he bit off their nipples, their nose and the tip of their tongue before stabbing them in the eyes.

Before long, Andrei quit his teaching job to become a factory clerk. His job involved travelling from his home town of Rostov in order to collect parts for the factory. Throughout his travels, he found many fresh victims to prey upon, and the fact that they lived often hundreds of miles meant that any connection between the murders and Andrei went undetected for some time.

In the early summer of 1983, Chikatilo murdered a 16-year-old American girl. He followed this with the murder of a 13-year-old Russian girl, a 24-year-old vagrant woman, an 18-year-old boy, a 19-year-old prostitute and a 14-year-old schoolboy.

The following year saw him slay an 18-year-old girl, an alcoholic who was found with her nose and upper lip bitten off. Two months later, the body of an 11-year-old boy was discovered near Chikatilo's home with 54 stab wounds.

In May 1984, while on his travels, Andrei met and befriended Tania Petrosan and her 11-year-old daughter Sveta. He arranged to take the unsuspecting mother and child for a picnic at an isolated beauty spot. Tania merrily unfolded the tartan blanket and laid it down on the ground in a small wooded copse. The child wandered off to pick wild flowers, leaving her mother with the fiend. Tania lay down next to

Andrei and started to fondle him. But once again Andrei was incapable of getting an erection. Tania taunted and giggled: 'Are you gay? Are you a poofter?' Those were the last words she ever spoke.

Andrei reached over into the wicker picnic basket, pulled out a kitchen knife and drove it into the side of Tania's head. The blood sent Andrei into a frenzied attack. Like a wild dingo he gnawed, bit and ripped at the helpless body until Tania was dead.

Sveta, the little girl, skipped back into the clearing clutching a bunch of wild flowers. On seeing her mother's bloodied body lying in a heap on the ground, she froze. Andrei was beside her wild and bloodied and Sveta started to scream. The little girl was later found beheaded. Chikatilo went on to kill three more victims, each of which had their uterus cut out.

During the post mortems of Andrei's victims, the police found one important clue. The semen belonged to a man with the blood group AB, a rare group shared by only about 6 per cent of Russians.

On 14 December 1984, Chikatilo was brought in for questioning because he had been acting suspiciously at a bus stop. He was given a blood test but was released because he had blood group A. What medical examiners didn't realise was that Chikatilo's semen contained a weak B antibody, which made it appear as if his blood type was group AB, even though it wasn't. Relieved to have been let off, he began his reign of terror again, killing an 18-year-old girl who he strangled and stabbed 34 times. He also gouged her eyes out.

As pressure mounted from the authorities, Andrei took a year off from his killing spree to let the heat die down, only to start again with six more horrific murders.

The whole of the Rostov area was put under surveillance from undercover police in order to catch the monster. Andrei became aware of this trap, and decided to go out of the danger zone where he killed a 22-year-old woman. Police found her body later, her nipples and genitalia removed.

Later, in the town of Novoshakhtinsk, Andrei abducted a ten-year-old boy, who was found three days later, mutilated and stabbed. The tip of his tongue and penis were missing. Semen on the dead boy's shirt was linked to two previous crimes, and this time the killer had left a fresh clue. Near to the body the Police found a large footprint. Witnesses told police they had seen the boy being followed. A tall, hollow-cheeked, bespectacled man with large feet shadowed the boy's every move.

With the body count escalating police felt the murder spree was getting out of control. Andrei had stepped up his pace from five victims in the first year to two every week. Andrei began shifting his pattern. He now removed the upper lip and sometimes the nose, and left them in the victim's mouth or ripped open stomach.

Andrei Chikatilo had become public enemy number one. Dozens of new detectives were brought in on the case and a task force of some 200 men and women became involved in the investigation. Detectives were assigned to work undercover at bus and train stations, and to be keep vigilance in parks. With all the surveillance, it was inevitable that certain suspicious men would be followed and detained. Police built up a profile of the man they wanted to apprehend. He was between 25 and 30, tall, well built, with blood type AB. He was careful, had at least average intelligence and was probably verbally persuasive. He travelled and lived with either his mother or wife.

He might be a former psychiatric patient or substance abuser and he might have some knowledge of anatomy and skill with a knife. Anyone who generally matched these characteristics would have to submit to a blood test.

Finally the break they had all been waiting for came through – an undercover officer spotted a man acting strangely in the Rostov bus station. Something was wrong with the way he spoke to a female adolescent and when she left him and got on her bus, he circled around and sat next to another young woman. The officer decided to question the man. His name was Andrei Chikatilo, and he was the manager of a machinery-supply company. He said he was there on a business trip but lived in Shakhty.

The officer asked why he was approaching young women, and Chikatilo replied that he had once been a teacher and missed talking to young people. The officer had an uneasy feeling in the pit of his stomach but had no choice but to let him go.

Later that day, the same officer again spotted Chikatilo. This time he decided to follow him. The suspect boarded a bus and seemed very ill at ease, twisting his head from one side to the other. This was a very different person to the one the officer had spoken to earlier in the day. He knew he was on to something and stayed close. When the bus arrived at the next bus station Chikatilo got off and approached various women. The officer kept his distance and saw Chikatilo solicit a prostitute. He disappeared with her down an alleyway between two derelict buildings. The officer radioed for backup while Chikatilo received oral sex under his coat. Police cars arrived and officers swooped and arrested Chikatilo for indecent behaviour in public. While two officers handcuffed him another went through his briefcase. Inside was a jar of Vaseline, a long kitchen knife, a piece of rope and a dirty towel. Chikatilo was led to the station. The Rostov Ripper had finally been caught.

Andrei Chikatilo admitted that he was the murderer they were looking for and was guilty of the crimes. He wanted to tell the truth about his life and what had led him to these atrocities. Among his admissions was that of his first murder, nine-year-old Yelena Zakotnova who he had killed in 1978. The police were shocked. They had already arrested, tried and executed for a man for that crime.

Chikatilo said that he had moved to Shakhty in 1978 in order to teach. Before his family arrived, he had spent his free time watching children and feeling a strong desire to see them without their clothes on. To maintain his privacy, he purchased a shack on a dark dirty street opposite a school.

One day, on his way to the shack he came upon a girl and was seized with an urgent sexual desire. He took her to the shack and attacked her. When he couldn't achieve an erection, he used a knife as a substitute. During his frenzy of strangulation and stabbing, he also blind folded the girl. Once she was dead, he tossed her body into a nearby river.

Officers asked him to explain the blindfold, and Chikatilo told them that he had heard that the image of a killer remains in the eyes of the victim. It was a superstition, but he had believed it. That was why he had gouged out the eyes of many of his victims. Then he had decided that it wasn't true, so he stopped doing it, which explained the change in the pattern of killings.

Chikatilo also described how his fantasies became more and more violent. In 1981 he attacked a vagrant girl who was looking for money. He used his teeth to bite off her nipples and then swallowed them. At the moment of slicing open her body, he said, 'I ejaculated.'

Chikatilo remembered the details of each of the 36 murders and went through them one by one. Some were premeditated, where he learned a person's route and habits, finding a way to get that person alone. Others were victims of opportunity who happened to come along at the wrong time. His stabbings were almost always a substitute for sexual intercourse that could not be performed. He had learned how to squat beside them in such a way as to avoid getting their blood on his clothes, which he demonstrated with a mannequin. At any rate, he worked in a shipping firm so there was always an excuse for a cut or a scratch. It seemed that his impotence generally triggered his rage, especially if the woman made demands or ridiculed him. He soon understood that he could not get aroused without violence. 'I have to see blood and wounds on the victims,' he said.

With the boys that he abducted, it was different. Although Chikatilo enjoyed seeing them bleed just as easily as the women, he would fantasise that these boys where no good and he was a hero for torturing and doing them in. He could not give a reason for cutting off their tongues or penises, although at one point he said he was taking revenge against life on the genitals of his victims. He also said that he would place his semen inside a uterus that he had just removed, and as he walked along would chew on it. He called it 'the truffle of sexual murder'.

He never admitted to actually consuming these organs, but searches never turned up any of the discarded remains.

Chikatilo said 'the cries, the blood and the agony of his victims gave him relaxation and a certain pleasure. He liked the taste of their blood and would even tear at their mouths with his teeth.' It gave him animal satisfaction 'to chew or swallow nipples or testicles'.

To corroborate what he was saying he drew sketches of the crime scenes the facts all fitted. Then he announced what everyone had feared. He added more victims to the list, many more.

In the end, Andre Chikatilo confessed to more murders, although there was corroboration for only 53: 31 females and 22 males. He confessed that he ate many of victims and mutilated their sexual organs, but he told police that he never set out to kill them. He pointed at his genitals and said, 'Look at this useless thing, what do you think I could do with that? I am not a homosexual, I have milk in my breasts. I am going to give birth.'

Andrei Chikatilo was considered a crazed beast and was put into a steel cage to await his fate. His trial lasted six months. Andrei Chikatilo was convicted on all counts of murder and sentenced to death.

On 16 February 1994, Andrei Chikatilo was led into a bare concrete room with a drain in the centre of the floor. Instructed to kneel down, stare at the wall and not to turn, he was then shot with a single bullet in the back of the head Russian style. The Rostov Ripper was finally dead.

THE CANDY MAN

Name: Dean Corll
Date of birth: 24 December 1939
Location: Houston, Texas, USA
Type of murderer: Homosexual predator
Body count: 27-plus
Sentence: Never lived to stand trial
Outcome: Murdered by one of his intended victims

'I'm gonna kill you all. But first I'm gonna have my fun.'
DEAN CORLL

Wednesday, 8 August 1973 looked liked being a particularly hot day in Houston, Texas. As early as 8am, Velma Lines, chief telephone operator in the Pasadena Police Department, was glad to walk out of the heat into the air-conditioned police headquarters. She'd been seated in front of the switchboard for only a couple of minutes when a call came through. A boyish voice with a broad Texan accent said, 'Y'all better come down here now. I just killed a man.' The caller gave the address as 2020 Lamar Drive. Within a couple of minutes, two squad cars were on their way. Lamar Drive was in a middle-class section of Pasadena, a southeastern suburb of Houston, and 2020 Lamar was a small nondescript wooden bungalow with an overgrown lawn and a broken fence. Three , three teenagers – two boys and a girl – were sitting on the step by the front door. The girl's clothes were torn to shreds and looked as though she had been mauled by a grizzly bear, all three were red-eyed, as if they'd been crying.

A skinny pimply youth with a wispy blond moustache said he had made the phone call. He pointed at the front door and said, 'He's in there.'

Lying against the wall of the corridor was the naked body of a well-built man. His face was caked with blood from a bullet wound. There were more bullet holes in his back and shoulder. He was very obviously, dead.

The teenagers gave their names as Elmer Wayne Henley, Timothy Kerley and Rhonda Williams. Elmer Henley or Wayne, as he liked to be called, was the boy who had made the call. He explained that he had shot his friend whose name was Dean Corll.

The bedraggled teenagers were driven to the Pasadena Police headquarters and an ambulance summoned to take the corpse to the morgue while detectives began to search the house. It was obvious from the state of the place that Dean had moved in recently. Half-empty boxes were strewn about the house, furniture was wrapped in plastic and decorating material lay in the hallway. Detectives carefully made their way through the corridor, trying not to breathe too deeply as a strong smell of acrylic paint made them quite giddy.

The bedroom close to where the body was lying contained only a single bed and a small table. The room was dominated by a huge poster of a Jesus-like face and the caption 'LOVE' The carpet was covered with transparent plastic sheeting. Beside the bed was an 8ft-long piece of plywood with handcuffs attached to two of its corners and nylon ropes attached to the other two. A long hunting knife in its scabbard lay near by. A black box contained a 17in-long dildo and a huge tube of lubricant. The sinister props clearly pointed to sadistic sexual practices. The seasoned detectives shook their heads in disbelief a look of horror frozen on their craggy faces.

The new Ford van parked in the drive gave the same impression. It had heavy navy-blue curtains which could be drawn to block out the back windows. A piece of carpeting covered the floor and rings and hooks were attached to the walls. There were also several rolls of nylon rope.

In a large box covered with a piece of carpet, the police found strands of human hair. Another similar box had air holes drilled into its sides.

Back at the police station, Elmer Wayne Henley was explaining how he had come to shoot his friend, Dean Corll. He was nervous and chainsmoked while he made his harrowing statement. He had met Corll he said, when both he and Corll lived in a run down area of Houston known as the Heights.

Corll, who was 16 years older than him, had only recently moved into the house in Pasadena. On the previous evening, Henley and Timothy Kerley, had been invited to a paint-sniffing party at Corll's house. Around midnight the two boys left to buy beer and cigarettes promising not to be long. When they returned, they had a friend with them, Rhonda Williams. She had decided on the spur of the moment to run away from home. Rhonda had been in a terrible state and had been totally miserable ever since her boyfriend had vanished a year before. A little after midnight she met Wayne and Timothy at the liquor store and when they invited her to the paint-sniffing party she readily accepted. Corll was furious when the two boys arrived back at the house with Rhonda in tow.

'You weren't supposed to bring a girl!' he yelled, 'Now you've spoiled everything.' But after a while he calmed down and seemed to be in a better mood. The four of them settled down to a paint-sniffing session in the living room. Acrylic paint was sprayed into a paper bag and passed around so they could all breathe in the fumes. Within an hour all four were stretched out unconscious on the floor.

When Wayne came round daylight was filtering through the drawn curtains. He realised with a jerk, that Corll was snapping handcuffs on his wrists. His ankles were already tied together.

The other two were also cuffed and bound, and Timothy had been stripped. As they began to recover their senses they started struggling to get free. It was clear that Corll's good humour of a couple of hours earlier had been an act. He was seething with resentment raving like a rabid dog. He waved a knife at them and told them he was going to kill them all: 'But first, I'm going to have my fun.' Then he dragged Wayne into the kitchen and pushed a .22 pistol against his belly.

Wayne panicked, but then quickly decided that his only

chance of escape was to sweet-talk Corll and persuade him that he'd be willing to join him in murdering Rhonda and Timothy. It took some time, but finally Corll removed the handcuffs and untied Wayne's feet. It was agreed that Wayne would rape Rhonda while Corll raped Timothy.

Corll carried Timothy and then Rhonda into the bedroom. He turned the radio on high to drown any screaming. Corll placed the pistol on the bedside table and began to undress. He handed Wayne the knife and ordered him to cut off Rhonda's clothes. The girl, still dazed from the paint fumes was only half-aware of what was happening. Knowing that Corll was watching him closely, he began to cut away Rhonda's clothing. Meanwhile, Timothy was struggling desperately trying to push Corll off him. Wayne shouted above the music: 'Why don't you let me take her out of here? She doesn't want to see what you are doing.'

Corll ignored him. He was far too busy abusing Timothy. Wayne saw his chance, jumped to his feet and grabbed the pistol. 'Back off, Dean!' he yelled above the radio. 'Stop it!'

Corll lurched to his feet, wide-eyed with rage. 'Go on, Wayne, kill me. Why don't you?' he screamed.

As Corll got closer and closer, he shouted louder and louder: 'Go on… Go on… be a man… pull the trigger…'

Elmer Wayne Henley had a little smirk on his face and a big grin inside as he fired the gun. The first bullet struck Corll in the head and he staggered a couple of paces – a look of surprise on his face as he clutched his head. Wayne stepped forward raised the gun and fired another shot into his shoulder. Corll fell through the door and hit the wall of the corridor. There was no stopping Wayne. With his legs spread apart and both hands gripping the gun he emptied the rest of the bullets into Corll's back. The dying man fell as if he had been filleted, his body slithering down slowly to the floor until he lay with his cheek and shoulders against the wall.

Wayne quickly found the handcuff keys and released his two friends. Rhonda was struggling to take in what had happened, but when she saw Corll lying in a pool of blood she began to scream. Wayne calmed her down and they all dressed, Rhonda making do with her slashed clothes.

They discussed what to do next. Neighbours had probably seen them entering the house and so could identify them, and the corpse was bound to be discovered sooner or later. If they fled now, it would be unlikely that their version of events would be believed. Wayne dialled 911 and his call was put through to the Pasadena Police Department. Still in shock, all three were unable to stop sobbing.

It took Wayne Henley an hour and a half to make his statement. Rhonda and Timothy were also questioned. Timothy mentioned something that the police found very interesting: 'While we were waiting for the police, Wayne told me that if I hadn't been his friend he could have got fifteen hundred dollars for me.'

Questioned about what Timothy had said and the plywood and the dildo, Henley told the police that Corll liked to use them to abuse young boys and had been paying Henley to find them.

Why, then, did Henley decide to kill Corll?

'He made one mistake,' said Henley. 'He told me that I wouldn't be the first one he'd killed. He said that he'd already killed a lot of boys and had buried them in a boatshed.'

The detectives interrogating Henley glanced at each

other. So far, they had assumed that they were dealing with a case of drug abuse and sexual perversion, and that Corll's threats to kill the teenagers had been intended merely to frighten them.

Henley's words raised a far more unpleasant suspicion. For nearly three years, boys had been disappearing from the Heights. The police had registered them as a matter of course as runaways, but many parents had claimed that their sons had disappeared too abruptly for this to be the case. The police were aware that Corll had lived in the Heights just before moving to Pasadena, and had lived opposite one of the missing boys.

'Where is the boatshed?' one of the detectives asked softly.

Henley said that he had only been there once, but it was somewhere in southwest Houston. He was able to recollect three of the names that Corll had mentioned: Marty Jones, Charlie Cobble and David Hilligiest. All three boys were listed as missing.

Even now, none of the detectives really believed that they were dealing with a mass murderer. It was more likely that Henley was still stoned from the acrylic paint he had been sniffing the night before, but his claims had to be checked out. Detectives asked Henley, 'Can you remember how to get to this boatshed?'

'I think so. It's near Hiram Clark Road.'

'OK. Let's go.'

Henley was transferred to Houston Police headquarters, where he was shown pictures of two boys who had been missing since 27 July, 13 days before. Henley identified them as Charlie Cobble, 17, and Marty Jones, 18. Two of the boys Corll claimed to have killed.

The Pasadena detectives, now accompanied by two of their Houston colleagues, headed south to Hiram Clark Road. Another group of detectives were ordered to gather diggers, spades and ropes and meet them there.

It was already late in the afternoon when the two cars arrived at the rendezvous. From here Henley took over the navigating, chainsmoking and chattering non-stop, pointing at this and that, and umming and aahing, much to the annoyance of the sheriffs.

Eventually they pulled up beside a barbed-wire fence on Silver Bell Street and Henley pointed to a row of corrugated-iron sheds standing well back from the road.

'That's it,' he said pointing. 'That's it...'

Southwest boat storage consisted of 20 roofed sheds, mostly used to house boats. The police drove into the compound and Henley directed them to shed number eleven. The double doors were padlocked and the owner of the complex – a Mrs Meynier, who lived in a large house next to the compound, told them detectives that she didn't have a key.

'Renters provide their own padlocks,' she told them.

When the police explained that the man who rented shed number 11 was dead, however, she gave them permission to break in.

Inside was a half-dismantled car, a child's bicycle and a large iron drum, along with some cardboard boxes, water containers and ominously, two sacks of lime. The earth floor was covered by two long strips of old carpet and a large plastic bag containing a collection of men's clothing. The place was stifling hot like a baker's oven.

Wayne Henley stood at the door nervously peering inside. He knew it was only a matter of time before the truth came out. Slowly he walked back towards the cars, sat down on the ground and buried his head between his knees.

The first task was to move everything out of the shed. While this was being done a detective noted the registration numbers on the car and bicycle and radioed the information back to police headquarters. It was soon established that the car had been stolen from a used car lot and the bicycle belonged to a 13-year-old boy named James Dreymala, who had vanished less than a week before.

Once the shed was empty, the two strips of carpet were rolled up. The detectives looked around for a good point to start digging. They chose a place where the earth seemed softer. Two trusted convicts who had been brought along from the local jail were ordered to begin digging.

Even with the doors open, the heat was unbearable. Both men were soon sweating heavily. Six inches down in the sandy earth, they uncovered a white substance. 'That's lime,' said the detective, 'keep digging.'

Suddenly, the shed was filled with a sickening stench. The detectives held their noses. One of the convicts carefully removed another shovel full of earth. There, staring up at him was a boy's face. The convict dropped his spade and rushed outside, heaving and retching. A sheriff picked up the spade and carefully went on with the job himself.

Minutes later, the police found themselves looking down at the body of a boy. He looked about 12 or 13 and was naked. The boy had probably only been in the ground a couple of days. One of the detectives immediately radioed police headquarters and requested a team of forensic experts.

A second body was soon discovered. As it began to grow dark, a fire engine with floodlights and two air extractors was brought in. The bodies of two more young boys were uncovered. One youth had been shot in the head and the other strangled with the cord from a set of Venetian blinds that was still knotted around his throat.

At 10pm, a silent and ashen-faced Henley was driven back to the police station. Two hours later the body count had risen to eight.

The men digging were exhausted and it was decided to stop for the night and resume work in the morning.

At 10am the next morning, after a visit from his mother, Wayne Henley was again sitting opposite a detective in the Pasadena Police's interview room. 'Tell me about the boys you procured,' the detective began.

Henley explained that he had first met Dean Corll two years earlier, while Dean was working in a candy factory. Dean had offered him $200 for every young boy he could bring along. At this point, Henley made a very significant admission: that he had been present when Dean Corll had killed some of the boys. This changed the whole situation. Until then, the police had assumed that they were dealing with an insatiable homosexual rapist and a youth who he had persuaded to help him procure boys. Now it looked as if Elmer Wayne Henley had been an active participant in the murders.

They were interrupted by a call from Houston Police headquarters. A man named Alton Brooks had turned up at the police station with his 18-year-old son David. He explained that David had known Dean Corll and wanted to tell the police about it. David Brooks was now giving a statement that implicated Henley in the murders.

When the detective hung up the phone he told the team manager on the other side of the desk, 'That was the lieutenant at Houston Homicide, who says he has a kid named David Brooks there, and Brooks is making a statement about you and Dean Corll.'

Strangely, Henley looked relieved, 'Good,' he said. 'Now I can tell you the whole story.'

The detectives did their best to show no emotion during the statement that followed, but it was difficult to look impassive while Henley described how he had lured boys he had known all his life into Dean Corll's lair.

There'd be liquor there, of course drugs. The boys would be plied with intoxicants until they could barely speak, and often they would simply pass out. When they woke up, they'd discover they were strapped and handcuffed to a 2in-by-4in wooden board. Here they'd be abused, tortured, and sexually assaulted for days.

Their pubic hairs were plucked out one at a time. Objects were inserted into their rectum and glass rods were shoved into their urethra and smashed. Genitals were removed, and all were sodomised. Sometimes they were strangled, other times they were shot. When a victim died, his body was discarded like yesterday's newspaper and the process of finding a new boy would begin again.

Detectives were stunned into silence. Henley was apparently an intended victim when he was taken to meet Corll in 1971. However, Dean Corll soon realised that Henley would make a good accomplice. He had lots of friends and would do anything for money.

The usual method of obtaining victims was to drive around until they spotted a likely victim and Corll would spin them a well-rehearsed line. Since there was already a teenager in the car, the boy would suspect nothing.

That was how Corll had picked up 13-year-old James Dreymala, a couple of days before. They had been parked in front of the grocery store when the boy rode past on his bicycle.

Dean Corll called him over and told him he had a lot of Coke bottles in his garage and if the kid would like to come along he could collect the deposits on them. So James Dreymala allowed Corll to put his bicycle in the back of his van. They drove to Corll's house on Lamar Drive, where the boy was raped, tortured and strangled.

At this point detectives received the latest report from the boat shed. Four more victims had been found in the last two hours, bringing the total to 12. Beside one of the bodies a set of genitals had been found in a plastic bag. It seemed that Corll did like to castrate some of his victims.

Henley's confession went on for two more hours. It was rambling and often incoherent, but detectives gathered that Henley had been present at the murder of at least nine boys. He admitted shooting one of them. The bullet had gone up the boy's nose and, stunned, the boy had looked at Henley and asked, 'Wayne, why did you shoot me?' Henley had simply pointed the gun at the boy's head and pulled the trigger again. This time, the boy died.

Detectives wanted to know whether Corll had buried any bodies in other places besides the boatshed.

'Yes,' Henley replied, 'there were some on the shores of Lake San Rayburn, and more on the beach at High Island some miles along the coast.'

An hour later, Henley had led the police into the woods by the shores of Lake San Rayburn. He showed them the sites of six graves before darkness made further digging impossible.

The latest news from the boatshed was that the parts of 17 bodies had now been found. Some of the bodies were so old that little more than bones remained.

The following morning the body count rose to 25 with the uncovering of another two bodies at Lake San Rayburn. By midday, a convoy of police and reporters were on their way south to High Island where Henley insisted more victims were buried. Two more bodies were found that afternoon, making the total 27.

Later, four more would be uncovered on the beach. Two others mentioned by Henley were never discovered.

On Friday morning while Elmer Wayne Henley was still at Lake San Rayburn, police back in Houston were taking a second statement from David Brooks. He gave the police a detailed account of Dean Corll's career of homicidal perversions. Though Brooks maintained that he had never taken an active part in the killings detectives suspected that he was lying. Brooks was eventually convicted of participating in one of the murders.

Brooks and Corll first met in 1967 when Brooks was 12 and Corll was 30. Corll gave Brooks, whose parents were splitting up at the time, something he needed badly – affection. Brooks began to see a great deal of his friend, treating Corll's apartment as his second home. It is probable that 1970 was the year that Corll committed his first murder.

Jeffery Alan Konen, a 21-year-old student at the University of Texas Austin disappeared on 20 September 1970 while hitchhiking to his parents' home in Houston. He was last seen at 6pm thumbing a lift. It seems likely that Corll picked him up and took him home.

Jeffery Konen's body was found three years later on High

Island beach. It was so decomposed that forensic scientists were unable to determine the cause of death, but they were able to establish that his body had been bound hand and foot, and that Konan had probably been brutally raped.

What made Corll's murderous missions so easy was the teenage drug culture of the Heights. In that poor rundown district, most of the kids were bored and discontent. The mere suggestion of a party was enough to make their eyes light up. They smoked pot when they could afford it and popped pills. Acrylic paint was the cheapest way of getting a quick high. The fact that most of the kids were permanently stoned gave another big advantage to a predatory pervert like Dean Corll who would get his perverted kicks for a couple of dollars. Occasional disappearances in the area caused little stir because the rate of runaways from the Heights was so high.

Not long after the murder of Jeffery Konan, David Brooks walked into Corll's apartment unannounced and found Corll naked. In another room were two naked boys each strapped to a plywood board. Corll demanded indignantly to know what Brooks was doing there and ordered him to leave. Later, he told Brooks that he had killed both boys and offered to give him a car as a price for his silence. He made good his promise and bought Brooks a green Corvette.

One unknown youth was picked up sometime in November 1970 and taken back to Corll's apartment. Corll raped and murdered the boy while Brooks looked on.

The Candy Man's appetite for murder was growing. Many of the boys he had befriended in the days that he worked in a candy factory – hence the nickname –now noticed that he was becoming bad-tempered and secretive and stopped calling round.

On 15 December 1970, two boys were enticed to an apartment that Corll had rented on Columbia Street. They were 14-year-old James Glass and his 15-year-old friend Danny Yates. Both had been to church with James Glass's father. Glass had already been to Corll's apartment once and had taken a great liking to Corll. This time, both boys ended up on the plywood board after which they were strangled. By this time, Corll had decided that he needed to rent somewhere closer than High Island Beach and San Rayburn to bury his bodies, so he rented the boat shed on Silver Bell Street. The boys were buried there.

Corll had enjoyed the double murder so much that he was eager to try it again. Six weeks later in January 1971, two brothers Donald and Jerry Waldrop, aged 17, and 13, were strangled and buried in the boat shed. Brooks admitted, 'I believe I was present when they were buried'.

On the 29 May 1971, 13-year-old David Hilligiest disappeared on his way to the swimming pool, his friend George Winkle aged 16, vanished the same day.

Ruben Watson, 17, went to the cinema on the afternoon of 17 August 1971 with a couple of dollars borrowed from his grandmother. He later called his mother at work to say that he would meet her at 7.30pm. He never showed up. Brooks later admitted being present when Ruben was murdered.

Another friend of Elmer Wayne Henley's was 14-year-old Rhonda Williams. She was a typical Heights teenager, living with a one-parent family and determined to leave home as soon as possible. Rhonda craved affection and security and thought she had found them in 18-year-old Frank, her boyfriend. He was a strong-willed young man who was saving up so they could get married as soon as possible.

On 24 February 1972, Frank failed to return home from work and was never seen again. Rhonda was shattered and indeed, over a year later, was still depressed. On the evening of 7 August 1973, she told Elmer Henley that she intended to run away from home that very night, and Henley took her over to Corll's house in Pasadena.

On Monday, 13 August 1973, five days after the death of Dean Corll, a grand jury began to hear evidence against Henley and Brooks. The first witnesses were Rhonda Williams and Tim Kerley, who had almost been Corll's latest victims. It was clear that Henley had brought Tim to Corll's house to be raped and murdered which is why he had told Tim that he could have got fifteen hundred dollars for him. When Corll had snarled, 'You've spoiled everything,' he had meant that the arrival of Rhonda Williams now made it impossible to murder Tim.

Then it seems Corll had thought of another solution, to kill all three of them. After listening to the evidence of the various teenagers, the jury indicted Henley and Brooks on various murder charges.

The trial was held in San Antonio, Texas. It began in June 1974 and ran into July. The jury rejected the insanity pleas put forward by the defence. Henley was convicted on nine counts of first-degree murder and sentenced to six consecutive 99-year life imprisonments, a total of 594 years in prison. Brooks was convicted on only one count and received only one term of life imprisonment.

THE MILWAUKEE
MONSTER

Name: Jeffrey Lionel Dahmer
Date of birth: 21 May 1960
Location: Milwaukee, USA
Type of murderer: Cannibal
Body count: 17
Sentence: 15 life sentences
Outcome: Murdered in prison by fellow inmates

'I really screwed up this time.'
JEFFREY DAHMER

Milwaukee is one of the most beautiful cities in the American Midwest, with wide tree-lined avenues and a stunning harbour on Lake Michigan. It is a city created by wealth, but it also has its slum areas. One of the seedier districts of Milwaukee is 25th Street, with the population mainly underprivileged Blacks and Asians. Most of the people who live here, rent cheap one-room apartments for under $300 per month. It's also an area of boarded-up shops, homosexual bars, sleazy strip joints, midnight muggers and mini-skirted hookers.

Robert Rauth and Rolf Mueller, the two police officers in the patrol car cruising along 25th Street were looking forward to getting off duty in half and hour. It was 11.30pm, and although it was July, the night was cool. A figure in the distance made them screech to an abrupt halt. A slim naked black man was running towards them, a look of horror on his face. Handcuffs were hanging from his left wrist. His relief when he saw the police car was almost hysterical and the tale he babbled out was so extraordinary that the officers had difficulty following it. All they could gather was that a madman had been trying to kill him.

The police officers accompanied the man, who gave his name as Tracy Edwards, to the white two-storey Oxford Apartments. It was a government subsidised rooming house occupied almost exclusively by African-Americans. Edwards told them that he had been abducted by a man living in apartment 213, and since it would clearly not be a good idea to ring the doorbell of that apartment, they rang a different door bell.

They told the resident who answered the intercom that they were the police. The door lock released and the two police officers accompanied by Edwards, entered the building.

The tall good-looking white man who answered the door of 213 had blond hair and a wispy moustache. As he stood aside politely to let the police in he seemed perfectly calm and looked at Edwards as if he'd never seen him before. Both officers had a feeling that this was a false alarm, until they smelled the unpleasant odour of decay. It was not dissimilar to rotten eggs and wafted throughout the whole apartment. When they asked the man, who gave his name as Jeffrey Dahmer, why he had threatened Edwards, he looked contrite and almost sorrowful, explaining that he had just lost his job and had been drinking. They asked him for the key to the handcuffs and Dahmer looked nervous and tried to stall. When the police insisted, Dahmer refused and became hysterical. A violent struggle started and a resident from an adjoining apartment, who had come out to hear what all the ruckus was about, heard one of the policemen shout, 'The son of a bitch scratched me!' Moments later, Dahmer was face down on the floor in handcuffs and his rights were being read to him.

One of the officers called head quarters on his portable radio and asked them to run a check on their detainee. The answer came back quickly. Dahmer had a felony conviction for sexual assault on a 13-year-old boy. That supported the story that Edwards, now able to speak calmly, went on to tell them.

Thirty-two-year-old Tracy Edwards, a recent arrival from Mississippi, had met Dahmer about four hours earlier in a shopping mall. Edwards had been drinking with friends at the time and, when the tall man asked them back to his apartment for a party, they all agreed. Dahmer and Edwards had gone on ahead in a taxi to buy some beer while the others were told to follow on. What Edwards did not know was that Dahmer had deliberately given his friends the wrong address.

Edwards didn't like the smell in Dahmer's tiny apartment, nor the male pin-ups hanging on the wall (his own preference was for women), but he was fascinated by a fishtank

69

containing Chinese fighting fish. Dahmer told him that he liked to watch them fighting and that the combat always ended in one of the fish being killed. They sat on the sofa and drank beer. Edwards felt uncomfortable and kept glancing at the clock wondering what had happened to his mates. When the beer was finished, Dahmer handed him a rum and Coke. Not wanting to be a party pooper or offend, Edwards gulped down the ice-cold drink.

The movement of the fighting fish was hypnotic and, with all the alcohol, Edwards was beginning to feel drowsy. Dahmer kept asking him how he was feeling, then put his arm around him and whispered a suggestion about sexual foreplay. Edwards was instantly wide awake and announced that he was going. That was a mistake. Seconds later a handcuff was snapped around one of his wrists. Edwards struggled as Dahmer attempted to handcuff the other wrist. He felt a large butcher's knife push against his chest and Dahmer told him that he would kill him unless he undressed. Edwards knew that his only chance of survival was to agree to his demand.

Dahmer's face had changed from a charming drinking buddy into a frightening monster with piercing wild eyes. As Edwards began to slowly unbutton his shirt, trying to act naturally, Dahmer began to get aroused. He prodded the knife into Edwards's back and motioned towards the bedroom. Edwards walked towards it.

The smell in the room was nauseating. On the wall were numerous photographs, amateur shots that showed dismembered bodies and chunks of meat that looked like joints in a butcher's shop. Edwards struggled to breathe through fear of what was about to happen. The unpleasant smell seemed to come from a blue plastic barrel with a black lid that stood beneath the window. By now, the petrified Edwards had made a good guess as to what it contained.

Dahmer pushed Edwards on to the bed without uttering a word. He shoved a video of *The Exorcist* into the recorder, and proceeded to watch it. It was clear that Dahmer had a taste for the gruesome and the bizarre as he relished each and every violent scene. Edwards's only thought was of escape. Without daring to move a muscle, he slowly scanned the room looking for a way out. He noticed that there was an electronic lock on the bedroom door, but to his relief the door had not been closed. Edwards chose his moment carefully and asked Dahmer if he could use the toilet.

Dahmer reluctantly agreed and unlocked one side of the handcuffs, but first he insisted that he was going to take some photographs. If Edwards did not comply, he told him, he would cut his heart out and eat it. Edwards knew this was his one and only chance to escape and probably his last.

As Dahmer stood up to get his camera, his prisoner seized his opportunity. He swung his fist in a punch so hard that it knocked Dahmer sideways. Dahmer fell to the floor. The adrenaline ran through Edwards's body like an electric current as he attacked Dahmer with ferocity, kicking him in the stomach and leaving him on the floor like a wounded animal. He wrenched open the door and fled for his life.

When Edwards had finished telling his story to the shocked police officers they told him to stand outside in the hallway. Edwards wanted to leave, to go home to safety, but the police insisted he wait amongst the growing crowd of curious neighbours who had gathered in the dimly lit corridor. As the nosey neighbours tried to peer into the room, they saw

Dahmer lying on the floor, handcuffed. Then one of them saw a policeman open the door of the refrigerator and gasp, 'Oh my God, there's a goddamn head in here!'

That was the moment Dahmer began to scream, a horrible, bloodcurdling scream like a dying animal. His body contorted in convulsions, thrashing around on the floor and spitting and snarling like a rabid dog. One of the police officers rushed into the hallway shouting at the crowd to 'Get out of the way...' as he rushed downstairs to collect more shackles. When Dahmer's writhing body was finally secure, the officers resumed their search of the apartment. Within minutes, they realised they had discovered a gruesome mixture of slaughterhouse and torture chamber.

The freezer compartment of the refrigerator contained meat in plastic bags, one of which looked like a human heart. Another freezer contained three plastic bags, each one with a severed head inside.

Each face had a look of frozen horror, stiffened, motionless, silent witnesses to whatever bizarre fantasies Dahmer had indulged in. A filing cabinet contained three skulls, strangely, some had been painted grey. A box contained two more skulls and an album was full of more gruesome photographs. Two more skulls were found in a saucepan, while another pan contained severed hands and male genital organs. The stinking blue plastic barrel contained three male torsos. There was also a large vat of murky hydrochloric acid and an electric saw stained with blood made it clear how Dahmer had dismembered his victims. The stench was sickening. The shocked officers heaved and retched, unable to believe what they were seeing.

It was a matter of minutes before three detectives from the

homicide unit arrived at the apartment along with more uniformed police. The wide-eyed Dahmer was led away in handcuffs, still cursing, and screeching.

At the police station, Dahmer fully co-operated and confessed freely to his crimes. He told the police that over a period of 13 years he had murdered more than 17 young men. He also confessed that he was a cannibal. The black bags of meat in the freezer were intended to be eaten. He described how he had fried the biceps of one of his victims in vegetable oil. The threat to eat Tracy Edwards's heart had been no bluff. The only food in Dahmer's apartment had been potato chips, human meat and a jar of yellow mustard.

It had all started, Dahmer admitted to the police, in 1978 when he was only 18 years-old. His first victim had been a hitchhiker. He waited almost ten years before committing his second murder, but recently the rate of his killings had accelerated. He'd done three murders in the last two weeks and had attempted to kill Tracy Edwards only three days after his last murder. Dahmer was able to help the police establish the identity of the victims which comprised of 12 Blacks, one Laotian, one Hispanic and three Whites. Some of the names he remembered and some he did not. One victim Dahmer did remember was a young lad, a 14 -year-old Laotian called Konorak Singthasomphone.

The youngster had met Dahmer in front of the same shopping mall where the killer had later picked up Tracy Edwards. The boy agreed to return to Dahmer's apartment to allow him to take a couple of photographs. Unknown to the boy, Dahmer was the man who had enticed and sexually assaulted older brother three year earlier when he was 13. In September 1988, Dahmer had asked Konorak's brother back to his apartment. He had slipped a powerful sleeping drug into his drink and then sexually fondled him.

Somehow, the boy succeeded in staggering out on to the street and back home. The police were notified and Dahmer was charged with second-degree sexual assault and sentenced to a year in a correction programme which allowed him to continue to work during the day at a chocolate factory.

Now his younger brother, 14-year-old Konorak, found himself in the same apartment. He was also given drugged coffee and when he was unconscious, was stripped and raped. Once he'd had his way with him, Dahmer went out to buy some beer.

On the way back to his apartment, Dahmer saw to his horror that his naked victim was talking to two black teenage girls, obviously begging for help. Dahmer rushed over and tried to grab the boy. The girls clung on to him. One of them rang the police and within minutes two squad cars arrived. The irritable officers wanted to know what all the trouble was about. When Dahmer told them that the young man was his lover and they had merely had a quarrel, the police officers were inclined to believe him. He looked sober and because of the drugged coffee, Konorak looked drunk. The police officers decided to take Dahmer and his friend back to the apartment where Dahmer said they lived. While they waited on the doorstep, Dahmer then showed the police the Polaroid pictures of the boy in his underwear, convincing them that they really were lovers. The police had no way of knowing that the photographs had only been taken that evening and Dahmer told them that the 14-year-old was in fact 19. Meanwhile, Konorak sat on the sofa, dazed, but believing that his ordeal was over. His failure to deny what

Dahmer had been saying convinced the police that Dahmer must be telling the truth.

They left Dahmer with the 14-year-old in his apartment. The moment the police were gone Dahmer strangled Konorak, violated his corpse and took photographs as he dismembered it.

Jeffrey Dahmer was charged with 12 counts of murder all of which had taken place at Oxford Apartments since May 1990. But, according to Dahmer, his first murder had taken place 13 years earlier at his childhood home in Bath Township, northeastern Ohio.

At the time his parents were in the process of a bitter and messy divorce. Jeffrey had become accustomed to the sight of his parents quarrelling and had already learned to take refuge in alcohol. According to Jeffrey's confession, one day he'd found himself alone in the family house at 4480 West Bath Road. His father had already left and his mother and younger brother David were away visiting relatives. He'd been left with no money and there was very little food in the broken refrigerator. That evening, he explained, he decided to go out and look for some company.

It was not hard to find. A 19-year-old youth who had spent the day at a rock concert was hitch hiking home to attend his father's birthday party. Dahmer's battered, rusting Oldsmobile pulled up beside him and since the driver looked about his own age, he had climbed in. The two went back to Dahmer's house and drank some beer and talked about their lives. Dahmer found he liked his new friend a lot but, when the teenager looked at the clock and said he had to go, Dahmer begged him to stay. The boy told him he couldn't, so Dahmer picked up a dumbbell, struck him on the head and strangled him. He then dragged the body to the crawlspace under the house and dismembered it with a carving knife.

It may sound a formidable task but Dahmer was not entirely without experience of dissecting bodies. As a child he had been fascinated by road-kills and would take the dead animals' bodies and cut them up. He felt like a doctor or pathologist, stripping the animals of their flesh. He had day dreamed of dissecting a human being. Now he had had his wish. Dahmer wrapped up the body parts of the teenager in plastic bags and hid them under the house. After a couple of days the smell began to escape and Dahmer's mother, who was due back soon, was sure to notice the stench. So, under cover of darkness he took the plastic bags out to the wood, dug a shallow grave and buried them. But he was worried that even though the bags were now underground, children might come across the grave. He dug them up again, tipped out the body parts, stripped the flesh from the bones and smashed the bones to pieces with a sledgehammer. He scattered the fragments around the garden and the property next door. When his mother returned a couple of days later there was nothing to reveal that her son was now a killer.

Unfortunately, Dahmer was unable to recall the name of his victim. The Milwaukee Police telephoned the police of Bath Township and asked them if they had a missing-person case dated from mid-1978. They had. On 18 June, a youth named Stephen Hicks had left his home in Coventry Township to go to a rock concert. Friends had driven him there and they agreed to meet up with him that evening to take him home. Stephen failed to turn up at the meeting place and no trace of him was ever found. The Bath Township police had two photographs of Stephen Hicks on file. When they showed them to Jeffrey Dahmer, he casually said, 'Yes, that's him'.

The police went to Dahmer's old house to check his story. In the crawlspace under the building, the used a blood-detecting compound commonly known as luminal. Particles of blood can cling to surfaces for years and, although invisible to the naked eye, the luminal will make them glow. Sure enough, there were traces of human blood under the Dahmer house.

The following day more bones and three human teeth were found. Dental records eventually revealed that they had belonged to Stephen Hicks.

For nine years after the killing of Stephen Hicks, Dahmer had managed to keep his homicidal impulses under control. Three years in the army ended with a discharge for alcoholism. After a short stay in Florida Dahmer moved in with his grandmother in West Alice, south of Milwaukee, but he was still drinking heavily and had been in trouble with the police for causing a disturbance in a bar. The family were relieved when at last he found himself a job at the Ambrosia Chocolate factory in Milwaukee.

Jeffrey Dahmer soon discovered Milwaukee's gay bars, where he became known as a loner. It was not long before the regular customers noticed that he had a sinister habit. He would chat-up men and offer to buy them a beer, then drug them by spiking their drinks. Yet Dahmer's intention was clearly not to commit rape. He simply wanted to try out the drugs as a kind of experiment to find out how much he could administer and to see how fast they worked. When one of his drinking buddies ended up in hospital, the owner of the club told him he was barred.

Dahmer began building up resentment and frustration which would explode into murder.

On the 15 September, Jeffrey Dahmer was drinking at a gay hang-out called Club 219 and met a 24-year-old named Stephen Tuomi. They decided to go to bed and went to the Ambassador Hotel where they took a cheap room which cost $43.00 for the night. Dahmer claims that he could not recall much about that night and admitted that they drank themselves into a stupor. When Dahmer woke up he said that Tuomi was dead.

He had blood coming from his mouth and strangulation marks on his throat. For Dahmer it was a terrifying situation. He was alone in a hotel room with a corpse and the desk clerk was likely to call up at any moment to see if the room had been vacated. Dahmer solved his problem by going out and buying a large suitcase into which he stuffed Tuomi's body. He then took a taxi back to his grandmother's house where he had his own basement apartment. The taxi driver helped him drag the heavy suitcase indoors. Once alone, he dismembered the body, put the parts into plastic bags and put them out for the garbage collector. He performed his task of disposal with such efficiency that when the police were investigating the disappearance of Stephen Tuomi they were unable to find the slightest sign of any crime and so was unable to charge Dahmer with the murder.

Clearly, this second killing was a watershed in Dahmer's life. Dahmer realised that murder and dismemberment were necessary to satisfy his deviant, sexual impulses. The fifteen murders that followed leave no possible doubt of it.

Ernest Miller was a student dancer and was 22 years old. He was from Chicago. Dahmer picked him up outside a bookshop in Milwaukee and took him back to his apartment. After drugging Miller, Dahmer cut his throat and reduced his body to a skeleton.

Nineteen-year-old gay model, Curtis Straughter, was strangled by Dahmer in February 1991. His body was dismembered.

Errol Lindsey, 19; Tony Hughes, 31; Matt Turner, 20; Oliver Lacy, 23; Joseph Bradeholt, 25; Jeremiah Weinberger, 23; all six of these men were killed by Jeffrey Dahmer between 7 April and 15 July 1991. Parts of their bodies were found in his apartment.

In January 1992, Jeffrey Dahmer was tried for the murders of seventeen boys and young men. He pleaded guilty but insane. On 15 February, he was found guilty and sentenced to fifteen consecutive terms of life imprisonment, which meant that he could never be released.

In a grisly postscript to the case, Dahmer was beaten to death at the Columbia County Correctional Institution in the early-morning hours of Monday, 28 November 1994 by fellow inmate Christopher Scarver.

THE STOCKWELL STRANGLER

Name: Kenneth Erskine
Date of birth: Unknown
Location: Stockwell, London, England
Type of murderer: Sadist
Body count: 7 murders, 1 attempted
Sentence: Life
Outcome: Imprisoned in Broadmoor Hospital

'It tries to think for me. It says it will kill me if it can get me.'
KENNETH ERSKINE, ON BEING HAUNTED BY A WHISPERED FEMALE VOICE
THAT HE SAID HE HEARD EMANATING FROM WALLS AND DOORS

It was summer – the dead of night. Frederick Prentice, a 73-year-old pensioner, was lying in bed in a South London old people's home where he lived when he heard footsteps in the passage outside. As quickly as he was able he got up and sat on the bed and saw a shadow through a glass door – a stranger was opening his door and entering his room. The old man shouted at the person to get out but the shadowy figure gestured to him to be quiet and ran to his bed and jumped on top of him.

'I was absolutely petrified,' said the frail Mr Prentice, 'but there was nothing I could do, he was sitting on my chest with his fingers clutching my neck, I thought I was a goner.'

As if in a dream Mr Prentice remembered screaming as loudly as he could, but the door had closed and no one could hear him. He was disabled and barely able to struggle, while the stranger was young and strong. 'I kept pleading with him to let me go,' said Mr Prentice. '"Take what you want and leave", but he took no notice, it was a nightmare.'

Mr Prentice recalled the terrifying moment when the stranger was trying to strangle him. Three times he felt pressure being applied to his throat and on the final occasion as Mr Prentice recalled, 'the stranger threw my head against the wall and ran off'. Mr Prentice's attacker had hauled him from the bed and thrown him against the wall. The blow almost knocked him out, he had slumped to the floor too petrified to move. He was even too frightened to watch him leave. Later he recalled his ordeal. He said it brought back horrible memories of that night, and the horror will always stay with him. There was one other detail he remembered about his attacker. He said the stranger had a terrifying toothy grin.

Mr Prentice was attacked at 3am on 27 June 1986. The strangler's reign of terror had begun just three months earlier. It developed into a short and brutal killing spree. After carrying out two killings in two months, the strangler murdered six people within a space of a month. All of his victims were pensioners and five were sexually assaulted before or after they were strangled.

Victim number one was 78-year-old spinster Nancy Emms, who lived in West Hill Road, Wandsworth. Miss Emms was strangled and sodomised in her bed on 9 April.

Victim number two was 67-year-old widow Janet Cockett, who was strangled in her bed in her first-floor flat on the Overton Road Estate, Stockwell, on 9 June.

Mr Prentice was attacked, but survived his ordeal on the night of 27 June. The following night the strangler carried out two murders, strangling two elderly residents at the same old folks' home in Stockwell Park Crescent. The victims were 84-year-old Valentine Gleim and 94-year-old Zbigniew Stabrawa. The strangler had claimed four victims over a period of eleven weeks. The Police now realised there was a serial killer on the loose and intensified their efforts to find him.

For his fifth murder, the strangler travelled north of the Thames to the fashionable London borough of Islington, where he murdered 82-year-old William Carmen in his bed at his flat in Sybil Thorndike House, Clephane Road, on 8 July, four days before his sixth victim, 75-year-old Trevor Thomas, who was found dead in his bath at his home in Barton Court, Jeffreys Road, Clapham.

On 20 July, the strangler returned to the scene of his second killing at Overton Road Estate in Stockwell, where he had murdered Mrs Cockett. This time the victim was 75-year-old pensioner William Downs.

Two days later, the strangler attacked his final victim. She was Florence Tisdall, an 80-year-old woman who was partially deaf and blind and who could only move around with the help of a walking frame. Mrs Tisdall lived alone in a flat in fashionable Ranelagh Gardens Mansions near Putney Bridge on the Thames. She too, like most of the victims, was found strangled in bed.

All in all, it was a horrifying catalogue of crime. Here was a serial killer – a man who, not content with a single murder, was searching for more victims to satisfy some inner craving which had to be, partly at least, sexually motivated. The string of deaths was big news in South London as soon as a murder occurred. But it was not until Florence Tisdall was found strangled that the killings hit the headlines nationally. Suddenly, people were told, there was a gruesome killer on the loose, strangling and sexually assaulting helpless pensioners.

The man was nicknamed the Stockwell Strangler, because most of the murders had occurred in and around Stockwell, a small corner of South London consisting of a mixture of rundown council estates and rows of small terraced houses. The newspapers were quick to print every gory detail they could uncover. The killer, they told their readers, put some of his victims through a bizarre ritual after they died, folding their arms across their chests and tucking them up neatly in bed.

By this time, more than 150 detectives were working on the case. But they had a serious dilemma. On the one hand, the last thing they wanted to do was to frighten elderly people by publicising the killings. On the other hand, the killer clearly had to be caught, and to do that, the public's help was needed. So the national papers went big on the story. Help the Aged set up a special help line for elderly people who were scared by the killings. Newspapers reported that the 'Stockwell Strangler' had struck terror into the hearts of pensioners throughout South London, and that detectives feared he was growing more dangerous and desperate by the day.

Little was know about the Stockwell strangler's earlier life before he was caught. Some psychologists thought that the killer might be a man who hated his parents. Leading psychologist had a theory that the murderer had developed a homicidal hatred of old people when he speculated that the killer probably bore a deep-seated grudge against his own parents, who were probably elderly, or against his grandparents. He seemed to want revenge on perfectly innocent old people, probably for some incident in his past. It could be that he suffered at the hands of his mother or father that could have led him to take terrible revenge.

Kenneth Erskine was finally identified as the Stockwell strangler. He was brought up in Putney, in a council flat by his English mother, Margaret, after she and her Antiguan husband, Charles were divorced. Margaret had three other sons and, at first, Kenneth seemed to be a perfectly normal chubby cheerful little boy. But Kenneth soon became difficult to control and received his education at a series of schools for maladjusted children.

This time in his life was marred by outbursts and unprovoked violence against the teaching staff and other pupils. He appeared to inhabit a fantasy world where he took on the role of Lawrence of Arabia, attacking and tying up smaller, weaker children. He even tried drowning them on trips to the swimming pool, holding their heads under the water until staff intervened. Homicidal tendencies were already there. As he grew into a teenager, Kenneth twice tried to hang his younger brother John.

On one occasion, he attacked a teacher stabbing him in the hand with a pair of scissors. The psychiatric nurse, who tried to examine him, was taken hostage by him as he held a pair of scissors to her throat. Whenever female staff tried to show him affection, he would do his best to shock them by rubbing himself against them or exposing his genitals.

By the time he was 16 Kenneth had turned to drugs and it all became too much for his mother, who kicked him out of the family home and disowned him. He never saw any members of his family again, and his tendency towards violence grew worse and worse.

After leaving home, Erskine spent seven years drifting through the twilight world of London's homeless and rootless. He lived mainly in squats in Brixton and Stockwell, indulging in petty crime. He carried out several burglaries and significantly preyed on elderly people. He appeared in court eight times, served four jail terms, and his life was so empty of friends and meaning that detectives were unable to trace a single possession of his, or find any friends. When his photograph was finally released to the press in an attempt to obtain evidence, there were scores of phone calls, but not single person came forward to say they had know him.

While in Borstal for burglary in 1982, Erskine shocked staff by painting pictures of elderly people in bed with gags in their mouths, or burned to death or had daggers in them. Other drawings showed headless figures with blood spurting from their necks. He pinned the ghoulish drawings above his bed. It was a chilly taste of what was to come. It alarmed the prison doctors enough for them to ask the authorities not to free him, but he was released, and four years later embarked on his killing spree.

THE STOCKWELL STRANGLER

1986 was a terrifying time for pensioners in South London. Their terror was made worse by descriptions of the killer as 'the faceless monster', so called because detectives had built up an idea of what the strangler wore, but did not know what he looked like.

Mr Prentice, the only man who had survived the attack by the strangler, said that the assailant was white, aged between 20 and 30 years old, five foot eight inches tall, with short dark hair and a face reddened by suntan.

Detectives confirmed that elderly people were right to feel frightened. Police patrols were stepped up and Scotland Yard appealed to friends and neighbours to check on old people living alone. People were warned to lock doors and secure windows.

The police and the public had been particularly shocked by Florence Tisdall's death. Mrs Tisdall, a long-time widow was 80 years old, half-blind and defenceless. Her body was discovered in a flat in Ranelagh Gardens Mansions, Putney Bridge, where she had lived for the past 60 years. The day she was killed Mrs Tisdall had enjoyed watching the royal wedding of Prince Andrew and Sarah Ferguson on television. She had even had her hair done especially for the occasion.

As she was frail, any shouts for help she might have uttered would have been drowned out by the noise from the celebration disco in the Eight Bells pub opposite her Fulham home. Like many old ladies, Mrs Tisdall loved cats. She had three of her own, and regularly took in strays. Tragically, the police reckoned that her cats might have indirectly led her to her death, because the strangler climbed into her flat through the window she used to leave open to allow them in.

There was another lead the police were following at the time. They had thought it was possible that the strangler was someone who had regular access to old people's homes. They paid particular attention to anyone who was known to have recently lost his job at an old people's home.

At one point, more than 150 detectives were working on the inquiry logging details from five incident rooms throughout London on to the Home Office computer. Then suddenly the police got the breakthrough they needed. A palm print found at the scene of one of the murders matched prints already on police files. A squad of 20 officers swooped and arrested Kenneth Erskine, a 23-year-old man. Erskine was arrested collecting benefit at Keyworth House, a DHSS office in Southwark, South London, on the morning of 28 July 1986. He surrendered without a struggle and was taken to nearby Clapham Police Station for questioning.

The Stockwell strangler was behind bars, but problems still remained for police. For one thing, virtually nothing was known about Kenneth Erskine. The police had no idea where he had been living, or where his possessions were. The only clothes and shoes they had of his to match up with forensic evidence discovered at the scenes of the crimes were the ones he was wearing when he was arrested. Secondly, the inquiry team quickly realised that Kenneth Erskine was mentally subnormal. He behaved strangely when being questioned and denied all knowledge of the killings. It became obvious that there was going to be absolutely no possibility of a coherent confession from the Stockwell Strangler.

On 30 July 1986, Kenneth Erskine was charged with the murders of Janet Cockett and William Downs, both of whom had lived in the Overton Road Estate in Stockwell. Shortly afterwards, he was also charged with the murders of William Carmen, Valentine Gleim and Zbigniew Stabrawa. He was also charged with the attempted murder of Frederick Prentice, the only witness able to make an identification of the suspect.

On 13 April 1987, Kenneth Erskine was sent for trial at the Old Bailey, accused of strangling seven pensioners. In court, Kenneth presented a pathetic figure, grinning and nodding when he meant to say no, and shaking his head when he meant to say yes. When questioned by lawyers Kenneth stayed stubbornly silent and fantasised.

He told the psychologist he was haunted by a whispering woman's voice which came out of the walls and doors and gave him dizzy spells. He claimed the voice tried to control him and that he couldn't fight it. 'It tries to think for me,' he said. 'It says it will kill me if it can get me. It blanks things out from my mind. I don't remember killing anyone. I may have done it without knowing it.'

A further nine months passed until, on12 January 1988, the jury had been selected and the Old Bailey trial began.

The prosecutor described Erskine as 'a killer who liked killing'. The killing he said was 'wanton'. He said that, Erskine had apparently played with his victims, strangled them slowly with one hand, while uttering the word 'kill'. He would place the other hand over their mouths. When he murdered Florence Tisdall, he used enough pressure to break her neck. In each case but one, where a victim was found in the bath, the victims were found lying in bed, the bedclothes having been tidied and the bed clothes had been pulled up to the chin. He said this was apparently done to prevent anyone suspecting foul play.

In five of the cases, involving two of the women and three of the men, there was evidence of sexual assault or interference. It is not generally possible to say whether that had occurred before or after the victim was dead, but in each case it took the form of buggery.

In the summing up, it was said that Kenneth Erskine had the mental age of 11, and a very poor memory, but this did not render him incapable of testifying on his own behalf. Those who are simple and children of 11 and younger can, and do, give evidence in court.

But he gave a warning to the jury, the only question for you is 'did he do these things, that is something you must decide on the evidence, coolly, without emotion, unaffected by the horrific nature of some of the things you have heard.'

The jury found Kenneth Erskine guilty on all seven counts of murder, and on 29 January 1988, he was sent to jail for forty years.

'I recommend to the Secretary of State that you serve a minimum of forty years.' He added, 'I waste no further words in cataloguing the chilling horror of what you did.'

Kenneth Erskine, who had repeatedly smiled and grinned during the trial, appeared close to tears, then seemed to control himself. After grimacing slightly, the Stockwell Strangler was led away to the cells to begin the longest minimum term for murder in the history of British crime.

THE BROOKLYN VAMPIRE

Name: Hamilton Albert Fish
Date of birth: 19 May 1870
Location: Brooklyn, USA
Type of murderer: Masochistic cannibal
Body count: 16
Sentence: Death
Outcome: Executed

'The supreme thrill of my life!'
ALBERT FISH, ON LEARNING THAT HE WAS TO BE ELECTROCUTED

'My dear Mrs Budd,

'In 1894, a friend of mine shipped as a deckhand on the steamer *Tacoma*, Captain John Davis. They sailed from San Francisco to Hong Kong, China. On arriving there, he and two others went ashore and got drunk. When they returned, the boat was gone. At that time, there was a famine in China.

Meat of any kind was from one to three dollars a pound. So great was the suffering among the very poor that all the children under twelve were sold to the butchers to be cut up and sold as food in order to keep others from starving. A boy or girl under fourteen was not safe in the street. You could go to any shop and ask for steak, chops or stew meat. Part of the naked body of a boy or girl would be brought out and just what you wanted cut from it. A boy's or girl's behind, which is the sweetest part of the body and sold as veal cutlets, brought the highest price. John stayed there so long he acquired a taste for human flesh. On his return to New York, he stole two boys – one seven and one eleven. He took them to his home, stripped them naked, tied them in a closet, and then burned everything they had on. Several times every day and night he spanked them, tortured them, to make their meat good and tender. First he killed the eleven-year-old boy, because he had the fattest ass, and of course the most meat on it. Every part of his body was cooked and eaten except the head, bones and guts. He was roasted in an oven, boiled, broiled, fried and stewed. The little boy was next. He went the same way.

'At that time I was living at 409 East 100th Street. John often told me how good human flesh was and I made up my mind to taste it. On Sunday, June 3rd 1928, I called on you at 406 West 16th Street, brought you a pot of cheese and strawberries. We had lunch. Gracie sat on my lap and kissed me.

'I made up my mind to eat her. On the pretence of taking her to a party, you said, yes, she could go. I took her to an empty house in Westchester. I had already picked it out. When we got there, I told her to remain outside. She picked wild flowers. I went upstairs and stripped all my clothes off. I knew if I did not I would get blood on them. When I was ready, I went to the window and called her. Then I hid in the closet until she was in the room. When she saw me all naked she began to cry and tried to run downstairs. I grabbed her, and she said she would tell her mamma. First I stripped her naked – how did she kick, bite and scream! I choked her to death, then cut her in small pieces so I could take the meat to my rooms, cook and eat it. How sweet and tender her little ass was, roasted in the oven. It took me nine days to eat her entire body. I did not fuck her, though. I could have. I wished I had. She died a virgin.' – *Letter written by Albert Fish to the parent of one of his murder victims*

Albert Fish looked like every child's favourite grandfather, but behind the quiet façade of his silver hair and moustache lay a hideous monster that preyed on the young and the innocent with his horrific instruments of hell – a meat cleaver, a butcher's knife and a saw. He later admitted to molesting more than 400 children over a twenty-year period, and, one of the shocked psychiatrists who examined him described his life as one of unparalleled perversity.

After his capture, Fish blamed the conditions of his childhood for his crimes. He was abandoned at the age of five and placed in an orphanage where he saw and experienced his first brutal acts of sadism. Fish had been born into a respectable family, in 1870 in Washington DC, and later married and raised six children. He had little education and mostly worked as a handy man or painter.

In January, 1917, Albert Fish's wife ran away with a man called John Straube, a slow witted handy man who lodged with the Fish family. Albert returned from work one day to find the house deserted and stripped of its furniture. Mrs Fish was apparently a bit odd herself. She once returned to her husband with John at her side, and asked if they could move in with her family. Albert said that she could, but her lover could not, so she agreed and sent John away. Days later, Albert discovered that she had actually hidden John in the attic and he had lurked there while she had smuggled food up to him. Again, Albert told her that she could stay but John had to leave. They both left and the family never saw Mrs Fish again.

Soon after, Albert began to behave very strangely. He took his young family up to their summer house, Wisteria Cottage, in Westchester County, New York. They would watch terrified as he climbed the nearby hill, shook his fist at the sky and repeatedly screamed, 'I am Christ'.

But the sensation of acute suffering, torment, torture, agony and pain seemed to delight Albert, whether inflicting it on him self or others. He took strange pleasure in being whipped and paddled on the backside with a rowing oar.

Albert encouraged his own children to paddle his backside until it bled, often using an oar that was studded with 1.5in nails. He even answered classified ads placed in windows by lonely women seeking husbands. Albert told the lovelorn ladies that he was not interested in marriage but in their willingness to paddle him. Albert was a weirdo and behaved in a bizarre, creepy, spooky way. He had peculiar, abnormal, deviant habits, the more distressing and painful the better he liked it. One of Albert's pleasures was inserting a large number of needles into his body, mostly into his genital region, losing track of some as they sank out of sight. At one time, when inserting needles under his own fingernails, Albert said, 'If only pain, were not so painful'.

He also burnt himself with hot irons and pokers, while on others he would soak cotton balls in alcohol, insert them into his anus and set them on fire.

On nights of the full moon, Albert's children said that he would eat huge quantities of raw meat. Over the years, he collected a great number of books and magazines, and anything he could lay his hands on regarding cannibalism. He carried the most gruesome article on the subject with him at all times. Before he turned to murder, Albert had been examined by psychiatrists several times, but he was always released and judged disturbed but sane.

Although he never divorced his first wife, Albert married three more times, enjoying a sex life which court psychiatrists would describe as 'unparalleled perversity'.

In jail, authorities compiled a list of 18 sexual perversions practised by Fish including coprophagia (the consumption of human excrement), scarification (mutilating yourself during sex), bestiality (having sex with animals), necrophilia (having sex with dead bodies), and paedophilia (having sex with children). Tracing his sadomasochism back to the age of five or six when he began to relish bare-bottom paddling in the orphanage, Albert's obsession with pain was focused primarily on children. He maintained that he was ordered by God to castrate young boys, and he molested children of both sexes as he travelled around the USA. Police confidently linked him with at least 100 sexual attacks in 23 states, from New York to Wyoming, but Albert felt slighted by their estimate, declaring, 'I have had children in every state,' and placing his own tally of victims at closer to 400.

When or where Albert Fish first became a murderer is unknown. He confessed to six killings and referred vaguely to dozens more. Although the victims, dates and places were lost to his hazy memory, he did confess to murdering a man in Wilmington, Delaware; mutilating and torturing to death a mentally retarded boy in New York in 1910; killing a Negro boy in Washington in 1919; molesting and killing four-year-old William Gaffney in 1929, and strangling to death five-year-old Francis McDonald on Long Island in 1934. But the most shocking murder carried out by Albert Fish was the abduction and horrific slaughter of Gracie Budd in 1928. Her abduction led to a manhunt that lasted for six years.

The police had given up hope of ever solving her mysterious disappearance, until they got a slender clue from an anonymous letter sent to Mr & Mrs Budd six years after their daughter's disappearance.

The first time Albert Fish met the Budds, a hardworking New York family, he introduced himself in a way that never raised their suspicions. Albert Budd, Gracie's father, earned a modest living as a doorman, and there never seemed to be enough money with which to take care of his entire family, which comprised his wife, Delilah, 18-year-old Edward, ten-year-old Albert Jr, ten-year-old Grace and the youngest child, five-year-old Beatrice. To help his father make ends meet, Edward advertised in the 27 May 1928 issue of the New York World Telegram, for a job. His ad read, 'Young man, 18, wishes position in the country', followed by his name and address.

That same afternoon, a smartly dressed Albert Fish answered the ad and showed up at the Budds' home in the Chelsea district of Manhattan. He introduced himself as Mr Frank Howard, a farmer from Long Island who was willing to pay

$15 a week to a strong young worker. The family could scarcely believe Edward's luck and good fortune, and quickly invited Fish into the house. After hearing Albert's description of the farm, Edward readily accepted the position. Fish promised to return next week and take not only Edward out to the farm, but his friend Willy, as well. Howard stressed that he had enough work for both young men.

Albert did not return as promised the following Saturday, 2 June, but he did send an apologetic telegram and arrived on Monday instead. Impressed by his manners, the Budds greeted him warmly and invited him to stay for lunch.

Albert behaved just like a visiting grandfather and passed out treats and dollar bills to the young children, who squealed with delight. He gave two of the bills to Edward and Willy so they could go to the movies, and promised to return after he had attended a prior engagement later that evening to take them to his farm. But it was Gracie, the radiant little ten-year-old, who caught Fish's eye. He watched mesmerised like a stoat to a snake as Gracie danced and hummed a song. Her huge brown eyes, pale skin and soft pink lips were hypnotic as he leered, 'Let's see how good a counter you are' as he handed her a huge wad of bills to count. The Budds were a poor family and flabbergasted by the amount money that the old man was carrying around with him.

'Ninety-two dollars and fifty cents,' Gracie squealed.

'My, my. What a bright little girl!' 'Mr Howard' said giving her the fifty cents to buy candy for herself.

He then asked Gracie's trusting parents if they'd permit him to take her to a children's birthday party at the home of his married sister at 137th Street and Columbus. The Budds agreed and Gracie left with Albert, holding on to his hand

and still wearing the white dress that she'd worn to church that morning. The Budds waved goodbye to their little girl as she skipped alongside Fish down the street and out of sight. They never saw her again.

When Gracie did not return that evening with Mr Howard, the Budds were concerned but assumed that perhaps the party had gone on late and she had most likely spent the night with Mr Howard's sister. They tried hard to convince themselves of this, even into the following morning when there was still no sign of little Gracie.

Finally, Albert Budd decided to go to the address himself and find his beloved daughter. Frantically he scoured the streets until he found that the address where Frank Howard's sister supposedly lived did not exist. Albert Budd was beside himself. Breathless he ran up and down the streets searching for Gracie. Stopping anyone willing to listen to his crying, babbling story of his missing daughter.

By the time he reached the police station the distraught Albert Budd was at his wits' end. He shook uncontrollably as he told his story to veteran detective, William King. It didn't take the police long to find that there was no Frank Howard with a farm on Long Island. This also meant that there was no real clue to the abductor's true identity. The man had covered his tracks well. He even retrieved his telegram that had been sent to the Budds, telling them that he was going to complain to Western Union because the telegram had been addressed incorrectly. The detective and other members of the bureau started a long and arduous search for the Western Union's copy of the telegram. It was the only link that they had with Gracie's kidnapper, and three postal clerks spent more than 15 hours sifting through tens of thousands of telegrams with detectives before they found the one that Howard had sent. The only clue it provided was that it had been sent from an office in East Harlem.

The idea of searching every home in that part of the city was at first considered, but then abandoned. It was a physical impossibility. Detectives then focused on another slim lead, a small piece of cheese and a carton of strawberries that Howard had purchased for Mrs Budd. He had told her that they were fresh from his farm.

Investigators scoured the East Harlem area until they found the delicatessen where Howard had bought the cheese and they also found the street peddler who had sold him the strawberries. The peddler described the man in detail, but could recall nothing else significant about him, so that trail also went cold.

Little Gracie Budd's disappearance started a wide-scale search through New York City, particularly when the detectives and the family went to the media with the story. Gracie's photo appeared on the front page of the newspapers and hundreds of tips and leads were sent in from an angry and panicked public. Thousands of circulars were printed and sent out to police departments throughout the United States and Canada but without any real result. The Budds grew more and more despondent when lead after lead went nowhere. A couple of months after Gracie had vanished all of the most experienced investigators had given up the case as hopeless. All, that is, except William King.

King was already a legend in New York's law-enforcement circles, and was the only investigator not to give up hope on Gracie. A day never went by when he didn't think of the little girl or her grieving parents. He promised to follow up on any long shots and to look into every lead that crossed his desk.

At one point, King was sure that he was on to his man when he received a file on a grey-haired conman and forger called Albert Corthill who was on the run for trying to abduct a little girl from an adoption agency. King tracked Corthill for months, chasing him from city to city. He finally caught up with him, but was crushed to find out that Corthill had been in prison in Seattle when Gracie had been taken.

Corthill was to be one of two strong leads that King pursued over two long years. Another suspect, Edward Pope, was also arrested and charged with Gracie's kidnapping, however, Mrs Budd – the principal witness in the case – admitted in court that she had picked out the wrong man. It turned out that Pope had been blamed for the kidnapping by his vindictive ex-wife. Pope was subsequently released.

Around the same time that Corthill and Pope were being investigated by the police, another grey-haired old man was arrested in New York and charged with sending obscene materials, mostly letters, through the mail. The letters were sent by a man pretending to be a well-known Hollywood movie producer. In the letters he offered to give large amounts of money to women who agreed to engage in sadomasochist orgies. After his arrest he was committed to the psychiatric ward at Belle Vue for a ten-day period of observation. While there, the letter-writer claimed that while his friends knew him as Albert, his real name was Hamilton Fish.

Albert Fish remained at Belle Vue for nearly thirty days in the winter of 1930. He was polite and co-operative and his doctors deemed him sane, although his sexual problems they attributed to dementia caused by advancing age. He was thought harmless and was released from hospital into the care of his daughter, Anna.

Meanwhile, years were passing in the Gracie Budd case, and despite Detective King's ongoing efforts, it seemed that the mystery of Gracie's disappearance would never be solved. Then on 11 November 1934, six years after her daughter had been abducted, Mrs Budd received an unsigned and anonymous letter in the mail.

The letter claimed to be from a friend from someone named, Captain John Davis. According to the letter-writer, Captain Davis was a seafaring man, and on one trip to China developed the taste for human flesh, mainly the flesh of children. His letter then described in graphic terms how, after returning from New York, Captain Davis had kidnapped and murdered two young boys, cooking their flesh and eating it. After learning from Davis that the flesh of children was good and tender, the deranged letter-writer had decided to try it for himself. He had visited the Budds' home for lunch and taken the girl home with him.

Mrs Budd sobbed hysterically as the letter went into great detail of how little Gracie had been killed – the sick killer was actually bragging about what and how he had snubbed out the little girl's life and ate her bit by bit. After the horrific letter, investigators went into action, pulling out all stops to find the monster who had written it.

The investigation was again led by Detective King who had delayed his retirement, two years earlier, so he could continue to work on the Gracie Budd case. King immediately found Mr Howard's original telegram, and there was no doubt about it, the handwriting was the same. King used a microscope on the letter and discovered an almost indiscernible design – 'NYPCBA' –on the flap of the envelope. A quick search in the Manhattan telephone directory revealed the letters to stand for the New York Private Chauffeurs' Benevolent Association headquarters at 627 Lexington Avenue. King wasted no time and the association

The NYPCBA willingly opened its files to detective King. He spent hours checking the backgrounds and handwriting of the association's 400 employees but sadly did not come up with a match.

Undaunted, he questioned all of the employees rigorously. He asked the drivers for any shred of information that might help him with the case. He offered immunity to anyone who may have stolen any letter-writing materials, all he wanted was to catch the sadistic child killer. Following his desperate appeal to the drivers, Detective King went back to a private office at the association's headquarters and waited, hoping that his assurance would pay off. A few minutes later an ordinary-looking man in a chauffeur's uniform named Lee Sicowski, knocked on the door. He told Detective King that he had a habit of taking the company's stationary home with him and using it. In fact, Sicowski explained he had left some of the unused paper and envelopes in a room that he had occupied at 622 Lexington Avenue. Detectives raced to the rooming house, but there was nothing there. Police then urged Sicowski to think of anywhere else the stationary could have been left.

Sicowski then remembered that he'd also spent some time in a cheap boarding house at 200 East 52nd Street and confessed that he might have left some there. The address turned out to be that of a flophouse, a cheap bed and breakfast used mainly by door-to-door salesmen, drifters and manual workers. Mrs Frieda Schneider told the police that Sicowski's old room had recently been occupied by a man who fitted Frank Howard's description. His name was Albert Fish.

King carefully checked the signature on the room's register. Running his stubby nicotine-stained finger along the paper, he painstakingly checked and rechecked the signature until he was convinced that the handwriting was the same as the letter-writer.

Although Albert Fish was no longer staying at the flophouse, the landlady told them that once a month he would collect his mail from there and was due there any day soon. Detective King was determined to catch the killer, and so took a room at the flophouse which gave him a view of the entrance as well as the upstairs and downstairs hallways. He waited for three long days and nights. Nothing. He felt deflated and believed the killer may once again have slipped through his fingers. He had almost given up and returned to the station to file some paper work when on 13 December 1934, he received an urgent call from the flophouse, it was the landlady. Albert Fish was back.

Detective King raced to the house. A very flustered and crimson-necked Frieda Schneider met him at the door. Feverishly she whispered and pointed telling the detective in a nervous and agitated tirade that Albert Fish had come back half an hour earlier and to stall him, until the detectives could get there, she had given him a cup of tea and a digestive biscuit.

'He's in there…' she pointed.

Detective King drew his revolver and walked into the room, where Albert Fish waited. What he found was a harmless-looking, white-haired old man with a straggly moustache and watery blue eyes.

'Hamilton Albert Fish… You are under arrest for murder… you do not need to say anything…but if you do… it will be taken down and used as evidence against you…'

Detective King was shocked and stunned when the seemingly harmless old man reached into his pocket and lunged at King with a vicious-looking cutthroat razor in his hand.

Albert Fish was no match for the solidly built officer. King grabbed and twisted Fish's wrist until the razor dropped to the floor. He quickly handcuffed the old man and searched his pockets. To his horror he found that Albert Fish's pockets were crammed with an assortment of deadly knives and razors. He then turned the old man to face him, and stared into his withered face. 'I've got you now' he hissed in triumph.

He had ended a six-year manhunt.

At the police station, Albert Fish became more resigned to his arrest and confessed to first succumbing to his blood thirst in the summer of 1928. His original victim, he explained, was intended to be Edward Budd, who had placed a classified ad, but when he got to the Budds' house and saw the size of the stocky teenager, he changed his mind and set his sights on pretty little Gracie. He confessed to kidnapping the girl and taking her to Wisteria Cottage in a place called Worthington Woods in Westchester County. His recall of the day when he kidnapped the girl was still clear after six years. The old man had no doubt relived it in his mind over and over again. He had bought a round trip train ticket to Worthington Woods for himself and a one-way ticket for Gracie. He had also remembered that when they were changing trains he had left a bundle behind on the seat. Gracie, trying to be helpful, had run back and retrieved it for him. Inside the bundle were Albert Fish's grisly tools of death — a cleaver, saw and butcher's knife. Gracie happily handed them over never knowing they would cut into her flesh a short time later.

After arriving at Wisteria Cottage, Albert Fish systematically strangled the young girl, beheaded and dismembered her body. He then ate her over a nine-day period. Albert Fish grinned as he described draining her blood and drinking it. The horrified detectives then made their own trip and discovered the skeletal remains of Gracie Budd buried in pieces behind a stone wall at the back of the cottage. Detective King finally had his killer, but Albert Fish could not stop confessing. He described other murders which he had committed between 1910 and 1934.

He provided enough details to convince the investigators that he had killed before, and perhaps killed dozens of people. Detectives were also chilled to discover that Albert Fish had been arrested in the New York area six times since the disappearance of Gracie Budd on charges that ranged from petty larceny to vagrancy and sending obscene letters through the post office. Three of his arrests occurred in a three-month period after Gracie had been kidnapped, but each time the charges against him were dismissed. As for the other arrests, he walked free each time after either a short period of incarceration or a fine. No one ever guessed that the old man was a depraved killer.

One of the few people unsurprised by the arrest of Albert Fish was his son, Albert Fish Jr, who said, 'That old skunk. I always knew he'd get caught for something like this.' He went on to tell of his father's appetite for raw meat and how he had come home one day to find his father stripped naked, beating himself with a heavy board studded with sharp nails. Albert Fish Jr concluded that his father disgusted him, that he had never wanted anything to do with him, and he would not lift a finger to help him.

Albert Fish was examined by teams of doctors and he relished his notoriety. He described his fetishes and perversions to the fascinated psychiatrists, telling of inserting needles into his scrotum. One psychiatrist in particular, Dr Frederick Wertham became close to Albert Fish before and after his trial. Wertham wrote that Albert Fish looked like 'a meek and innocuous little old man, gentle and benevolent, friendly and polite. If you wanted someone to entrust your children to, he would be the one you would choose.' However, he then went on to describe Albert Fish as the most complex example of perversion he had ever known. Someone who had practised every perversion and deviation known to man, from sodomy to sadism, eating excrement and self-mutilation. He even confessed to Wertham that he'd carried Gracie's ears and nose back to New York with him, wrapped in newspaper, the bundle placed on his lap as he travelled on the train, and quivered with excitement as he thought of what was inside.

Like the other psychiatrists who examined Albert Fish, Wertham judged him to be insane. He said that Fish was a sadist of incredible cruelty, a homosexual and a paedophile with a penchant for young children. For 50 years Albert Fish had preyed on scores of innocent children. He could not begin to guess how many victims the man had claimed, but:

'I believed to the best of my knowledge,' the psychiatrist stated, 'that he had raped at least one hundred children.'

At his trial a plea of insanity was entered, but this did nothing to sway the jury, they wanted to see Hamilton Albert Fish punished. He was found guilty and sentenced to die in the electric chair. Hamilton Albert Fish had only one response to the verdict:

'Going to the electric chair will be the supreme thrill of my life'.

Albert Fish, now dubbed the 'Brooklyn Vampire', was taken to Sing Sing Prison in 1935. Handcuffed and shackled he carried only a Bible. Dozens of appeals to save Albert Fish were rejected and he was scheduled to die on 16 January the following year. As his appointment with the electric chair grew closer, Albert told warders that he was looking forward to his execution:

'It will be the only thrill I've not tried', he said.

On 16 January 1936, Fish ate his last meal: a raw steak. Without aid he entered the death room and walked briskly towards the electric chair. He climbed into the seat and readily helped the guards to fix the electrodes to his legs. The reporters and witnesses who were present there were aghast at his behaviour as he could barely disguise his joy of going to a violent death. But death didn't come quickly for Albert Fish. When the switch was pulled the first massive jolt of over 3000 volts failed to kill him. Blue smoke appeared around him and flames shot 2ft into the air, but that was all. It was thought that the needles which he had put into his body had created a short circuit. Another prolonged and massive charge had to be put through his body in order to execute him. The current raced through him. Moments later the doctor on duty pronounced that Albert Fish, the oldest man to be executed in Sing Sing, was dead.

POGO THE CLOWN

Name: John Wayne Gacy
Date of birth: 17 March 1942
Location: Chicago, USA
Type of murderer: Sexual predator
Body count: 34
Sentence: Death
Outcome: Lethal injection, 19 May 1994

'A clown can get away with murder.'
JOHN WAYNE GACY

It was a bone-chillingly cold night and snow was hard packed on the frozen ground. Chicago can be one of the coldest cities in America, and Mrs Piest did not like the idea of her son walking home alone in the heavy snow. Elizabeth Piest sat on a stool at the candy counter wishing that her son would appear. She'd come to collect him from his evening job, but 15-year-old Robert had asked her to wait while he went to talk to some guy about a summer job. The mother was getting more and more distraught. She kept looking at her watch, at the clock above the counter, every time the door went she looked around thinking it was Robert. She shivered whilst talking to the lady behind the counter, but still no Robert. It was her 46th birthday and there was a big family party planned that night. She knew that Robert didn't want to miss it and she couldn't understand why he hadn't come back. In the end, she got fed up waiting and decided to go home. She asked the lady behind the counter to phone her as soon as Robert came back.

Back home, Elizabeth told her husband Harold, 'There's something wrong, I can feel it.' At 9.45pm, she rang the candy store, but there was still no sign of her son. She asked the owner if he knew the name of the man that Robert went to see. 'Yes,' he replied, 'John Gacy.' But there was no John Gacy listed in the telephone directory.

At 11.30 that night – 11 December 1978 – Elizabeth and her husband went to the Des Plaines Police Station to report their son missing. The whole family spent the rest of the night driving slowly through the local streets, peering down dark alleyways in case Robert had been in an accident and was lying unconscious.

At 8.30 the next morning, the Des Plaines Police Department began searching for Robert Piest. A check with the telephone information service revealed that John Gacy's telephone number was listed under the name of his building company, PDM Contractors, at 8213 West Summerdale Avenue Norwood Park. Detectives ran a check on Gacy to see if he had a criminal record. The answer, which came within minutes, was shocking. Gacy had a record of sodomy involving teenage boys and was known to be capable of violence. In 1968, he had been sentenced to ten years in jail on a charge of handcuffing a youth and sexually assaulting him; he had been released for good conduct after only 18 months.

At 9.30 that morning, Lieutenant Joseph Kozenczak called on John Gacy. The detective had a 15-year-old son of his own which is why he took charge of the case personally. The door of 8213 West Summerdale Avenue was opened by a short, fat, sweaty man in his mid-thirties, with a moon face and sagging belly. When the police said the reason why they were there, he smiled and invited them in. When asked if he had offered Robert Piest a summer job, he shook his head – no, he did not even know the boy. But he had been in the candy store at 6pm the previous evening, when Robert Piest came in to work, and had been seen talking to him.

'Oh, that boy,' said Gacy. Yeah, they had exchanged a few words. But there had been no offer of a job, and he certainly hadn't agreed to meet him later. The detective asked him if he would mind coming down to the station. Gacy replied calmly that it would be impossible right now – a beloved uncle had just died, and he was awaiting a call from his elderly mother.

The officer suggested he ring his mother, the come to the police station. Gacy's niceness suddenly switched to anger:

'Ain't you got no respect for the dead?' he yelled.

After making Gacy promise to come to the police station as soon as his mother had called, the detective left. But the interview had set off an alarm bell in his mind. Of course, it was possible that Robert Piest had run away from home, but it seemed highly unlikely.

Robert Piest's frantic parents were waiting for the

detectives at the station. His mother had already talked to the candy-store owner about Gacy and was convinced that her son was being held against his will in Gacy's house. She wanted the police to storm it immediately. Officers soothed her, pointing out that, at this stage, they had no evidence.

Detectives waited all day and until 1am the following morning, but the moon-faced contractor failed to appear. When Lieutenant Kozenczak came in to his office the next day, he was told that Gacy, covered in mud, had finally turned up at 3.30am saying he had had a car accident.

Gacy then returned to the police station just before noon. He apologised for failing to turn up the previous day – his car had got stuck in the snow. Once again, he flatly denied knowing anything about Robert Piest. But he seemed in no hurry to leave, and talked about his highly successful building business – worth a million dollars a year, and claimed his friends included the mayor of Chicago, and Rosalyn Carter, wife of President Jimmy Carter. It seemed he worked for the local Democratic Party as a volunteer and was well known for his charitable work. He even visited a local hospital and entertained sick children, dressed as 'Pogo' the clown.

While detectives encouraged him to talk. Kozenczak was obtaining a search warrant. At 3.30 that afternoon, they informed Gacy of the warrant and asked him for his house keys. Something in Gacy's manner as he handed over the keys told Kozenczak that they would not find the missing boy at Gacy's home.

He was right. But the first five minutes in the house confirmed the lieutenant's worst suspicions. The place was full of books on homosexuality and pederasty (sexual relations between men and boys), with titles like *Tight*

Teenagers and *The American Gay Guide*. There were pornographic homosexual videos, a pair of handcuffs and a length of nylon rope. But as far as they could see, there was nothing to suggest that Robert Piest had been in the house. However, the investigators did find one item that looked as if it might provide a clue – a receipt from the Nisson Pharmacy for a film that was being developed. When they showed it to Robert's mother, she told them that she thought it belonged to Robert's girlfriend, Kim Beyers. The 16-year-old girl confirmed this. She had borrowed Robert's jacket a few days before – the same one he had been wearing when he disappeared – and had left the film receipt in the pocket.

Now Kozenczak had proof that Robert Piest had been inside Gacy's house. Meanwhile, John Gacy was showing signs of strain. But officers had no choice but to let him go – for now.

The police who had been assigned to follow Gacy made no attempt to hide their presence. They stuck like glue to him, trailing him day and night.

A week after Robert Piest had vanished, it was clear that Gacy was starting to crack; he looked tired and unshaven and on one occasion drove so erratically that the surveillance team had to stop him and caution him for dangerous driving.

Then, one day, Gacy took a long aimless drive. At the end of his journey, he invited the two police officers, who had followed him, to visit his home. This was a mistake. As soon as the officers walked into his house, they recognised the sickly sweet smell that hung in the heated atmosphere – it was the smell of death. The officers who had previously searched the bungalow had failed to notice it because on that occasion the house had been freezing cold.

Kozenczak decided it was time to arrest John Gacy – he

was taken back into his own home, Gacy was told that the police intended to tear-up the floorboards. Turning pale, he told them it would not be necessary. He had, he explained, buried the body of a man he had killed in self-defence under the floor of his garage. At this stage, the police were not going to be bamboozled into drilling up a concrete floor. Back in the house, in a closet, they found a trapdoor. When they opened it, they found themselves staring into a dark pool of stinking water. It took a quarter of an hour for the water to be drained away, when it did, an officer dropped 3ft into the mud of the crawlspace under the house. When he sank his shovel into the mud, he was almost overpowered by a sickening stench of decay. As he heaved and retched he lifted a shovelful of a lard-like soapy substance that he recognised as rotting flesh. Seconds later his shovel levered up a human arm bone.

This was obviously not the body of Robert Piest, which could not have decayed to such an extent in the time since his disappearance. But if it wasn't Robert's body, whose was it?

The arrival of police cars and ambulances outside the house of John Gacy caused a tremendous stir. The neighbours were absolutely shocked. They all knew Gacy as a nice, good-natured and helpful guy. He seemed a likeable, affable man, widely respected in the community, charming and easy to get along with. He was a good Catholic and a sharp businessman. He also businessman who spent much of his free time hosting elaborate street parties for his friends and neighbours, serving the community groups and entertaining the children as Pogo the clown. He was a generous, hardworking, friendly family man. Everyone knew that, but that was a side of John Wayne Gacy that he allowed people to see, underneath the smiling mask of the clown was the face of a depraved fiend.

As the facts about Gacy began to emerge, the officers of the Des Plaines Police Department found it hard to conceal their embarrassment. Gacy's record, it turned out, was so appalling that it seemed incredible that he was still at liberty. Gacy was handcuffed and taken away to be interviewed. He knew his time was up. Knowing he was caught banged to rights – Gacy went on to tell the police what had happened to Robert.

He said that Robert had approached him about a summer job in his construction company. Gacy had told him to jump in the back of his car and took him home so that they could discuss the job. Once he got him inside, he started to make sexual advances towards him, but Robert was straight and was not interested.

Then Gacy picked up a pair of handcuffs and toyed with them. Robert was fascinated and asked him what they were for. Gacy told him that they were trick handcuffs and offered to show him.

'Put your hands behind your back.' Robert did as he was told. Once Robert was handcuffed Gacy said, 'It's not John any more, it's Jack. Now I'm going to rape you.'

As the police dug in a stench-filled space underneath the house, investigators were learning for themselves that John Wayne Gacy was one of the worst serial killers in American history. Conditions that the investigators had to work in were terrible. They had to take all kinds of medical precautions wearing disposable overalls and gas masks. Even so the methane gas in the air made them feel sick and dizzy. It also meant that anyone who struck a light would cause an explosion. Afterwards they had to have a bath in disinfectant.

Gacy was taken off to the police headquarters and he sat and confessed to seven years of brutal killings. As the horrific story started to unfold Gacy's face was strange and lifeless as if he was in shock or on some kind of drugs. Occasionally he lapsed into a semi-comatose state and would wake up with a jerking movement, not sure where he was. But this was all acting according to John Wayne Gacy he had not committed the murders. The culprit was a sinister alter ego named Bad Jack.

In the murderer's house two bodies were removed that day, one of them encased in concrete, the second in a plastic wrapper. Three more bodies were found the next day, one under the concrete of the garage floor. A few days later ten bodies were removed, and after that, six more.

Three of them were placed so close together and were in such a similar state of decomposition that the police surmised that they had all been killed together. The lifeless body of Robert Piest was eventually found. He has been raped and killed. He was 15 years old.

The murders created a nationwide sensation. The house was permanently surrounded by television cameras and news men, and every news bulletin showed pictures of an ordinary-looking bungalow with Christmas lights twinkling outside. Parents all over the country were suddenly terrified that their missing son might be buried under the concrete of 8213 West Summerdale Avenue. A few had already had their worst fears confirmed these included the families of teenagers John Butkovich (who had been missing since August 1975), Gregory Godzik, John Szyc and Rick Johnston. A week after the search began, the Cook County medical examiner had 27 corpses in the morgue. The count of those recovered from Gacy's house would eventually reach 34 with another five discovered dumped in the river.

John Wayne Gacy's trial opened on 6 February 1980. He decided to plead insanity. On 12 March 1980, the jury took just two hours to decide that Gacy was not insane. The following day Judge Garippo sentenced Gacy to death. The courtroom applauded.

THE PLAINFIELD BUTCHER

Name: Edward Gein
Date of birth: 27 August 1906
Location: Wisconsin, USA
Type of murderer: Cannibal
Body count: 15
Sentence: Life imprisonment at a hospital for the criminally insane
Outcome: Died of cancer on 26 July 1984

'She's at the farm right now. I went and got her in my pickup truck and took her home.'
EDWARD GEIN

Hogan's Tavern was a rough-and-ready drinking den owned by Mary Hogan, a large, vivacious, rotten-toothed German woman. Mary had made a big impression on the conservative, God-fearing farming families of the area. While the men liked the warm but faintly illicit atmosphere of the tavern, it earned the outright disapproval of their wives and girlfriends. Late on the afternoon of 8 December 1954, a freezing winter's day, a local farmer named Seymour Leicester stopped by the tavern for a drink. He found the doors open with all the lights left on, but the place deserted. When his calls for service remained unanswered, he began to grow suspicious. Then he noticed a huge bloodstain by the door leading through to the back room. Sensing that something was seriously wrong, Seymour panicked and hurried to telephone for help. Soon there were sheriffs and deputies everywhere, all looking for Mary.

Behind the bar was a large patch of blood which had soaked into the floorboards and had begun to dry. The blood was streaked as if something had been dragged through it. Nearby lay a spent .32-calibre rifle cartridge. Beyond the patch, a bloodstained trail led through the back door and out towards the customers' parking area where it ended abruptly by deep, freshly made tyre tracks. The sheriff recognised them as the tracks of a pickup truck. It was obvious that someone, almost certainly Mary Hogan, had been shot where they stood and their body dragged outside to a waiting vehicle. Yet there was no other sign of a struggle. No evidence or motive for the crime. The cash register was full and nothing appeared to be missing.

The aptly named town of Plainfield is a flat, featureless place that even the official state guide book called 'nondescript'. Little more than a group of clapboard stores and houses, life here was mundane. Nothing exciting or out of the ordinary ever happened, so, when the news of Mary's disappearance broke, it became the talk of the town. The question of 'What happened to Mary Hogan' cropped up in talks all over the area. Weeks went by without the authorities turning up a single shred of evidence.

A month or so after her disappearance a conversation took place between a Plainfield saw-mill owner, Elmo Ueeck, and a shy odd-job man who had called in to mend a couple of fences. The fence mender's name was Edward Gein. Eddie had lived on his farm miles west of Plainfield since he was seven years old. His old ramshackle farmhouse was an isolated building surrounded by nothing but woodland. The farmhouse itself had no mod cons, electric light or gas. Eddie had lived there alone since his mother died in 1945. He was a shy rather awkward man who kept to himself. He was a small, slightly built bachelor in his early fifties, with thin fair hair and watery, cornflower blue eyes and became well known to residents as a lonely odd job man who lived in the spooky farmhouse on the edge of town.

Ueeck, the saw-mill owner, didn't really bother with Eddie much although he'd known him for years. The only thing he ever did was tease him, just like everyone else. Most of the residents in Plainfield teased him. They thought he was an odd bod, a bit eccentric. But on this occasion – particularly as Eddie was known to be awkward when talking about women – Ueeck couldn't resist the temptation to tease Eddie on the subject of Mary Hogan.

Ueeck had seen Eddie at Hogan's Tavern on several occasions, sitting alone in the back of the bar, clutching a glass of beer. He and his friends had noticed the way Eddie sat there staring at the bar owner, lost in a world of his own. They supposed, with much amusement, that he was in love. Ueeck teased Eddie and said that, if he'd made his intentions to Mary Hogan a little plainer, she might at that very moment be cooking him supper back at his farmhouse instead of being missing. Eddie rolled his eyes and nervously scratched behind his ear before shifting from one leg to the other and lapsing into one of his creepy grins.

'She isn't missing' Eddie replied and after a couple of second of thought looked up and said, 'She's at my farm house, right now'.

Ueeck shrugged. 'Yeah, right, in your dreams Ed.'

He laughed at what seemed like Eddie's pathetic attempts at humour and although Eddie repeated the claim to several other residents in the weeks that followed, not one of them took it the least bit seriously. It was, after all, just the kind of crazy thing he would say.

Three years after Mary Hogan's disappearance, on the day that Wisconsin's annual deer-hunting season began, Eddie Gein went on a hunt of his own. However, his quarry was not deer. Eddie's prey was another citizen of Plainfield.

Like Mary Hogan, Bernice Worden was a well-upholstered, rather plump woman in her late fifties. Unlike Mary, the bar owner Bernice was a devout Methodist who enjoyed an almost spotless reputation and had taken over as sole proprietor of Worden's Hardware following the death of her husband.

Bernice and her son, Frank, had built the hardware store into a thriving business, a sort of 'open all hours' store to which every farmer in the area would turn at some time or another for everything from agricultural machinery, rolls of floral material, ground flour, liquorice sticks and candy to rifle cartridges and, of course, hunting rifles.

Early in the morning of Saturday, 16 November 1957, Bernice opened the store as usual, expecting a slow start to the day's trade. It was the first day of the nine-day deer-hunting season and most of the town's male residents – including her own son, Frank – were already out in the surrounding woodlands. The rest of the town was deserted and most of the shops closed, but Bernice Worden decided to keep her shop open thinking that there would be a steady stream of visitors eager to replenish their supplies.

She soon had a customer. A little after 8.30 in the morning the small figure of Ed Gein shuffled up to the hardware store. Like everyone in Plainfield Bernice found it hard to regard Edward Gein as anything other than a simpleton, but lately he'd taken to troubling her over the most trifling of details without ever buying anything. Only the night before Eddie had stopped off at the store to check the price of anti freeze and having been given the answer he stood there for several seconds with an idiot grin on his face before shuffling off into the darkness.

Bernice had also been taken aback a few weeks earlier when Eddie, out of the blue, turned up at the store and asked Bernice to go ice-skating with him. The offer had been blurted out in a nervous, half-joking way and she had simply shrugged it off.

Yet she was scared enough to tell her son and to point out that since then she had seen Eddie Gein staring at her from inside his pick up truck or from the other side of the street.

Frank Worden, Bernice's son, was a part-time deputy sheriff and, like his mother, a steady, reliable person. When Frank returned from a long day's deer hunt, he was cold and hungry. He called out to his mum as he unlocked the door of the hardware store and stepped inside. Instinctively he knew there was something wrong. The cash register was gone, torn from its place on the counter, and towards the back of the shop was a large pool of blood.

Frank phoned the country sheriff and carried on searching the store for his mother. When the sheriff and another deputy arrived a quarter of an hour later, Frank had already made up his mind what had happened.

'He's done something to her,' Frank told them confidently.

'Who?' they asked.

'Eddie,' said Frank. 'Eddie Gein!'

While waiting for the sheriff and the deputy to arrive, Frank Worden had replayed over and over in his mind the conversation with his mother about Eddie. How he'd been staring at her of late, how he had pestered her to go out with him and how, the previous night, he'd stopped off to enquire about the price of antifreeze.

Frank also recalled that Eddie had asked him if he had intended to go hunting the very next day. Could it be that Eddie Gein was checking to see if the coast would be clear? What clinched it for Frank was the discovery of a handwritten sales slip next to the pool of his mother's blood. The sales slip was for two quarts of antifreeze and was dated 17 November – that very day. It was made out to Eddie Gein. The sheriff put out a general alert on the radio to bring Gein in for questioning.

Eddie Gein meanwhile had just finished eating, when a neighbour burst in to report the news of Bernice's disappearance. Eddie's only response was 'It must have been somebody pretty cold-blooded'. The neighbour was puzzled by the response but suggested that Eddie drive them into town to see what was going on. Eddie happily agreed and the two men stepped out into the freezing snow-covered yard to start his truck.

At that point, two deputies arrived looking for Eddie. One of the deputies stepped quickly across the yard and tapped on the window of Eddie's truck, just as he was about to pull away. Gein was ordered to get out and was escorted back to the squad car for questioning. The officer asked Eddie what he had been doing all day and where he had been. Immediately, it became apparent that Eddie was involved.

'Somebody framed me!' he snapped.

'Framed you for what?' the deputy asked.

'Well, about Mrs Worden.'

'What about Mrs Worden?'

'Well, she's dead, ain't she?'

'How do you know she's dead?'

'I just do,' said Eddie. 'I just do.'

As soon as the town sheriff heard over the radio that his chief suspect had been apprehended, he and his deputy went to Eddie Gein's isolated farm house. The kitchen door at the back of the house gave way easily. Switching on their flashlights, the two men stepped inside.

A moment later, the sheriff felt something brush his right shoulder and he whirled round instinctively to see what it was. As his flashlight played across the object he gasped in horror. There before him, hanging upside-down from the ceiling, was the headless corpse of a woman with a large gaping hole where her stomach had once been. The sheriff's first thought was that the body had been hung up, gutted and skinned like an animal. It took some time for the two police officers to get a grip of themselves and for the full horror of what they were seeing sink in. The officers made it back to the car and managed to radio for help. Both men then braced themselves and prepared to set foot inside the house again.

A second look at the body revealed that it was hanging from a branch which had been sharpened and driven through the tendons of one ankle. The other foot had been slit below the heel and was secured to the pole with a wire. The body itself had been slit from the breast bone to the base of the belly, and the inside glistened as if it had been scraped and cleaned. There was no head, it had been completely severed. Only once before the officer had seen anything like this, and that was in an abattoir. There is no doubt that it was Bernice Worden and that she had been slaughtered and expertly cut up as if she were a side of beef.

As the officers shone their torches small beams of light danced around in the darkness. It was hard to believe that a human being could live in such conditions. Everywhere were piles of stinking, rotting rubbish, with furniture, kitchen utensils and dirty smelly clothes strewn about. Cardboard boxes, empty cans and rusting farm implements littered the floor, giving the impression that the room had been overrun by some wild untamed beast leaving a trail of filth and excrement in its wake.

Shining their flashlights around hardly daring to let their eyes follow the beams, the officers soon became aware of stranger sights. There were Detective magazines and Horror comics piled into boxes and dropped on the floor. A sink filled with sand, spat-out chewing gum in old coffee tins and rows of dentures were displayed on the mantelpiece.

It wasn't long before Eddie Gein's farm was choked with squad cars. At first, the search through the house continued by flashlight and paraffin lamps, but then a generator was brought in and as the house was bathed in the glare of police arc lights, the full horror of what was inside became apparent. Scattered about the kitchen were a number of skulls, some intact, others sawn in half and used as crude soup bowls. Two of them had even been used to adorn the posts at the foot of Eddie's festering, rag-strewn bed. On closer inspection, one of the chairs by the kitchen table turned out to have a seat consisting of strips of human skin. There was a kind of vest fashioned from the skin of the top portion of a woman's body and several pairs of human leggings. As the investigators poked around they found boxes containing various body parts. Each part had been cut away from an unidentified corpse with the skill and precision of a surgeon.

Most horrifying of all for the police searching the house was the discovery of a collection of death masks – real shrunken heads, more usually associated with the most lurid tales of tribal cannibalism. Each of the nine masks consisted of the face and hair of the victim which had peeled away from the skull. The gruesome masks had then been stuffed with rags or newspapers to keep their shape.

Four of these masks were found hanging on the walls around Eddie Gein's bed, silent witnesses to what ever bizarre fantasies he had indulged in. The others were found in bags, old cartons and sacks scattered around the house. Some had been treated with oil to keep the skin smooth and one still showed traces of lipstick. Another one, although shrunken, was still recognisable to one of the officers present. It belonged to Mary Hogan, the bar owner who had vanished three years before.

By this time, the assembled company of policemen, forensic experts and detectives on the scene were stunned into silence. Many of them were long-serving officers who had seen all types of gruesome crimes in their time, but nothing could have prepared them for the house of corpses, bones and other human remains they saw before them.

Even in the harsh frost of the November night, the stench was unspeakable. A nauseating, sweet, sickly smell of death hung in the air like a cold Victorian foggy night. The searchers found the heart of Bernice Worden in a plastic bag in front of the kitchen stove, and her still-warm entrails wrapped in an old suit near by. But still the police searched on, grimly determined to find the one piece of evidence which had so far eluded them, the head of the corpse hanging from the rafters.

Beyond the kitchen was the sleeping area which led off into the ground floor of the house a door was securely boarded up, but within minutes the investigators had prised away enough of the planks to gain entry into the main living room. Their torch beams shone down onto an orderly and perfectly normal family room in which the only thing out of place was the thick layer of dust which covered everything from the furniture to the ornaments above the fire place. It was a tomb which had been closed up exactly the way it was the day his mother had died 12 years before.

Back in the kitchen, an officer attempting to catalogue the ghastly remains, spotted steam rising from an old feed sack lying in a heap of rubbish in the corner of the room. Pulling the sack out into the middle of the floor, he opened it up and found what everyone had been looking for, the head of Bernice Worden. It was covered in dirt and blood was congealed around the nostrils. The hair was matted and her eyes were wide open. The expression on the face seemed reassuringly peaceful but the investigator was taken aback by the sight of hooks driven through the ears with a chord connecting the two of them.

Gein had obviously intended to hang Bernice's head on the wall along with all the other ghoulish trophies.

As the night wore on the search of Gein's farmhouse finally drew to a close. Bernice Worden's corpse was taken down from the rafters and labelled along with the other remains which were then packed into plastic sacks and taken for a proper post mortem examination. It was clear that there were many more body parts, heads and skins to the grisly cachet than just those of Mary Hogan and Bernice Worden.

The big question still left in the minds of the stunned, sickened police officers as they left Eddie Gein's farm that cold night was, who did the other corpses belong to?

Edward Gein sat quietly in the Wautoma County Jail, guarded by arresting officers. At 2.30 in the morning on Sunday, 17 November 1957, the sheriff returned from the nightmare scene in Plainfield. Over the next 12 hours, Eddie was questioned almost continuously. He stayed silent. By the following morning, Monday, 18 November, Eddie broke his silence. Eddie was asked to account for the numerous skulls, pieces of skin and other human remains found at the farm. He was adamant that he had murdered no one else besides Bernice Worden and Mary Hogan.

Gein told astonished detectives that he had obtained the other body parts from grave yards. He explained that over the last few years he had, on occasion, been gripped by a sudden compulsion to rob graves. In many cases he had know the victims while they were alive and had read about their deaths in the local paper. He would drive to the cemetery on the night of the burial, remove the bodies from the freshly dug graves and fill the graves in again to leave it in what he cheerfully described as 'apple-pie order'. Eddie admitted that on many of these nocturnal expeditions he'd panicked and on reaching the grave had driven straight home again. He could not remember how many bodies he had actually obtained and once more offered the excuse that he was 'in a daze'.

When asked if he had ever enjoyed any kind of sexual relationship with the stolen corpses, a question in the foremost of the minds of the interrogators, he shook his head and cried, 'No! No! No!', before adding that they 'smelled too bad'.

Later in the interview, the question returned to Eddie's grave-robbing exploits. If the soil was soft enough he would remove it by hand and prise open the lid of the burial casket with a crow bar to expose the body. Sometimes Eddie only removed the head by sawing across the neck and then snapping the spinal cord. On other occasions he would remove other parts as well. A few times he had removed the entire body then replaced the casket lid and refilled the grave. Throughout the interrogation, Eddie remained his usual quiet, co-operative self.

On the 16th January, 1958, Eddie sat impassively in the dock chewing gum while three psychologists gave evidence. After listening to the evidence the judge had no hesitation in recommending that Eddie Gein be committed indefinitely to the State Mental Hospital for the Criminally Insane.

But the Gein story was not yet over. In May 1960, dogs scrabbling in a trench on what had once been Eddie's farmland, discovered a fresh pile of human bones, including arms, leg bones and a pelvis.

The mad little handyman's eventual total, once all the remains had been catalogued and analysed, came to fifteen bodies, including the two murder victims Bernice Worden and Mary Hogan.

Eddie flourished in his new home in the mental hospital and was a model prisoner. He got on well with the warders and never showed signs of requiring sedation. He also demonstrated considerable skill at handicrafts in the prison work shop, and with the small salary he was paid, he bought a short wave radio becoming something of a radio buff.

In January 1968, the district judge received a letter from the hospital authorities stating that, in their opinion, Eddie was now mentally fit to stand trial. The trial took place the following November and lasted just a week. For the first time a jury and public gallery were to bear witness to the gruesome findings at Eddie Gein's farmhouse. The jury heard numerous psychologists recall their interviews with Eddie, and how, on the subject of grave-robbing the little man seemed hardly aware that he had done anything wrong.

When the verdict came in it wasn't a surprise to anyone. Eddie Gein was the first person to be found guilty and not guilty on the same day. Guilty of murder. Not guilty because of his obvious insanity. Eddie himself remained, as always, quiet and docile throughout. After the case was declared finally closed, Eddie rose from the dock and shuffled through the assembled ranks of reporters and photographers. The Plainfield butcher was on his way home to the central state hospital for the criminally insane in Waupun.

THE COED KILLER

Name: Edmund Emil Kemper III
Date of birth: 18 December 1948
Location: Burbank, California, USA
Type of murderer: Headhunter and sex maniac
Body count: 10
Sentence: 8 consecutive life terms
Outcome: Imprisoned at the California Medical Facilit
State Prison in Vacaville, California, USA

'When I see a pretty girl walking down the street, one side of me says I'd like to talk to her. The other side of me says I wonder how her head would look on a stick.'
ED KEMPER

At 15, Ed Kemper was different. Already a 6ft 4in knuckle-dragger, he was given to brooding silences and fixed stares. Other kids tended to stay out of his way. His mother thought he was a nutter, a real weirdo'. She didn't want him to go and live with her and her new husband in Los Angeles and his father told him he couldn't stay with him either, so he ended up staying with his grandparents in what must have seemed like the middle of nowhere – a farmhouse in the foothills of California's Sierra Nevada.

His grandparents were from his father's side of the family and they were stricter and dished out more punishment than his own parents had done. His grandma, Maude Kemper, particularly disliked the way her grandson looked at her. He was always watching her, staring and peeping. It made her feel uncomfortable and ill at ease and she would threaten to call his father about it. Ed was a big fella who ate like a horse. He knew his way to the pantry alright and Grandma complained non-stop about how much he cost to feed. Ed got on ok with his grandpa, even though Ed Kemper, Sr, was a little senile and a boring colourless man.

On the morning of 27 August 1964 – a stifling hot summer's day – while his grandfather was at work, Ed and his grandmother were sitting at the kitchen table, chatting and drinking coffee, when abruptly Ed got up from the table and grabbed his rifle from the rack by the kitchen door, telling his grandmother that he was going out to shoot some rabbits. 'Don't you go killing any birds,' she told him without looking up.

Ed stopped on the porch and without turning he dropped his huge shoulders and sighed. A surge of anger began to well up through his body like an electric current.

He turned around, lifted the rifle to his shoulder, aimed at the back of his grandma's head through the kitchen window and fired. 'Bang'. Grandma slumped forward and, as if in slow motion, her lipstick-smeared coffee cup fell to the floor. Emotionless, Ed stepped forward into the kitchen. He shot her twice more in the back, picked up a hunting knife and plunged the serrated blade deep into Grandma stabbing her again and again until his frenzied anger had stopped. Then he paused. The only sound he could hear was the pounding of his heart. Ed stared down at the lifeless body of Grandma and grabbing a towel he wrapped it around her head to soak up the blood and dragged her blood soaked body into the bedroom. He started to undress her. He had an insatiable curiosity about sex, and about the way woman looked without clothes.

At that point, he heard his grandfather's old car cough and splutter to a halt outside. Ed peered through the grubby window and watched as the old man bent over to get the box of groceries from the front seat. He raised the rifle and aimed a single shot to the head. Grandpa was dead.

With a cool, almost arrogant indifference, Ed grabbed Grandpa by his skinny legs and as if dragging a rag doll, pulled him into the garage leaving a deep crimson tide bleeding into the dusty yard. With a large blood stained hand Ed picked up the telephone receiver and dialled. The phone was answered and Ed whispered, 'Grandma's dead and so is Grandpa.'

Ed Kemper's mother was on the other end of the line. She knew in her heart that Ed had killed them. She was shocked at the news but not really surprised. She had warned Ed's father that something like this might happen.

Ed's mother told him to call the local sheriff, who drove out to arrest him. Ed freely admitted to the killings and when he was asked 'why?' the only thing he could say was: 'I just wondered how it would feel to shoot Grandma and Grandpa.'

On 6 December 1964, Ed Kemper was sent for assessment to the California State Hospital at Atascadero which catered for sex offenders, as well as the criminally insane. A team of psychiatrists interviewed Ed and pronounced him a 'paranoid schizophrenic'. He was committed and spent the next few years in the psychiatric hospital. It was to prove a real learning experience for Ed. The hospital specialised in treating sex offenders and, along with fellow inmates, the teenage Ed was given both group therapy sessions and private consultations where he absorbed highly graphic information about sex. He learned about rape, listening to convicted rapists, and he began to indulge in violent sexual fantasies of his own. Ed noted how many rapists had been caught after being identified by their victims.

Ed worked hard at presenting a dynamic, intelligent image that eventually resulted in his release after only five years. In 1969, he was taken into the care of the California Youth Authority and placed in a halfway house. Here he stayed for three months, attending college and achieving high marks.

On his release, the doctors at the hospital in Atascadero had recommended that Ed be kept away from his mother, whom they thought had been the cause of all Ed's problems, but through some bureaucratic error Ed was sent back to live with Clarnell, who had since married and divorced for the third time and was now living in the coastal town of Santa Cruz and working at the local campus of the University of California.

In Santa Cruz, Ed found it harder than ever to fit into the outside world, largely because by this time he'd grown to a giant and weighing more than 20 stone. He also found it difficult to fit in at home. He and his mother had argued constantly from the moment he arrived. He took refuge in nearby bars, especially the Jury Room, where he was known as 'Big Ed' and where no-one enquired too hard into his past.

By 1970, Ed had left his mother's house and was living in a shared apartment in Alameda in the Bay area of San Francisco. He spent much of his leisure time cruising the highways and the freeways of California. After his release from the mental hospital he had become fascinated by the number of young girls hitchhiking and he now made a point of stopping to pick them up. He practised chatting to them, gaining confidence. He knew that his sheer size and strange looks put many of them off getting into his car, but he learnt how to make himself appear harmless and pleasant. He had persuaded his mother to get him a University of California car permit, giving him access to the many campuses up and down the state. In the spring of 1972, Ed was ready to strike.

On Sunday, 7 May, Ed was in San Francisco cruising the roads and freeways looking for the right girl to pick up. He had selected special clothing for the occasion – a light-brown jacket, checked shirt, dark jeans and a buckskin jacket.

Mary-Ann Pesce and Anita Luchessa were both 18 and were first-year students and room-mates in Fresno State College. They were on their way to visit a friend at Stanford University, an hour's drive away. On the spur of the moment they decided to hitch a ride.

Ed's yellow-and-black Ford Galaxy pulled up. The girls were giggling and chatting as they climbed into the back seat. Ed pushed an Eagles tape into the cassette player and dropped the car into gear, gently pulling away. Instead of heading South to Stanford, he drove around the freeway system for a while and headed East. As he pulled off into a side road, the girls realised that they were in big trouble. One of them screamed at him, 'What do you want?'

Ed reached under the seat for his gun, a Browning 9mm pistol that he had borrowed from a workmate. He lifted it up so they could see it and coolly said, 'You know what I want.'

Anita cowered in her seat, petrified. Mary-Ann tried to reason with Ed. Keeping a cool head she tried to get him to see reason and to visualise her as a person rather than a victim. Ed felt some sympathy for her, but from his days at the psychiatric hospital he recognised what she was doing and wasn't taken in by her feeble attempts for compassion.

Finally, he found somewhere off the beaten track where he could park. He told the girls that he was going to lock one of them in the boot of the car and hide the other on the back seat. Then he was going to take them both back to his apartment. Ed handcuffed Mary-Ann to the seatbelt while he put the meekly, unresisting Anita into the boot. He had no intentions of taking either of them anywhere. He had only one thing on his mind – murder.

Returning to Mary-Ann he handcuffed her hands behind her back. As he did so the back of his hand brushed against her breast and he apologised for accidentally touching her. He then put a plastic bag over her head and a belt from a dressing gown around her neck, and began to strangle her. Mary-Ann fought for her life; she bit a hole in the plastic bag and manoeuvred her head so that the ligature went into her mouth rather than around her neck. Frustrated, Ed took out a knife and stabbed her twice in the back. She moaned, and he told her to 'shut up', but she wouldn't. As Mary-Ann continued moaning Ed repeatedly stabbed her. She struggled fiercely, turning over on the seat and shaking the bag from her head, but Ed stabbed her again and again. Still she refused to die. In desperation, Ed grabbed her by the chin and cut her throat. Mary-Ann was finally quiet.

Ed got out of the car and went to the boot. He knew the other girl would have heard the struggle. He knew he would have to kill her quickly. When he opened the boot, Anita saw his bloodied hands and screamed. Ed explained to her that he had broken Mary-Ann's nose because she had talked back. He ordered the petrified Anita out of the boot of the car. As she climbed out of the boot, Ed lifted up another of his knives – a longer one with a jagged edge – and thrust it down into her body.

As the deranged maniac stabbed her again and again Anita began screaming and fighting with all her might. In the frenzy Ed's hands became cut and bleeding. Finally, the girl's resistance ended and she fell back into the boot. Ed tossed the knife in after her and slammed the boot shut. On the back seat of the car Ed pushed Mary-Ann's body on to the floor, and covered it with a coat. Then he drove off.

Ed drove around with the bodies for a while before returning to his apartment. His flatmate was out. Ed wrapped the bodies in a blanket and carried them inside, where he undressed them and set about dissecting and decapitating them. As he worked he photographed his handiwork using a Polaroid camera. He went through the bags that the girls had been carrying and took out and kept what little money they had had – 8 dollars and 28 cents. Pouring over their personal papers, he copied down the information on their ID cards and then destroyed everything. When he was finished, he hid the heads in a cupboard and took the torsos back to the car.

He then drove to the wild mountainous country behind Santa Cruz and buried them knowing that without their heads it would be impossible to identify them through their dental records.

At first, Ed kept the girls' heads in his room, partly as a sexual trophy and partly to delay identification. A few days later he drove into the hills and threw both heads into a ravine.

Four months went by without Ed searching for any more victims. When he felt his sadistic urges rising, he contented himself by re-running, moment by moment in his memory, the killing of the two girls and gazing at the photographs he had kept of their dismembered bodies.

By 14 September, Ed was ready to strike again. As the sun set, Ed was cruising University Avenue in Berkeley looking for students to pick up. He spotted a petit Oriental girl thumbing a lift by a bus stop. Aiko Koo was on her way to a dance class in San Francisco. She was just 15 years old. In the half-light Ed took her for a student. Aiko wasn't a regular hitchhiker, but she had waited in vain for a bus and was worried that she would be late for her class, so had decided to try and hitch a lift.

Ed picked her up and then used the same method he had used with Mary-Ann and Anita. He drove around the freeway system and disorientated his passenger, then set off South down the coast highway. When Aiko realised that he was not taking her where she wanted to go she began to scream and plead. Ed pulled out another borrowed gun – this time a .357 Magnum – and held it to her ribs with his right hand, as he drove with his left. He assured her that he would not hurt her and that he was in fact planning suicide, and just wanted to talk to someone.

Ed drove up into the mountains and pulled the car over. He became violent, punching and slapping the tiny frightened girl. As he did so he threatened her, then tied her up and gagged her. She tried to resist but was no match for massive Ed. He forced his giant 20st frame on top of her and covered her nose and mouth with his hand. The tiny girl fought back, grabbing his testicles, but as Ed pushed his weight down harder her little body soon went limp. Ed relaxed his grip and Aiko began to fight again. This time Ed didn't let go until he was sure she was unconscious. Then he dragged her out of the car and raped her. After he squeezed the last gasp out of her dying body he wrapped her body in a blanket and put it in the boot of the car.

On his way home Ed stopped off at a bar for a beer and then dropped in to see his mother. As he listened to his mother chatting on and on he had a little smirk on his face and a big grin inside, enjoying the powerful feeling his secret gave him. When Ed left his mum's house, he couldn't resist looking into the boot of his car knowing already that the poor girl was dead and feeling her body to see which parts were still warm.

Ed arrived back at his apartment later that evening. He placed the body on his bed and then pored over the young Aiko's personal possessions, trying to gain some impression of the life he had just ended. Later he dissected the body and disposed of the pieces in the Santa Cruz mountains. The young girl's severed head was still in the boot of his car two days later when he travelled to see a couple of psychiatrists. At the interview, they declared that he had made so much progress they would recommend his juvenile record be sealed. Later that month, a court ruling confirmed the psychiatrists' judgements. So far as the authorities were concerned, the slate had now been wiped clean. Ed Kemper could now walk into any gun shop, fill out a form, wait five days and buy a gun just like any other citizen.

However, money was proving a problem. Ed was not working. He had broken his arm in a motorbike accident and it was taking a long time to heal, keeping him off work. He could no longer afford to pay rent in Alameda and defeated, decided to move back to his mother's house at 609A Ord Drive in Aptos, not far from Santa Cruz. The arguments began almost immediately and Ed spent much of his time hanging around Santa Cruz, drinking in the Jury Room bar. Ed could feel the urge to kill resurfacing. On 8 January 1973, he bought a .22 Rutgers automatic with a 6in barrel. He had waited so long for the day when he could buy a gun of his own that he could barely contain himself.

At dusk, he went hunting for girls at the University of California campus at Santa Cruz. It was a rainy evening and there was no shortage of possible victims, all eagerly thumbing lifts. Ed picked up three different girls, two of them together, but decided not to do anything with them because too many people may have seen them get into his car. Ed had just about decided to give up and was driving home down Santa Cruz's Mission Avenue, when he spotted a short Buxom blonde girl thumbing a lift.

Cynthia Schall, known to her family and friends as 'Cindy', was on her way back from a babysitting job, to Santa Cruz's college where she was a student. As soon as she got into the car, Ed showed her his gun. To calm her down, he stowed it under his leg and told her the same tale he had spun to the young Asian girl. He told her that he was suicidal and just needed to talk to someone. Ed drove around, and then headed East along the highway to Watsonville turning into the hills at the small town of Freedom. Once he had found a deserted side road he pulled up. He told Cindy that he was going to take her to his mother's house to talk some more and that she had to get into the boot of his car. He gave a feeble excuse that he didn't want his mother's neighbours to see him drive up with a girl.

Cindy reluctantly climbed into the boot. As she curled up on her side he raised the gun. Catching the movement out of the corner of her eye, she turned to face him as he squeezed the trigger. A single shot to the head killed her instantly. Ed was amazed at how quickly she died. One second she was animated, the next second she was still. It was absolute.

Ed drove home. He knew that his mother was out for the evening. His arm was hurting and it was all he could do to manhandle the girl's body, which weighed about 11 stone, into the house before his mother returned. The plaster cast on his arm was splattered with blood so he covered it over with white shoe polish. Ed hid the body in the cupboard and waited for morning. Once his mother had gone to work, he pulled the corpse out, sexually abused it and dragged it to the bathroom for dissection. After cleaning the pieces, he put them in a plastic bag for disposal. The head, Cindy's head, he kept in his bedroom cupboard. He also kept her oversized woolly, checked man's shirt for his own use and took a small souvenir from her body; a small handmade silver ring. Ed then got rid of the rest of her belongings, before driving South. He went through Monterey and tossed the bags out of the car over a 300ft cliff along the coast.

The next day, a sharp-eyed highway patrolman saw an arm

sticking out of a bag beside the road. Looking over the cliff, he saw more human remains scattered down the drop including a hand, and portions of two legs. A week later, a rib cage was washed ashore. Enough of the body had been found for the dead girl to be identified as Cindy Schall.

As soon as Ed heard that the remains had been discovered, he buried Cindy's head in the back garden outside his mother's bedroom window.

Less than a month after killing Cindy, Ed had another argument with his mother and stormed out of the house saying he 'was going to see a movie'. Seething with rage, he drove off instead towards the university.

That wet night, there were plenty of people thumbing for lifts, including Rosalind Thorpe, who came out of her evening lecture just as Ed drove by. He stopped his car and she climbed in, then started chatting happily to him, assuming from the university parking sticker she'd seen on the car that Ed was a fellow student. As they drove slowly through the campus. Ed couldn't take his eyes off Rosalind's legs and breasts.

Then Ed saw a small Chinese girl thumbing a ride. He stopped and Alice Liu climbed into the back seat. As he drove past the campus security guard he glanced to make sure the guard had not noticed the two girls in his car. The road swept down in long curves from the hilltop campus to the town below. Ed slowed down to enjoy the view of the city lights and the ocean beyond.

They were alone on the road. Ed slowed to a halt and dropped his right hand on to his lap and pulled out his pistol from under his thigh. He lifted it up. Rosalind half-turned towards him, her mouth opened to say something and Ed shot her in the side of the head.

As she slumped over, he turned to Alice who was cowering, terrified in the corner of the back seat, trying to make herself as small as possible.

Ed's first two shots missed as Alice thrashed around trying to miss the bullets. Then Ed fired again and hit her. She stopped moving and Ed fired one more time. As the car rolled slowly down the hill, Ed dragged a coat over Alice, who although unconscious was moaning softly.

Then he tried to push Rosalind's body down out of site below the dashboard. He could barely move her so he just dragged a blanket over her and accelerated smoothly away. Alice was still moaning and gurgling on the back seat so Ed turned and shot her again. This time, point blank in the head. He pulled up in a quiet cul-de-sac and dragged the two bodies into the boot of the car before heading back to his mother's house. En route, Ed stopped at a petrol station and went into the toilet to wipe the blood off his plaster cast and wipe what he could from his clothes.

Returning home, he parked the car in the street outside the house and told his mother that he had fallen asleep at the cinema. He left her watching TV while he went out saying he had to buy some cigarettes. Before he went to the shop he opened the boot of his car and, using a hunting knife, decapitated both the bodies. Then he went to buy cigarettes, went home, watched TV and went to bed.

The next morning, Ed brought the heads into the house, washed them and removed the bullets. Then he brought in Alice's body and sexually abused it before washing that too, then putting it back in the boot of the car. There, he cut off her hands. This time though, he did not dissect the bodies. He no longer got a thrill from the task.

145

Now all Ed wanted to do was to get rid of the evidence. He headed North towards San Francisco, hoping that if he left the bodies around there the police would assume the killer was a local man. On the way he stopped off to see a friend and the drove into Eden Canyon in the early hours of the morning to dump the bodies.

Afterwards, he drove to the coast and tossed the heads and hands of the girl's over a cliff. The bodies were found in the canyon less than a fortnight later by workmen.

For the first time, Ed deviated from his master plan by keeping some of the evidence – the bags that Rosalind and Alice had been carrying. He spent weeks poring over the documents the girls had in their bags, which included family photos and letters, trying to get to know his victims. He decided to pack up all the papers, and the keepsakes he had taken from Cindy and the other three girls, plus the guns he had used to kill them and throw them into the ocean.

By now, Ed's nerves were shot and he was getting ulcers. It was time he felt to climax his career of crime and show the world he was a man to be reckoned with. For a while, he considered killing everyone who lived in the immediate vicinity – fantasising about creeping from house to house under cover of darkness silently slaying. He abandoned the idea as impractical. Besides, there was his mother to think about.

On Good Friday, 20 April, he went to see a friend and put in a few hours at his old job, but he was in a black mood and decided to go back home. His mother was still at work and he phoned to tell her he was at home. She told him she was going straight out from work and would not be back until late.

Ed spent the evening working his way through a six-pack of beer in front of the television. His mother had not returned by midnight, nor had she returned by the time he went to bed at 2am.

At 4am, Ed decided to get up and check if she had returned. As he wandered into her room, she was just getting into bed. She asked Ed what he was doing and he told her that he was simply checking to see if she was back. She asked if he wanted to talk and he said no. With that, she turned over to go to sleep saying, 'We'll talk in the morning.' Ed went back to his room glad that there hadn't been an argument. He didn't want to part from her on bad terms.

Ed lay awake for an hour or so until he was sure his mother was asleep. Then, carrying his pocket knife and a hammer, he went back into her room. His mother was fast asleep on her left side. Ed stood over her watching for a minute or two and then brought the hammer down on her right temple with great force. She didn't move, just lay there. Blood trickled from the wound, but she was still breathing. Ed turned her over onto her back and swept the pocket-knife across her throat, 'What's good for my victims is good for my mother', he said.

Working swiftly, with practised hands he removed her head, then dragged her body into the cupboard.

In the morning, by the time he had cleaned the blood off the walls and the carpet, he felt sick and giddy. He had to get out of the house. He loaded his knives and guns into the car and left.

Driving round town, he met a drinking buddy called Robert McFadzen. Robert had owed Ed ten dollars for some time which was a good enough reason for Ed in his current state of mind to decide to kill him. But before he could carry out the plan, Robert apologetically handed over the money. Ed brought them both five dollars worth of beer.

Back at the house, Ed worried about explaining away his mother's absence over the Easter weekend. It occurred to him to say that she had gone away with a friend. This flimsy story could be made more convincing if the friend were to go missing too. He searched out his mother's address book and called Sally Hallett, a friend and colleague of his mother, but there was no reply. Ed fretted around the house. Then at 5.30pm, Mrs Hallett rang and asked to speak to his mother. Ed told her that they were celebrating Ed's being back at work after a long lay off, and he had been trying to get in touch with her to come a surprise dinner for his mother. Mrs Hallett was delighted to accept his invitation and agreed to arrive at 7.30 that evening. Ed got the house ready for his guest. He closed the doors and windows, put a pair of handcuffs in his pocket and scattered assorted weapons around the place.

Mrs Hallett was half an hour late. Ed told her that his mother had been delayed and showed her into the living room. He wasted no time. He stepped in front of her, punched her in the stomach and chest, spun her around into a strangle hold and lifted her off the ground. She dangled, struggling in his arms for a while, then went limp. Ed had crushed her windpipe. He lowered her to the ground and wrapped paper bags around her head and tied them in place with a cord and scarf around her neck.

He put the body on his bed, covered it and then went out for a drink to the Jury Room bar. He sat there for a while, outwardly in control, if a little distracted, nursing a beer and eavesdropping on other conversations.

When he got back home, he cut off Sally Hallett's head and fell into a fitful sleep in his mother's bed. He knew it was over.

Ed had felt secure when he was stalking strangers but there

was no way he could brazen this one out. There was nothing for it but to go on the run.

First thing in the morning he transferred Sally Hallett's body to the bedroom cupboard and loaded his weapons into the car. He had no precise plan. At 10 that morning he headed east over the Sierra, driving more or less non-stop, drinking fizzy drinks and caffeine tablets to keep him going. He listened to the news reports on the car radio, alternating between fear that he would soon be the subject of a manhunt and disappointment that no one seemed to notice him.

Ed drove for two days and two nights, before pulling up at a pay phone. It was One in the morning. He dialled the number of Santa Cruz Police Department and said that his name was Ed Kemper. He was on the edge of hysteria. 'I have over 200 rounds of ammo in the trunk of my car and three guns. I have killed eight people. I need help...'

On 8 November 1973, Ed Kemper stood in the dock with bandaged wrists. He had tried to commit suicide for the second time since his arrest. The jury took five hours to find Ed Kemper guilty on eight counts of first-degree murder.

Ed Kemper was sentenced to life imprisonment, with a strong recommendation that he will never be released. There was no appeal.

THE SOUTHERN CALIFORNIA STRANGLER

Name: Randy Kraft
Born: 9 March 1945
Location: Long Beach, California, USA
Type of murderer: Homosexual psychopath
Body count: 16 murder charges (29 uncharged)
Sentence: Death
Outcome: Still on Death Row at San Quentin Prison

'How's my friend?'
RANDY KRAFT, ENQUIRING TO POLICE OFFICERS
AFTER THE CONDITION OF ONE OF HIS VICTIMS

Michael Howard heaved a weary sigh, and switched on the red light of his patrol car. It was 1am on the 14 May 1983 and he was just about to book his second drunk driver of the night. Sgt. Howard and his partner, Officer Michael Stirling had been watching an old battered brown Toyota Celica for some time. From their position in the far right hand lane, they had followed its unsteady progress as it weaved its way down a remote stretch of Interstate 5, the San Diego Freeway. When the driver made an illegal lane-change, the two police officers realised that the driver was drunk. The Toyota slowed from 45mph to 30mph and the driver steadied his steering but showed no sign of pulling over. Stirling flashed his head lights and shone a spotlight into the car. As he did so he noticed the driver reach over to the back seat and grab a jacket which he tossed onto the passenger seat. Sgt. Stirling's patience was wearing thin. He turned on the public address system and ordered the car to stop. The driver finally pulled over.

Randy Kraft, a thin wiry man, with receding sandy brown hair and a typical 'village people moustache'. Got out of his motor and walked briskly to the police car. Stirling, an officer with close to 5000 drunk-driver arrests in his three years with Orange County Police, immediately smelled a rat. He knew that drivers don't normally leave their cars unless they have something to hide. As Randy Kraft got out, he dumped a half-empty bottle on the tarmac, but the broken bottle was the least damning evidence that Stirling and Howard, and various other officers would eventually turn up. The 38-year-old admitted having had three or four drinks, but told the officers that he was sober. Stirling made him do a field sobriety test, walk in a straight line.

Sgt. Stirling noticed that Kraft's jeans were open, except for the top button. At that point, Stirling saw Randy Kraft as just another guy who could down a few beers in a local bar and still drive home safely. While the officer went through the routine of handcuffing Randy Kraft and telling him that he was under arrest, Sgt. Howard walked up to the passenger side of the Toyota and saw that Kraft had not been on his own. There was a figure sitting motionless in the car. Howard tapped on the car window to get the man's attention. When there was no response he tapped harder and shouted, his impatience wearing thin. Howard peered into the car.

Terry Gambrel, a 25-year-old Indiana farm boy who had joined the Marines and was stationed at nearby Marine Airbase, was slumped in the seat, a black jacket draped over his lap. He appeared to be sleeping. When the officer asked Kraft where his friend lived, Kraft said that he did not know. He explained that the man was just a hitchhiker who he had picked up. The passenger door was locked, so the officer went round to the driver's side. He saw a couple of pill bottles and some empty whisky bottles on the floor and resting on Kraft's seat was a folded 5in buck-knife. The officer gave a sigh of disgust. Gambrel was so obviously drunk that he had passed out, but the veteran patrolman recoiled when he leaned over and touched the clammy flesh of the Marine's forearm. It was obvious that the man was not just drunk. He was dead.

The stunned officer picked up the pill bottles and the knife and placed them on the car roof. After reaching across the body to unlock the door on the passenger side he walked around the car to check Gambrel's pulse and pupils for signs of life. Then he lifted the jacket.

Gambrel's flies were open. The crotch of his jeans pulled up so tight around his scrotum that his genitals were hanging out. His lap was wet, caused by him peeing himself as he died. His hands were bound with the laces from his shoes. His shoes had been removed and tucked under the front seat. There were also marks on Gambrel's neck, caused by the tightening of his own belt.

At 1.17am, the officers radioed for paramedics and then waited with Kraft. It took four minutes for the team of paramedics to get there. The two officers remained grim and silent. Kraft was equally silent, although at one point he did ask, 'How's my friend?'

At 3.45am, Jim Sidebotham's phone rang. The seasoned homicide investigator was no stranger to middle-of-the-night calls. In 25 years with the Orange County Sheriff's Department, the 48—year-old investigator had been called out of bed to dozens of killings. The caller told the investigator that there was a man in custody, 5' 10 tall, about 160lbs, and probably gay. He had been found with a dead Marine in his car.

It was the call Sidebotham had been waiting for for a long time. For years a string of bodies had been turning up on the freeways, often Marines, and always young men. The corpses had been tortured and defiled by what could only be a madman. It looked as though they had finally tracked down The Freeway Killer.

Jim Sidebotham acted fast. His first move was to get a supreme judge out of bed so he could obtain a search warrant for Kraft's home.

It would have been easy to just barge his way into Kraft's house, but the detective did not want any suggestions that his evidence had been obtained by illegal means when the case went to court. He wanted an airtight search warrant before going in. Sidebotham ordered an investigator to stand outside Kraft's home in Long Beach.

On Saturday afternoon, the Sheriff's Department's forensic expert and several other personnel joined Sidebotham in going through Kraft's Toyota. At first the vehicle appeared to contain nothing unusual: keys, chewing gum, a toothbrush, can opener, a cigarette lighter and old newspapers, just the ordinary bits and pieces that accumulate in many people's cars. In the glove compartment were matches from the Charterhouse Restaurant and a San Diego bar called The Hole. Investigators also found a half-empty bottle of Styx, a spray guaranteed to act as an aphrodisiac and relaxant used mainly by gays. Behind the driver's seat they found Gambrel's brown leather belt. It matched the width of the purplish mark that had been left around his neck by the ligature that had been used to garrotte him to death. Two unopened bottles of Mouse-head lager were still on the back seat. As well as the empty beer bottles the team discovered several more prescription drugs including Ativam, Valium (the anti depressant), Propranolol, and Inderal – a painkiller used in the treatment of angina and migraine headaches. Also found was a large well-thumbed paperback entitled *The Essential Guide to Prescription Drugs: What You Need To Know For Safe Drug Use*. Kraft had evidently done his homework.

Investigators lifted the floor carpet on the driver's side of the car and found an envelope. Inside were 47 photographs, all of young men, some were nude, some were clothed, some appeared to be dead. One photograph showed a naked young man draped on a couch with a distinctive floral pattern. He appeared either drugged or dead. His eyes were glazed and his mouth hung loosely open. Other men looked as if they were asleep. They were generally a similar height and build, many sported a distinctive close-cropped military haircut.

There were further shocks to be discovered. The seat that Gambrel had been sitting on was soaked in blood. It could not have been Gambrel's blood because the young Marine had no open wounds. By the time investigators went to open the car boot there was a feeling of dread in the air. What they found inside did nothing to dispel that feeling. Contained in a briefcase was a ring-bound file. In it they discovered a list bearing 61 neatly printed codes. At first glance they made little sense. The list began with 'STABLE', 'ANGLE', 'EDM', 'HARI KARI' and ended with 'ENGLAND', 'OIL', 'DART', '405' AND 'WHAT YOU GOT'. Officers had a fair idea these words meant. Each entry appeared to be a meticulous coded memory trigger for a murder, as in, '2 IN 1 HITCH', and '2 IN 1 BEACH'. Including four '2 IN 1' notations, the entries added up to 67 victims. It was a scorecard that made Randy Kraft a prolific serial killer.

A grim-faced Jim Sidebotham left the search and headed off to Randy Kraft's house at Long Beach, search warrant in hand. At 5.30pm he knocked on the door but there was nobody home except for Kraft's dog, Max, barking loudly. The police erected screens outside the house and Sidebotham let himself in, followed by a small army of police investigators.

Later in the evening, Jeff Seelig, who had been Kraft's lover for more than years, returned home from work to find the house that he shared with the suspected mass murderer being ripped apart by the investigators. Part of a wall had already been removed, as had a pair of couches with a distinctive pattern. The wall was stained with blood, and the couches matched the one in the photograph found in Kraft's Toyota. In the bathroom, the police found a camera that had once belonged to Michael Shaun O'Fallon, a dead Colorado youth. An electric shaver belonging to Eric Church, another dead youngster was also discovered. Also unearthed were a shoulder bag and a pair of Japanese sandals, once the property of Lance Taggs from Oregon. A signed sketchpad that belonged to Greg Jolley whose dismembered body had been found in a rubbish bag in the San Bernardino mountains. These were just some of the grim mementos that Randy Kraft had stored in his quiet suburban house.

By the time Sidebotham and his men left 824 Roswell at 2.15am the next morning they had enough evidence to fill a removal van. It was clear that they had stumbled upon the most terrifying of nightmares and it was only just beginning.

Jeff Seelig was taken into custody immediately. The police suspected that he and Kraft had been operating as a team, but it was clear from Seelig's shocked demeanour that the activities of the lover he had known for over a decade were a complete surprise to him. Seelig told his questioners that he and Randy were both gay and had lived together since 1975. Jeff said that he was into S & M, sadomasochism. But, as far as he knew, Randy had no other vices.

Seelig went on to explain that he and Kraft sometimes picked up hitchhikers on the freeway and took them home to have sex. However, whenever he and Kraft had an argument, Randy would drive the freeways by himself, sometimes bring back hitchhikers to the house.

The picture which emerged in dozens of lengthy interviews simply didn't fit. Randy Kraft it seemed was a mild-mannered computer programmer whose only vice was a Friday-night game of cards with his friends. Apart from his homosexuality,

Randy was the epitome of the all-American boy. Caring, polite and well respected by colleagues and friends.

Meanwhile, investigators were still going over the Kraft house with a fine-tooth comb. The mounting pile of evidence now included an unusual collection of belts, chains and shackles. There was also a pile of old shirts stored in the garage, one of them was found to belong to Chris Schoenburg, another youth whose mutilated body had turned up on the freeway years before. A yellow rug yielded nylon fibres which matched those found five years earlier on the body of a young Marine called Scott Michael Hughes. A harmonica was also found which was once owned by Eddie Moore, yet another unaccounted-for body.

The young man in the photograph was identified. He was Marine Corporal Wyatt Loggins. His body, stuffed in a rubbish bag, had been discovered in September 1980. Sidebotham now knew that his suspicions had been well founded. The 47 photographs found under the threadbare carpet of Randy's car had been taken by him as grim reminders of the victims.

In 1970s America, very few gay men openly admitted their sexuality, even in the more liberal California. The Marine Corps with its reputation for macho toughness seemed an unlikely choice for a career for a gay man. Eddie Moore's shyness did nothing to hide his homosexuality. The young, blond-haired, blue-eyed Marine felt trapped by his chosen profession.

Eddie hitched a ride with the freeway killer. The crumpled body of the 20-year-old Marine was found on the Westbound exit of the 405 Freeway. It was spotted by a passing motorist at about 1.15am on 26 December 1972. The body had no shoes or belt and wore only one sock. The other sock was jammed in his rectum. He wore a jacket with the USMC patch and the Confederate flag.

Eddie Moore was stencilled on to the waistband of his jockey shorts and the collar of his T-shirt. The corpse had been dumped from a car.

Signs on the body showed that the car had slowed down but did not stop. Moore's face had been beaten with a blunt instrument, possibly a piece of piping. The post mortem later showed that the facial injuries occurred minutes before death, and the actual cause of death was garrotting. Red ligature marks ringed his neck. Faint red marks also encircled his wrists and ankles. Investigators concluded that he had been tied up.

It was not long after Eddie Moore's body had been found that a regular roadside corpse parade began. On 29 December 1973, the body of 23-year-old Cruz Mestas, a Long Beach art student was found at the bottom of a ravine in the San Bernardino mountains. Except for the shoes and one sock, found forced inside his rectum, the body was fully clothed. After he was dead the killer had shaved Mestas's face and head and then cut off both his hands wrapping plastic bags around the stumps. A stick had been jammed into his penis before he died.

On 2 June 1974, the nude body of Malcolm Eugene Little was found propped up against a tree by the side of Highway 86. His legs were spread apart and his genitals were missing. A branch from the tree had been forced into his rectum. Little was an unemployed truck driver from Alabama who had arrived in Long Beach only a week earlier.

Twenty days later the body of 18-year-old Marine Roger E

Dickinson, was discovered near a cul-de-sac in Laguna Beach. His killer had chewed his penis and left nipple before sodomising him and strangling him.

On the 3 August 1974, workers at the Long Beach Harbor oil field found the body of Thomas Paxton Lee. The 25-year-old waiter was found lying halfway down a steep bank. His blood alcohol level showed that he had drunk more than a six-pack of beer the night before. He had also been strangled.

Only eight days later, the shoeless, body of Gary Wayne Cordova was found on an embankment in Southern Orange County. The cause of death was due to acute poisoning by a combination of alcohol and tranquillisers.

At sun rise on 29 March 1975, 19-year-old Keith Crotwell thumbed a lift to Orange County. After a game of pool, he found himself in a beach front car park where he met a friend, 15-year-old Kent May. May was in a depressed mood because he had just argued with his girlfriend. It was then that the pair noticed a man in a denim jacket and sailor's cap. Pointing to the black and white mustang car, he offered them a beer from his icebox. Within moments, Crotwell was sitting in the front seat of the car, his friend soon joined him sitting in the back. The stranger handed the pair a beer each and started the car. Later, he offered the boys some pills. May gulped them down obediently and, after holding one up to the light and recognising it as Valium, Crotwell followed suite. Before long, Crotwell had downed ten tablets while May had taken seven. May remembers driving for hours without stopping and then passing out. When he came to, he had a blinding headache, and sun was streaming through his bedroom window. Keith

Crotwell's step-parents were there, wanting to know what happened to their son.

On 8 May, three teenagers climbing rocks near Long Beach Marina spotted something wedged in the rocks. Weeks of decomposition in the sun and salt water had made the object almost unrecognisable. It was a green human skull. When police scoured the area, they could find no body to go with the head. Two days later, dental records confirmed that the head belonged to Keith Crotwell.

On the 25 February 1980, another body was discovered. On the short mountain landfall, just off the 125 freeway near Goshen, Oregon, the naked corpse of Michael Cluck was found by a passer-by. The 17-year-old hitchhiker was naked from the waist down and his T-shirt had been pulled up to his armpits to expose his chest. Blood had congealed in the pool around his skull which had been battered with a heavy blunt instrument at least 30 times. Blood covered the body, face and clothes. His anus was ripped and bleeding. The killer had also scratched his fingernails across the teenager's thighs and groin. There was an empty packet of Marlboros near the body, a bloodstained knife and some white pills strewn everywhere.

On 20 August 1981, 17-year-old Christopher Williams became the latest name on Randy Kraft's hit list. His body was discovered lying off a mountain road in the San Bernardino mountains, southeast of Los Angeles. His nostrils had been stuffed with paper, and the cause of death was certified as pneumonia due to asphyxiation. He had choked to death.

On Randy Kraft's next business trip, he chose a homophobic as his victim. Brian Whitcher was an outspoken 26-

year-old heavy drinker. He was found on the day after Thanksgiving in 1981, lying in a pool of blood with his sweater pulled up to expose his chest.

He had a lethal combination of beer and Valium in his blood. On the night that he had died, a drunken Brian had telephoned his friend Earl Davis, and told him that he was at someone's house at a party. Earl remembered drinking with Whitcher earlier that evening and noticed that he was getting friendly with a scruffy guy with blond hair and jeans. The man had been putting his arm around Brian's shoulder and continually asking for cigarettes.

One morning a week before Christmas, 1982, Randy Kraft struck again, this time the victim was 29-year-old Anthony Jose Silveira. The body was discovered in some wet undergrowth off the Boone's Ferry Road. He was stark naked and lying face down with a toothbrush rammed into his anus. In his bloodstream were large does of alcohol and Valium. He had been strangled. Even worse was to come.

The last time that anyone saw Christopher Schoenburg, a tall husky farm boy, he was standing at a boy talking to a short, blond-haired stranger. The man had been buying the handsome 20-year-old drinks. They had later driven off in the stranger's car. Somewhere along the way they picked up a friend of Schoenburg's, Dennis Alt.

A meter reader from an electricity-company found the two bodies the next morning. Christopher was naked, his legs splayed out to form a 'V'. Alt was still clothed. Both were frozen and covered with a layer of snow.

Randy Kraft trimmed his hair and moustache for his trial and looked reasonably comfortable as the courtroom drama unfolded around him. Listening to the evidence given by the prosecution's first five witnesses, he allowed himself an ironic smile. But four months in prison had already begun to take its toll.

Although outwardly Kraft had managed to maintain an air of quiet confidence, inside Randy was being torn to pieces. First there was the loss of partner, Jeff Seelig, who had finally realised that for years he had been living with a monster. Jeff's initial shock and disbelief at the accusations against Randy had been eroded away. The friends who had come to Kraft's assistance immediately after his arrest had also gradually disappeared.

On the first day of the hearing Michael Howard and Michael Stirling, the police officers who had arrested Kraft took the stand to tell their grim stories. But it was the veteran pathologist Walter Fischer's bland monotone descriptions of the violent deaths that captured the nightmarish horrors. The old man told the jury that it was one of the worst cases he had ever worked on. Fischer explained that most of the bodies he had examined had been emasculated, the nipples had been badly burned with a car cigarette lighter and they had suffered massive damage to the rectums from a large blunt object forced into them

By the third week, the daily stories of horror were beginning to sound commonplace. Even so, the harrowing tales told by the pathologist still brought a gasp from the jury. 'The trachea was packed with dirt', said the pathologist, describing the post mortem he had performed on the body of Mark Howard Hall in 1976.

He went on to explain that Hall had also had his penis chopped off and a cocktail stick jammed with such force into the penis that it was lodged in the bladder. He also described cuts and lacerations on the victim's legs caused by a sharp instrument such as a buck-knife. As with the other bodies, the nipples and face had been burned by a car cigarette lighter.

One eye had been completely burned away with the same instrument. All the signs pointed to the fact that the man was still alive during the terrible torture. Near to the body, a broken beer bottle had also been found. The dried blood that was caked over its shattered end indicated that it had, at one point, been forced into the victim' rectum. A thumbprint on it belonged to Randy Kraft.

At 9.45am on 26 September, 1988, Randy Kraft emerged into Orange County Court room dressed in a blue shirt, dark tie, jeans and white canvas shoes. Randy looked poised as he took his seat.

One of the main prosecution witnesses was the pathetic figure of Joseph Fancher, now serving time himself for petty crimes. Looking at the giant grizzly bear of a man who entered the court shackled to a police officer, it was difficult to believe that this was a teenager who Randy Kraft had drugged and sodomised years ago. The inarticulate Fancher struggled with his words in what was the most poignant moment of the whole trial. Tears welling up in his eyes, he recalled the nightmarish afternoon when he had first met the freeway killer. In lurid detail, he explained how a couple of hours in Randy Kraft's company had completely destroyed his life. By the end of the statement it was noticeable that one or two members of the jury were struggling to hold back their own tears.

More than any of the other horrific stories of torture and death, this was to be the one that proved the most damning.

It took 11 days for the ten women and two men of the jury to return their verdict. On 12 May 1989, they found Randy Kraft guilty of murdering 16 young men, and 29 uncharged murders remained on file. The jury recommended that he be sentenced to death.

THE DÜSSELDORF VAMPIRE

Name: Peter Kurten
Date of birth: 26 May 1883
Location: Düsseldorf, Germany
Type of murderer: Narcissistic psychopath
Body count: 9 murders and 7 attempted murders
Sentence: 9 consecutive death sentences
Outcome: Guillotined

*'I like to drink the blood from my victims. Once I gulped down
so much that I vomited.'*
PETER KURTEN

As the sun went down on the night of 23 August 1929, the
people of Düsseldorf in the German Rhineland could never
have imagined that the next few hours would demonstrate
the full bestiality of the man they had labelled the
Düsseldorf Vampire.

One bright and cheerful area of light that evening was in the suburb of Flehe where hundreds of people were enjoying the annual fair. Old-fashioned merry-go-rounds revolved to the heavy rhythms of German march tunes, stalls served tankards of frothy beer and there was a comforting feeling of safety and warmth in the closely packed crowd.

At around 10.30pm, two foster sisters, five-year-old Gertrude Hamacher and 14-year-old Louise Lenzen, left the fair and started to walk home through the adjoining allotment. As they did so, a shadow broke away from amongst the bean sticks and followed them along the footpath. Louise stopped and turned, and a gentle voice said, 'Oh dear. I've forgotten to buy some cigarettes. Look, would you be very kind and go to one of the booths and get some for me? I'll look after the little girl.'

Trusting Louise took the man's money and ran back towards the fairground. Quietly the man picked Gertrude up in his strong arms and carried her behind the bean poles. There was no sound as he strangled her and slowly cut her throat with a razor-sharp Bavarian clasp knife.

Louise returned a couple of moments later and handed over the cigarettes. The man seized her in a strangle hold and started dragging her off the footpath. She managed to break away and scream, 'Mamma, Mamma!'

The fiend grabbed her again and began to throttle her. She gasped and gurgled, eyes bulging. Veins in her delicate neck stood out like crimson crayons. The man in black never uttered a word as he dragged a blade silently across her pale thin neck almost decapitating her. Then he vanished into the darkness.

The following day Gertrude Schulte, a 26-year-old servant girl, was stopped by a man who offered to take her to the fair at the neighbouring town of Neuss. Foolishly, she agreed. The man introduced himself as Fritz Baumgart and suggested they first take a stroll through the woods. Gertrude and 'Fritz' chatted merrily about this and that – Gertrude was excited about going to the fair.

Suddenly 'Fritz' stopped chatting. He was no longer friendly. Lunging at the petrified girl he grabbed her by the hair and dragged her to the ground, roughly attempting sexual intercourse. Terrified Gertrude pushed him away and screamed, 'I'd rather die!'

The fiend yelled back, 'Well die then!' and began stabbing her frenziedly with a knife.

She felt searing pains in her neck and shoulder and a terrific thrust in her back.

'Now you can die,' said the man as he thrust with such force that the knife broke and the blade was left sticking in her back.

But Gertrude Schulte did not die. A passer-by heard her desperate screams and called for the police and an ambulance. By then, her attacker had disappeared.

In barely more than half a day, the Düsseldorf maniac had killed two children and had attempted to rape and murder a woman. The citizens were stunned as they read the following day's papers.

Day by day, the attacks continued. Their increasing frequency and ferocity convinced medical experts that The Vampire had lost control of his sadistic impulses. Over the next week and a half he attacked and wounded a girl of 18, a man of 30 And a woman of 37. He changed the tools that he murdered with, from a Bavarian dagger to a sharper thinner blade and then to some kind of blunt instrument. He bludgeoned to death two servant girls, Ida Router and

Elisabeth Dorrier and killed five-year-old Gertrude Albermann with a thin blade, shredding her body with 36 wounds.

Twenty miles away from Düsseldorf, in the cathedral city of Cologne, a 21-year-old domestic named Maria Budlick read the distressing headlines, and said to a friend, 'Isn't it shocking? Thank goodness we are not in Düsseldorf.'

Unfortunately for Maria, she lost her job a couple of weeks later and on 14 May set out to look for work in Düsseldorf. As she boarded the train she sealed her fate for an unwitting rendezvous with The Vampire.

On the platform at Düsseldorf station, Maria was approached by an easy-going man who offered to show her the way to a girls' hostel. For a while, the pair walked through the brightly lit streets, but when the man started leading Maria towards the dark streets of Volksgarten Park she became nervous, thinking of the stories of the 'vampire' and refused to go any further. The man insisted that this was the right way, and it was while they were arguing that a second man appeared, as if from nowhere and enquired softly, 'Is everything all right?' The man from the railway station ran away and Maria Budlick was left alone with her rescuer.

Somewhat relieved, tired and hungry she agreed to accompany him to his one-room flat in Mettmannerstrasse, where he gave her a glass of milk and a ham sandwich.

When Maria had finished eating the man offered to take her to the girls' hostel. She accepted and the pair happily boarded a tram to the northeastern edge of the city. The softly spoken rescuer sat next to Maria on the journey and when they arrived at their destination he led her towards a wooded area. Maria realised they were walking deeper and deeper into the woods and started to feel anxious and apprehensive.

Suddenly her companion stopped. 'Do you know where you are? You are alone with me in the middle of the woods. You can scream as much as you like but nobody will hear you.' The man lunged forward, seized her by the throat and pushed her against a tree. Maria struggled violently and was about to lose consciousness when she felt the man's grip relax.

'Do you remember where I live?' he leered.

'No!' gasped Maria, and in one word saved her own life and signed the death warrant of the Düsseldorf Vampire. As quickly as it had started Maria's ordeal was over. Clutching her neck, she fell to the ground gasping for breath. Her attacker had vanished into the night.

But Maria Budlick *did* remember the stranger's address. She vividly recalled seeing the street sign 'Mettmannerstrasse' under the flickering gas light and in a letter to a friend the next day she wrote of her terrifying experience in the Grafenburg Woods with the quiet softly spoken man.

The letter never reached her friend; it was misdirected and opened by a Frau Brugman who took one look at the contents and called the police.

Twenty-four hours later, accompanied by two plain-clothes detectives, Maria Budlick was walking up and down Mettmannerstrasse trying to pinpoint the quiet man's house. She stopped at number 71. It looked familiar and she asked the landlady if a fair-haired, rather sedate man lived there. The woman took her up to a room on the fourth floor. She recognised it as the same apartment in which she had drunk her milk and eaten her sandwich two night's earlier. Maria turned round to face even more conclusive proof. The man who had taken her to the woods was coming up the stairs towards her. He looked startled but quickly entered his front door and shut it behind him. Maria ran down the stairs to the waiting officers. A couple of moments later her assailant left the house with his hat pulled down over his eyes, walked past the plain-clothes officers standing in the street and disappeared round the corner. Maria told the officers, 'That's the man who assaulted me in the woods. His name is Peter Kurten.'

So far, nothing connected Peter Kurten to the Düsseldorf Vampire. His only crime was suspected rape, but he knew there was now little hope of concealing his identity. Early the following morning, after meeting his wife as usual at the restaurant where she worked overnight, he confessed to her, 'I am the monster of Düsseldorf.'

On 24 May 1930, Frau Kurten went to the police. She told them that her husband was the killer they were looking for and added that she had arranged to meet him outside St Rochus's Church at 3pm that afternoon. By 3pm the whole area around St Rochus was surrounded by armed police.

The moment Peter Kurten appeared, four officers rushed forward with loaded revolvers. Kurten smiled and offered no resistance.

'There is no need to be afraid,' he said.

The trial opened on 13 April 1931. Peter Kurten was charged with a total of nine murders and seven attempted murders. Thousands of people crowded into a converted drill hall at the Düsseldorf Police Headquarters, hoping to catch a glimpse of the depraved creature who had terrorised their city. A special shoulder-high cage had been built inside the courtroom to prevent his escape and behind the cage were arranged the grisly exhibits of the Kurten museum; the prepared skulls of his victims showing their various injuries, knives, scissors, a hammer, articles of clothing and a spade he had used to bury a woman.

The first shock was the physical appearance of the monster. Despite his appalling crimes, 48-year-old Peter Kurten was far from the maniac of the conventional horror films. He was no Count Dracula with snarling teeth and wide eyes, no lumbering stitched-together Frankenstein monster. There was no sign of a brutal sadist or dribbling degenerate. Instead, there stood a man with sleek, meticulously parted hair, in an immaculate suit and well-polished shoes, engulfed in a cloud of eau de cologne. He looked like a prim shopkeeper or civil servant, but it was when he started talking that a chill settled over the court. In a quiet matter-of-fact voice, as if listing stock of a haberdashery shop, he described his life of perversion and bloodlust in such clinical detail that even the most hardened courtroom officials paled. His crimes were more monstrous than anyone had imagined.

Peter Kurten was not just a mere psychopath. He was a walking textbook of perverted crimes; sex maniac, sadist, rapist, vampire, strangler, stabber and arsonist. A man who committed bestiality and derived sexual satisfaction from witnessing people injured or killed in street accidents. Yet he seemed completely sane. The most brilliant doctors in Germany testified that Kurten had been perfectly responsible for his actions at all times.

So how did this inoffensive-looking man become the Düsseldorf Vampire? In his flat unemotional voice, Peter Kurten described a life in which a luckless combination of upbringing, environment and the faults of the German penal system had conspired to bring out and foster the sadistic streak with which he had been born.

Kurten described how his childhood had been spent in poverty. He was one of a family of thirteen living in a one-room apartment. His father was a drunken brute and there was a long history of alcoholism and mental problems on his father's side of the family. His father frequently arrived home drunk, assaulted the children and forced intercourse with his mother. If his parents had not been married, it would have been rape, he said. His father was later jailed for three years for committing incest with Kurten's sister, aged 13.

Peter Kurten's sadistic impulses had been awakened by the violent crimes in his own home and at the age of nine Kurten pushed a boy off a raft as they played on the Rhine. When another boy dived in to rescue the drowning youngster, Kurten pushed him down and held him under the water until he drowned, too. The drowning was attributed to an accident. Around this time a further evil influence came into young Peter's life.

A dog catcher who lodged in the same house as the Kurten family, took Peter on as his apprentice. The man was a degenerate and showed Peter how to torture animals and how to masturbate them.

Kurten's sexual urges rapidly developed and, within five years, he was committing bestiality with sheep and goats in nearby stables. It was soon after this that he became aware of the pleasure at the sight of blood and he began to torture animals, achieving orgasms by stabbing pigs and sheep.

The terrible pattern of Peter Kurten's life was forming. It only needed one more depraved influence to transfer his sadistic urges from animals to human beings. That influence came in the form of a prostitute twice his age who lived with Kurten for some time. She was a masochist who enjoyed being ill treated and abused. Peter Kurten's sadistic education was now complete.

A two-year prison sentence for theft further added to Peter's anger and bitterness. The penal conditions were inhumane, particularly for adolescents, and the brutal treatment inside prison had introduced him to yet one more sadistic element to fuel his fantasies. He would achieve orgasm by witnessing the brutal, sexual acts that took place behind prison walls. He became so obsessed with these thoughts that he deliberately broke minor prison rules in order to be sentenced to solitary confinement. It was the ideal atmosphere for sadistic daydreaming and masturbating.

Shortly after being released from prison, he made his first murderous attack on a girl during sexual intercourse, leaving her for dead in the Grafenburg Woods. No body was ever found.

More prison sentences followed for assaults and thefts. At each jail term Peter Kurten's feelings of injustice were strengthened. His sexual and sadistic fantasies now involved revenge on society.

The court was hypnotised by the revelations. To them, Peter Kurten's narrative sounded like the voice of Satan. It was almost impossible to associate it with the mild figure in the wooden cage. While hysteria and demands for lynching, or worse, rained outside the court, the trial itself was a model of decorum and humanity, mainly due to the courteous and civilised manner of the presiding judge, Dr Rose. Quietly he prompted Kurten to describe his bouts of arson and fire rising. Kurten continued, 'When my desire for injuring people awoke, the love of setting fire to things awoke as well. The sight of the flames delighted me, but above all it was the excitement of the attempts to extinguish the fire and the anguish of those who saw their property being destroyed.'

The court was deathly silent, sensing that the most unspeakable was about to be revealed. Gently, Judge Rose asked, 'Now tell us about Christine Klein.' Kurten pursed his lips for a second as if mentally organising the details, and then, chillingly, in the unemotional tone of a man describing a minor business transaction, revealed the horrible circumstances of his first sex killing: 'On 25 May 1913, I'd been stealing, specialising in public bars or inns where the owner lived on the floor above. In the room above an inn at Klon-Mulheim, I discovered a child of thirteen asleep. Her face was facing the window. I seized it with my left hand and strangled her for about a minute and a half. The child woke up and struggled but lost consciousness.

'I had a small but sharp pocket knife with me and I held the child's head and cut her throat. I heard the blood spurt and drip on to the mat beside the bed. It *spurted* in an arc above my head.

'The whole thing lasted about three minutes. Then I locked the door again and went back home to Düsseldorf. The next day, I went back – there is a café opposite the Klein's place and I sat there and drank a glass of beer and read all about the murder in the papers. People were talking about it all around me. All this amount of indignation and horror did me good.'

In the courtroom, the horrors piled up like bodies in a morgue. Describing his sexual perversions, Kurten admitted that the sight of his victims' blood was enough to bring on an orgasm. On several occasions, he drank the blood, once gulping so much that he vomited. He admitted drinking blood from the throat of one victim and from the wound of the temple of another. In another attack, he licked the blood from the victim's hands. He also had ejaculated after decapitating a swan in a park and placing his mouth over the severed neck.

Everyone in the courtroom was stunned. Peter Kurten's detailed, almost fussy confession was the most damning of evidence. Never before had a prisoner convicted himself so utterly, and never before had a courtroom audience been given the opportunity to gaze so deeply into the mind of a maniac. Every tiny detail built up a picture of a soul twisted beyond all recognition.

Peter Kurten's face peeped through the wooden cage as he burst out his final statement before sentence was passed. Speaking hurriedly, and gripping the rail, he said, 'My actions as I see them today are so terrible and so horrible that I do not even make an attempt to excuse them. The real reason for my conviction is that there comes a time in the life of every criminal when he can go no further, and this spiritual collapse is what I experienced. I do feel that I must make one statement. Some of my victims made things very easy for me.'

At such self-righteousness, the judge's patience snapped. 'Stop these remarks!' he ordered, banging on his desk.

The jury took only an hour and a half to reach their verdict: guilty on all counts.

The judge sentenced Peter Kurten to death nine times over. On 1 July 1932, Peter Kurten was given a traditional *Henkers-mahizil* – a condemned man's last meal. He asked for

Wienerschnitzel, fried potatoes and a bottle of white wine, which he enjoyed so much he had it all again.

At 6 o'clock the following morning the Düsseldorf Vampire, a priest on either side, walked briskly to the guillotine erected in the yard of Klingelputz Prison. 'Have you any last wish to express?' asked the attorney general.

Without emotion, almost cheerfully, Peter Kurten replied, 'No.'

Just before the fatal blow that would sever his head from his body, Peter Kurten turned to the prison psychiatrist and asked, 'Tell me, after my head has been chopped off, will I be able to hear the sound of my own blood gushing from the stump of my neck? At least for a moment?'

The psychiatrist replied that, for a couple of seconds, he probably would.

Kurten savoured that thought and then added, 'That would be the pleasure to end all pleasures.'

THE MONSTER
OF THE ANDES

Name: Pedro Alonzo Lopez
Date of birth: 1949
Location: Tolmia, Colombia
Type of murderer: Psychopathic predator
Body count: 300-plus
Sentence: Life imprisonment
Outcome: Released from prison in 1998; current
whereabouts unknown

*'I look forward to the opportunity to feel my hands around the
throat of my next child.'*
PEDRO ALONZO LOPEZ

In the summer of 1998, a prison van slipped through the gates
of an Ecuadorian high-security jail in the dead of night and
made its way towards the Colombian border. For several hours,
it sped through the capital city, Quito, and through the quiet

Ecuadorian villages where children slept, unaware of the unimaginable horror that was passing briefly through their lives.

Later, as dawn was breaking, the vehicle pulled off the road. Pedro Alonzo Lopez was bundled out of the back door onto the soil of Colombia, his homeland.

'The Monster of the Andes', the worst and most feared serial killer in the world, had been released to strike again.

Pedro Alonzo Lopez was born in Tolmia, Colombia, in 1949, during the height of the country's 'la violencia' period. This was in fact the last place on earth anyone would have wanted to be born. The country was ruled by riots and unthinkable acts of violence. The troubles began just one year earlier, in 1948, when a popular liberal politician Jorge Elie'cer Gaita'n was assassinated and a civil war broke out. The war would continue for the next ten years and take over 200,000 lives before it was over.

The son of a penniless prostitute, Pedro was the seventh of 13 children, and his early years could be described as anything but happy. His mother was an overbearing woman who dominated her children with an iron fist. Regardless of his home life, anything was better than being out on the mean streets. In 1957, at the age of eight, his mother caught him having sexual intercourse with his younger sister and his worst nightmare became a reality – he was kicked out on to the streets and ordered never to return. Pedro became a beggar on the violent Colombian streets. As bleak as the situation was, things began to look up when an older man picked him up off the streets, and offered him a safe home and food to eat. Pedro was desperate and hungry and it didn't take him long to agree and go with the man.

But instead of going to a comfortable home, with food and a warm bed, he was taken to an abandoned building and repeatedly sodomised, before being tossed out on to the cold hard streets.

After being raped by the paedophile, Pedro became paranoid of strangers. He slept in alleyways and deserted buildings and would only venture out at night in search of food from trashcans and local dumps. It was almost a year before Pedro finally built up the courage to travel about the country leaving Tolmia, and wandered to the town of Bogota. After a few days of begging for food and scavenging dumpsters, a resident North American couple reached out to him, after feeling pity for the thin boy begging for food. They brought him to their home and provided him with a warm meal and asked him to come and live with them. With little other choice, Pedro accepted their kind offer and went home with the couple. He was provided with free room and board and enrolled in a school for orphans. Pedro couldn't believe his luck, but as with everything else in his life, it was not meant to be.

In 1963, at the age of fourteen, a male teacher sexually molested him at his day school. All Pedro's fears resurfaced and anger grew inside him. Shortly afterwards, Pedro stole money from the couple and fled back to the only place he knew – his first true home, the mean streets of Colombia. Pedro's lack of education and skill meant he survived the next six years in the streets begging and committing petty thievery.

By his mid-teens, Pedro turned to car theft to support himself. He had little to lose and local 'chop' shops paid him well for his services. In spite of his skills, in 1969, he was arrested by authorities for car theft and sentenced to seven years in prison. He had served just two days behind bars before being brutally gang-raped by four older inmates. The anger and rage he experienced as a child rose inside him again, consuming him. He made another vow to himself, to never be violated again. In retaliation, he made a crude knife from prison cutlery and spent the following two weeks seeking revenge for the rape by killing each one of the four men responsible.

Authorities added an additional two years to his sentence, deeming his actions as self-defence. Prison time, combined with his hardships, did irreparable damage to Pedro's mind and pushed him over the edge of what little sanity he still held. Due to the mental abuse he endured at the hands of his crazy mother during his early years, he had grown scared of women; he had time to think about his life, and a quiet rage towards his mother became monstrous. He dealt with his sexual needs by browsing through pornographic magazines. His prostitute mother and the pornography were Pedro's only knowledge of woman, and this fed his demented hatred for them.

In 1978, he was released from prison, and moved to Peru, and began kidnapping and killing young Peruvian girls. He was caught by a group of Ayacuchos Indians in North Peru, while attempting to kidnap a nine-year-old girl. The Indians stripped and tortured Pedro for hours before deciding to bury him up to neck in sand. However, luck was on his side, because an American missionary intervened and convinced the Indians that murder was ungodly and that they should turn Pedro over to the proper authorities. Reluctantly they agreed and handed over their prisoner to the Peruvian authorities. Not wanting to waste time investigating petty

Indian complaints, the Peruvian government deported Pedro back to Ecuador.

Experience in near death did not influence his murderous ways, and his killing of young girls continued. The increase of missing girls was noticed by the authorities, but it was thought that they had likely been kidnapped by South American sex-slave rings.

In April 1980, a flash flood near Ambato, Ecuador, made the authorities take a second look at their missing-person cases when the raging waters uncovered the remains of four missing children. Just days after the flash flood, a local resident, Carvina Poveda, was shopping at a local market with her 12-year-old daughter Maria, when a stranger tried to abduct the young girl.

Carvina screamed out for help as the man tried to flee the market with her daughter in his arms. An angry mob of market workers chased the man down before he could make his escape, holding him down until police arrived.

Pedro was rambling incoherently when police arrived at the scene. At first they thought they had a madman in custody. Back at police headquarters, Pedro refused to cooperate and remained silent throughout the investigation. So they enlisted the help of a local priest, Father Cordoba Gudino, dressed him as a prisoner and placed him in a cell with Pedro. The trick worked; Pedro was quick to share his brutal crimes with his new cellmate.

When confronted by the police about the crimes he had shared with his cell mate, Pedro broke down and confessed. His memory of the crimes was clear, which was remarkable since he confessed to killing at least 110 girls in Ecuador, 100 in Colombia and another 100 in Peru. Pedro confessed that he would walk the streets, looking for innocent good-looking girls who he would lure away with the promise of gifts. In his confession, Pedro told of having tea parties and playing morbid games with the dead children. He would prop them up in their graves and talk to them, convincing him self that his little friends liked the company. But when the dead children failed to answer, he became bored and would go off to find another victim.

The police found his ghastly confessions hard to believe, so Pedro agreed to take them to the graves of the children. Over 53 bodies were found, which was enough for the investigators to take him for his word. The public named him 'The Monster of the Andes', as more information about his crimes became known.

For his crimes of raping, killing and mutilating over 300 children, Lopez received life imprisonment. Pedro Alonso Lopez never showed any remorse for his crimes.

No one was concerned that Lopez would have the opportunity to kill again. If he was paroled from prison in Ecuador, he would still have to stand trial for his murders in Colombia and Peru, but after 20 years of solitary confinement, in the summer of 1998, Lopez was taken in the middle of the night to the Colombian border and released. Neither, Colombia nor Peru had the money to bring the madman to justice. Whatever happened to the Monster of the Andes is unknown. Many suspect and hope that one of the many bounties offered for his death eventually paid off and that he is dead. If Lopez has escaped his enemies and is still alive, there is little doubt that he has returned to his old ways.

THE CONFESSION
KILLER

Name: Henry Lee Lucas
Date of birth: 10 January 1937
Location: Blacksburg, Virginia, USA
Type of murderer: Psychopath
Body count: Admitted to 350; 150 confirmed
Sentence: Death, later commuted to life imprisonment
Outcome: Died in his cell due to heart failure on 13 March 2001

'To me, a live woman ain't nothing. I enjoy dead sex
more than I do live sex.'
HENRY LEE LUCAS

In the early hours of 15 June 1983, Joe Weaver, a jailer on duty in the Montague County Jail in Texas, was startled by shouts coming from one of the cells. Fearing that the racket would wake everybody in the block he rushed down the hallway to quieten the prisoner down. Weaver yelled at the prisoner, 'What are you doing?'

'There's a light in here!' cried the prisoner in a quivering voice.

In fact, the cell was in pitch darkness.

'There's a light and it's talking to me!'

'Just shut up,' said Weaver. 'You're just seeing things. Get some sleep.'

The prisoner was a dirty little man with only one eye. He was called Henry Lee Lucas. He was in jail for weapon offences but he was also suspected of having committed two murders. Only three nights before, Joe Weaver had found Lucas hanging from his cell, a makeshift noose around his neck and blood dripping from his slashed wrists. After a couple of days in the prison hospital, Lucas had been moved to a special suicide cell where he could be kept under close observation. Another yell echoed down the hall: 'Jailer, jailer, come here quickly!'

With a final drag on his cigarette and a sigh Joe Weaver made his way back down the hallway. He peered in through the observation hole in the door, known as a spy hole.

'What the hell is it this time?'

There was a long pause then Lucas spoke in a sad, quiet voice, 'Joe, I've done some pretty bad things.'

Joe Weaver huffed sternly, 'If it's what I think it is, Henry, you'd better get on your knees and pray.'

There was another long pause. Then Henry said, 'Joe, can I have some paper and a pencil?'

Half an hour later Lucas handed the letter through the cell door, it was addressed to Sheriff Bill F Conway, and it began, 'I've tried to get help for a long time and no one will believe me. I've killed for the last ten years and no one will believe me. I can't go on doing this. I also killed the only girl I ever loved.'

Joe Weaver hurried to the telephone. He had no hesitation about waking Sheriff Conway in the middle of the night. This, he knew, was the break Conway had been waiting for. The unshaven, smelly little man who now waited in his dark cell had been a hard nut to crack. Since the previous September he had been suspected of killing an 80-year-old widow called Kate Rich, who had vanished from her home. Sheriff Conway had learned that she had been employing an odd-job man called Henry Lee Lucas, together with his girlfriend, 15-year-old Becky Powell. Lucas had left Mrs Rich's employment under a cloud and gone to live in a local religious commune. Not long after that, Becky had also disappeared.

Sheriff Conway had arrested Lucas in the previous October and questioned him for days on end. Lucas was a coffee addict and a chain smoker, but even deprived of these Conway could not crack him. He insisted that he knew nothing about the disappearance of Kate Rich.

As for Becky Powell, Lucas claimed that she had run off with a truck driver while they had been trying to hitch hike back to her home in Florida. With no evidence against him, the sheriff had been forced to finally let him go.

A few hours later, Henry Lee Lucas sat in Sheriff Conway's office, a large pot of coffee and a packet of cigarettes in front of him. Lucas was a strange-looking man with a glass eye, a thin haggard face and a loose down-turned mouth like a shark. When he smiled he showed a row of rotten, tobacco-stained teeth.

'Right, let's get down to business then, Henry,' said the sheriff. 'You say on your note that you want to tell me about some murders.'

Henry's voice was eager. 'That's right, I do. The light told me in my cell that I had to confess all my sins.'

'The light?' The sheriff knew that Lucas had smashed the bulb in his cell so he could not be talking about the electric light.

'There was a light in my cell, and it said, "I will forgive you, but you must confess your sins." So that's what I'm doing.'

What followed was a chilling detailed confession. Lucas seemed to have total recall of the murder of the 80-year-old woman and the violation of her dead body. He described how he had gone to Kate Rich's house and offered to take her to church. As they were driving Kate asked him questions about his girlfriend, Becky Powell and at some point Lucas had made the decision to kill the old lady. He had taken the butcher's knife that lay between them on the bench seat of the old car and jammed it into her left side. The knife entered her heart and she collapsed immediately.

Speaking as calmly as if he was narrating some every day occurrence, Lucas described how he had dragged Kate's body down an embankment then undressed and raped her. After that, he dragged her to a wide drainpipe that ran under the road and stuffed her into it. Later, he returned with two plastic garbage bags and used them as a kind of makeshift shroud. He buried her clothes near by then drove Kate's body back to her prayerhouse, where he was living. He made a fire in the stove and burned the body. The bones that were left he buried in a compost heap outside.

Later that day, Sheriff Conway and Texas Ranger Phil Ryan,

who had also been working on the case, sat in Conway's office with a tape recorder running. Sheriff Conway asked Lucas what had happened to Becky Powell. This time, the story was longer and Lucas's single eye often overflowed with tears as he told the details. By the time he had finished, Conway and Ryan were trying to hide their nausea.

Lucas had met Becky Powell in 1978 when she was 11 years old. She was the niece of his friend, Ottis Toole, a transvestite. Lucas was staying at the home of Ottis's mother in Jacksonville, Florida. Becky herself was slightly mentally retarded. Even at the age of 11, she was not a virgin. The family situation was something of a sexual hothouse. He grew up bi-sexual and liked picking up lovers of both sexes including Henry Lee Lucas. He liked watching his pick-ups have sex with Becky. Ottis had another peculiarity; he liked burning down houses because it stimulated him sexually.

In December 1981, Becky's mother, Drucilla, committed suicide and Becky and her younger brother, Frank, were placed in juvenile care. Lucas decided to rescue her, and in January 1982 he and Ottis fled with them both, living off the proceeds of robberies, mostly of small grocery stores. Lucas felt heavily protective of Becky. He explained that she called him 'Daddy', but one night, as he was saying goodnight to her and was making her shriek with laughter by tickling her, they began to kiss. Becky raised no objection as he undressed her. Then he undressed himself. After that, the father/daughter relationship changed into something more like husband and wife.

In 1982, while living with Henry Lucas, Becky had become homesick and begged him to take her back to

Florida. Reluctantly, Henry agreed and they set off hitchhiking. Later on a warm June night, they settled down on blankets in a field but, when they began arguing over her decision to go home, Becky lost her temper and punched Lucas in the face. Instantly, like a striking snake, Lucas grabbed a carving knife that lay near by and stabbed Becky through her heart. After that, he violated her body and, then, because the ground was too hard to dig a grave, he cut her into nine pieces with the carving knife and scattered them in the woods.

The two police officers listening to the confession felt exhausted, but the night was only half over. They first had to check Lucas's story about Kate Rich. Lucas had pointed out on a map where the drainpipe was that he had stuffed her body. Still dazed from the lack of sleep, Sheriff Conway and Ranger Ryan drove there in the darkness. They quickly located the wide drainpipe that ran under the road.

Lying close to its entrance was a pair of knickers, the type that would be worn by an old lady and also a length of wood. Lucas had told them that he had used a piece of wood to shove the body up into the drain pipe. On the other side of the road they also found the broken lenses from a pair of woman's glasses.

Back at Henry Lucas's house the officers looked around the filthy room that Lucas had occupied. In the stove they found fragments of burned flesh and pieces of bone. Later that day they drove to Denton, a college town north of Dallas where Lucas had said he had killed Becky Powell. This time Lucas accompanied them.

In a grove of trees 50 yards off the main highway they found a human skull and various body parts in an advanced stage of decomposition. Becky's orange suitcase lay near by and articles of young girls' clothing and make up were strewn everywhere. So far, it was obvious that Lucas had been telling the truth. He had killed Becky Powell and Kate Rich as he had described. But what about all the other victims he had mentioned? After killing Becky, Lucas told them that he had murdered another woman. He said he had drifted west to California, then down to Mexico and then north again to Illinois and finally to Missouri. At a petrol station he saw a young woman waiting by the pumps. He went up to her pressed a knife in her ribs and told her he needed a lift. All that night, they drove south towards Texas. Lucas wanted money and sex. Just before dawn, he pulled off the road and plunged the knife into the woman's throat. Then he threw her out on to the ground, cut off her clothes – raped and sodomised her.

After that he dragged her into a grove of trees, took her money and then drove the car to Fredericksburg, Texas, where he abandoned it.

Lucas was unable to remember the woman's name, but the description of the car and where he abandoned it offered a lead. In fact, the Texas rangers near Fredericksburg were able to confirm the finding of an abandoned station wagon the previous October and a little further checking revealed that at about the same time in Texas they had found the naked body of a woman with her throat cut. Again, it was clear that Lucas was telling the truth.

On 17 June 1983, two days after he had started to confess, Lucas appeared in Montague County Court House accused of murder and of possessing an illegal firearm. He was indicted on both counts. When the judge heard the indictment concerning

Kate Rich, he asked if the prisoner understood the seriousness of the charges against him. Lucas quietly replied, 'Yes, sir, I have about one hundred murders to confess.'

It was said so casually, that for a moment the judge failed to grasp its significance. Was this man really saying that he had killed one hundred people? Apparently, he was. To the judge who was now asking if he had undergone a psychiatric examination, the little man replied, 'I know it ain't normal for a person to go out and kill girls just to have sex, but I didn't do all of these murders on my own. My lover helped me too, my lover, Ottis Toole.'

Ottis Toole, who had a gap in his front teeth and permanent stubble on his chin, looked even more like a hillbilly than Lucas. The two men had met in prison and become lovers. After their release from prison they had embarked on a murder spree that had shocked America.

There could be no possible doubt that Toole and Lucas had committed a great many murders between them. At one point, Lucas insisted that the total was about 360. He was able to detail 175 murders he had committed alone and 65 together with Ottis Toole.

Lucas was visited by many lawmen from all over the country, hoping that he could clear up unsolved killings. Sometimes, if he felt the police men failed to treat him with due respect he refused to utter a word. At other times he confessed freely. The problem was that he sometimes confessed to two murders on the same day in areas so wide apart that he could not have possibly committed them both. This tendency to lie at random led many police officers to believe that Lucas's tales of mass murder were mostly exaggeration, but none of the officers who knew him closely believed that for a moment. Too many of his confessions turned out to be accurate.

For example, on 2 August 1983, while he was being charged with the murder of a hitchhiker known only as 'orange socks', Lucas was taken to Austin to be questioned about another murder.

On the way there, sitting between two deputies, Lucas pointed to a building they had passed and asked if it had ever been a liquor store at one time. The detectives looked at each other. It had and had been run by a couple called Harry and Molly Schlesinger who had been robbed and murdered on 23 October 1979. Lucas admitted that he had been responsible and described the killings with so much detail that only the killer could have known.

He then led the deputies to a field where, on 8 October 1979, the mutilated body of a girl called Sandra Dubbs had been found. It was clear that Lucas had killed three people in Travis County in two weeks.

When asked whether Ottis Toole had committed any murders on his own, Lucas mentioned a man in his fifties who had died in a fire that had been set by Toole in Jacksonville. Toole had poured petrol on the man's mattress and set it alight. Then he had hidden and watched the fire engines. A 55-year-old man was carried out of the building, badly burned. He died a week later. Police assumed that the man had accidentally set his mattress on fire with a cigarette. Lucas's description led the police to identify the victim as George Sonenberg who had been fatally burned in a fire on 4 January 1982.

Police drove out to Ralford Penitentiary to interview Toole. He admitted the crime cheerfully. When asked why he did it, he grinned broadly. 'I love fires. I reckon I've started about a hundred of them over the years.'

Both men were sentenced separately. On 1 October 1983, the courtroom was hushed as Lucas was sentenced to 75 years for the murder of Kate Rich. Later he was sentenced to life imprisonment for the murder of Becky Powell. Before the courts had finished with him, he would be sentenced to another 75 years, four more life sentences and a further 66 years, all for murder. He was also sentenced to death. Toole also received life imprisonment and a death sentence.

Now in prison, Henry Lee Lucas seemed a well-satisfied man. He was plumper and his rotting teeth had been replaced or filled courtesy of the prison system. He no longer looked like an interbred hillbilly.

Lucas had a special cell to himself because the other prisoners had attacked him during the brief period he was among them. He had been moved for his own safety. Now inside, police officers turned up by the dozen to ask him about unsolved murder cases and were all told before meeting him to treat Lucas with respect in case he ceased to co-operate. Now he was receiving the attention he had always craved and revelled in it. He freely admitted that most of his crimes were opportunist, including the time he had offered a lift to a girl called Tina Williams near Oklahoma City after her car had broken down. He shot her and then had intercourse with the body. Police later confirmed Lucas's confession. He explained that once he paired up with Toole it seemed to be a turning point where they decided they would kill for fun.

According to Toole's confession they saw a teenage couple walking along the road in November 1978, after their car had run out of petrol. Lucas forced the girl into their car while Toole shot the boy in the head and chest. Lucas shot the girl six times and left the body by the road. The police were able to confirm the case. The youth had been called Kevin Key and the girl Rita Salazar.

The man in charge of the Key /Salazar murder investigation was Sheriff Jim Boutwell and the case was the first of more than a score of similar murders along Interstate 35 that kept him busy for the next five years. The victims included teenage hitchhikers, elderly women abducted from their homes, tramps and men. They were all killed for robbery. Lucas was later to confess to most of these crimes and many more.

Lucas and Toole began robbing convenience stores, forcing proprietors or store clerks into the back of the store. Lucas described how, on one occasion, they tied up a young girl but she continued to try to get free, so Lucas shot her through the head and Toole had intercourse with her body.

On 31 October 1979, the naked body of a young girl was found in Calvert on Interstate 35, her clothes were missing except for a pair of orange socks by the body. After his arrest, Lucas described how he and Toole had picked up orange socks, who was hitchhiking and, when she had refused to let Lucas have sex, had strangled her. Lucas eventually received the death sentence for the murder of the unidentified girl – known only as 'orange socks'.

Of the 360 murders, Henry Lee Lucas had confessed to an estimated 157 had been confirmed. Even if his claim of 360 victims is never substantiated, the little man with the glass eye has achieved what he wanted, a place in American history.

In 1999, the then Governor of Texas, George W Bush, Jr, commuted Lucas's death sentence to one of life imprisonment. Lucas's partner Toole died in prison some years earlier of cirrhosis of the liver.

THE MUSWELL HILL
MURDERER

Name: Dennis Andrew Nilsen
Date of birth: 23 November 1945
Location: Fraserburgh, Scotland
Type of murderer: Homosexual predator
Body count: 12
Sentence: Life imprisonment with a recommendation that
he serves no less than twenty-five years
Outcome: Imprisoned at HMP Whitemoor,
Cambridgeshire, UK

*'I am damned and damned and damned. How in heaven's name
could I have done any of it?'*
DENNIS NILSEN

The drains at 23 Cranley Gardens had been blocked for five
days when Dyno-Rod sent a couple of members of staff to
investigate. They arrived at the house in Muswell Hill,

London, at 6.15pm on Tuesday, 8 February 1983 One of the tenants at the house let them in. They soon found that there was a problem outside, so they went to the side of the house and removed the manhole cover that led to the sewers. There was a 12ft drop with iron rungs down one side. One of the men shone a torch while the other climbed down. At the bottom, he found a thick porridge-like gunk made out of numerous pieces of greyish-white substance – the smell was nauseating.

As the man from Dyno-Rod moved about in the drains more of the gunk fell out of the pipes – thick glutinous stuff falling on his shoulders and hands which made him heave and retch. As he climbed back out of the drain he told his mate that they'd better check this out in daylight. He phoned his boss saying, 'The stuff blocking the drains looks a bit naughty. I think it's human flesh.'

At 9.15 the next morning, the Dyno-Rod men returned to the house with their manager and went straight to the manhole. To their astonishment, the porridge-like stuff had totally disappeared. There had been no rain that day or the previous night so they knew that it could not have been dislodged.

One of the tenants, Fiona Bridges, arrived and asked what the men were doing. She said that late in the night she had heard footsteps and suspected that the 'odd' man in the attic had been to the manhole. She said, 'I dunno what he was doing… but he was doing it for a long time…'

As they looked closer, they noticed a small crack in the main sewer pipe, trapped inside was some pieces of meat and four small bones. They decided to call the police.

Detective Chief Inspector Peter Jay arrived at 11am. He

immediately took the meat and bones to Hornsey Mortuary where they were looked at by a consultant pathologist. He confirmed that the flesh was human tissue, probably from the neck and the bones were from a man's hand.

Inspector Jay soon found out that the occupier of the attic flat was Dennis Andrew Nilsen, an executive officer at the Jobcentre in Kentish Town. He lived alone in the flat with a mongrel bitch called Bleep and rarely spoke to the other tenants. Nilsen had left for work at 8.30 that morning after taking Bleep for a walk. The Inspector and two other detectives decided to wait at the house for Nilsen to return.

That evening, Dennis Nilsen came home, clutching his briefcase. The inspector introduced himself and said he wanted to talk to him about the drains. Nilsen replied that it was odd that the police should be interested in the drains and asked if the other two men were health inspectors. He allowed the three policemen to come up to his flat and it was then that the inspector revealed the drains had contained human remains.

'Good grief,' Nilsen gasped. 'How awful!'

The inspector told him to stop messing about and asked 'Where's the rest of the body?'

There was a short pause before Nilsen answered, 'In two plastic bags in the wardrobe. I'll show you.'

In the bedroom the smell was overpowering. Nilsen pointed to the wardrobe, inside which were several bags of male body parts in various stages of decomposition. The Inspector asked Nilsen if there was anything else he wanted to tell him.

He sighed. 'It's a long story, it goes back a long time, I'll tell you everything. I want to get it off my chest – but not here, please. Take me to the police station.'

Nilsen was arrested on suspicion of murder and was taken to Hornsey Police Station. The police officers sat next to him in the back of the car. Both policemen were troubled by what they had seen. One of them asked, 'How many bodies are we talking about, Dennis?'

With an expression of utmost serenity, Nilsen replied, 'Fifteen or sixteen.'

When they arrived at Hornsey the officer said to Nilsen, 'Let's get it straight, are you telling us that you have killed sixteen people?'

'Yes,' Nilsen said. 'Three at Cranley Gardens and about 13 at my previous address, 195 Melrose Avenue, Cricklewood.' The drab colourless man showed no emotion as he spoke.

The black plastic bags from Nilsen's wardrobe where taken to Hornsey Mortuary, where a full examination of their contents was conducted. In one bag they found four smallish shopping bags. The first contained a left side of a man's chest including the arm. The second: the right side of a chest and an arm. The third: a torso with no arms, legs or head, and the fourth shopping bag a mixture of human offal. The bags had been closed for some time and the stench made everyone gag.

In the second black bag, they discovered two heads and another torso with the arms attached but the hands missing. One head had the flesh pulled away. The other retained much of the flesh and some of the hair at the back, although the front hairline and oddly, the lips had gone. The head had recently been subjected to moist heat and although the police were not yet to know it, Nilsen had severed the head from the body four days earlier and had simmered it in a pot on the kitchen stove.

The head had belonged to Stephan Sinclair, a young drug addict who Nilsen had met on 26 January 1983 and killed that same evening. Nilsen identified the victim in the first five minutes of his interview with the police which was to last a total of thirty hours spread over the coming days. He told them his flat contained the remains of three more men. The second he called John and the third he couldn't remember the name.

Nilsen suggested the police should look inside a tea chest in the corner of the front room and under a drawer in the bathroom. The bathroom contained Sinclair's legs and pelvis and in the tea chest was another torso, a skull and bones, moth balls and air fresheners. It was now possible for the police to commence the grim task of assembling the pieces of Stephen Sinclair's body.

On 11 February, Nilsen went with the officers to 195 Melrose Avenue. He pointed out an area of the garden where they would find human remains. Between 1976 and 1981 Nilsen had lived in the ground-floor flat and during his final three years there he said he had murdered about 12 or 13 men. He had cut the corpses into pieces and burned them on huge bonfires.

A team of police investigators sealed off the garden and began the laborious task of sifting through the earth for clues. They found plenty of human ash and enough fragments of bone to enable forensic experts to declare that at least eight people, probably more, had been laid to rest in the top soil of a London garden.

As the questioning continued Nilsen indicated that he could not identify most of his victims. He saw them as props to his fantasies rather than people and was not interested in who they were and where they came from. There was one story in particular that made everybody feel quite ill in fact it was jaw-droppingly awful.

Nilsen had strangled a young man three times, yet his frail body still clung to life. Nilsen then dragged him into the bathroom, plunged him into the bath and held him under the water. The man had pushed himself up and pleaded for mercy, but Nilsen pushed him back down again. He took the body back to the bedroom and lit himself a cigarette. Bleep, Nilsen's dog began to lick the young man's legs and Nilsen realised that he was still alive. He could have finished him off in seconds, but instead, Nilsen rubbed the young man's legs to increase his circulation. He covered him with blankets and gradually brought him back to life. The man's name was Karl Stottor.

The police were doubtful whether Nilsen was telling the truth at all but were able to track Stottor down. Without revealing why, the police asked Stottor to remember an incident two years before when he met Dennis Nilsen in a pub in Camden Town. Stottor told a story that entirely corroborated with the one that they had heard from Nilsen himself.

Stottor explained that when he met Nilsen he had been feeling miserable and suicidal over a broken love affair. Nilsen had comforted him and tried to cheer him up. He told him that he mustn't think of suicide at his age. Karl Stottor had thought that Nilsen seemed a very nice person who had been very kind to talk to him when he had been so depressed. They took a taxi home to Cranley Gardens holding hands by way of comfort rather than any sexual nature. Nilsen had promised not to make any advances to Stottor and the young man had snuggled down to sleep in a sleeping bag on the living-room floor. When asked what he could remember of the night's events, he told the nightmarish tale.

'I woke up feeling something around my neck, my head was hurting, I couldn't breathe properly and I was wondering what it was. I felt his hand pulling at the zip at the back of my neck, he was saying in a sort of whispering, shouting voice, "Stay still! Stay still!" I thought perhaps he was trying to help me out of the sleeping bag because I thought I was caught up in the zip which he had warned me about. Then I felt the pressure increasing, my head was hurting and I couldn't breathe. I passed out. I remember vaguely hearing water running, being carried and then I felt very cold. I knew I was in water and he was trying to drown me. I tried to get up but he kept pushing me under the water. The third time I came up, I said, "No more, please! No more!" and he pushed me under again. I thought I was dying. I thought this man was trying to kill me and I was dying. I thought, "I am drowning. This is what it feels like to die." I felt very relaxed and I passed out. I couldn't fight any more.'

But Karl Stottor did not die. He was amazed to feel the dog licking his face as he lay on the couch and Nilsen rubbing him to make him warm. There was an ugly mark around his neck and broken blood vessels over his face.

Asked why he did not report the matter to the police, he said that he was afraid he wouldn't be believed and that the police would be unsympathetic. He thought they would see it as a homosexual squabble.

Nilsen's confession gave the police enough evidence to identify several victims. One of them an Irish boy he had met in the pub on New Year's Eve, 1979. The following morning Nilsen woke up to find the Irish teenager lying fast asleep beside him in his bed. The had left the pub the night before, returning to Melrose Avenue to see in the New Year together drinking until they were unable to walk. After clambering into bed they fell asleep. No sex had taken place. Nilsen was afraid that when he woke up the boy would leave him and Nilsen wanted him to stay. He saw his tie on the floor and knew what he must do. Straddling the boy in the bed, he placed the tie around his neck and pulled hard. Immediately the boy came to his senses and an almighty struggle broke out as they rolled on to the floor. Nilsen pulled tighter and after about a minute, the boy's body went limp.

Nilsen went to the kitchen and filled a bucket with water. He pushed the boy's head into it holding it there until he drowned. Nilsen ran a bath and carried the dead body into the bathroom to be cleaned. He spent a long time drying it to ensure that it was spotless and then dressed the boy in fresh underpants and socks. For a while he lay in bed holding the corpse. Then he placed it on the floor and went to sleep. The next day he wanted to put the body under the floorboards but rigor mortis had set in and it got stuck.

Nilsen pulled it out again and decided to wait until the limbs could be worked loose once the rigor mortis had lost its grip. He took Bleep for a walk then went to work. When the corpse could be manipulated Nilsen undressed it again, cleaned it, masturbated over it and admired it. He expected to be arrested at any moment and was amazed when no one came to the door. The person whose life he had taken was, it seemed, not missed by anyone.

The experience had satisfied the now dominant needs of his fantasies, but it had also frightened him and he was determined it wouldn't happen again. He decided to give up drinking. After a week of living with the corpse, Nilsen put it under the floorboards. The body remained there for almost eight months.

Nearly a year elapsed before his second murder occurred, and the victim was to be the only one whose disappearance was widely reported in the press – Kenny Ockendon. Kenny was a Canadian tourist on a visit to England. He was looking up his family relations and was staying in a cheap hotel near Kings Cross. On 3 December 1979, Ockendon met Nilsen in a pub in Soho. They fell into chatty conversation, each buying a round of drinks. As Nilsen had the afternoon off work they went on a tour taking photographs of the sights of London. Kenny agreed to go back to Nilsen's flat for something to eat. They stopped at an off licence, sharing the bill and returned to Melrose Avenue, where they sat in front of the television eating ham, egg and chips and drinking rum, whisky and beer. Nilsen began to think about Kenny going back to Canada and began to feel the same feelings of desertion he had before he killed the Irish boy.

He knew he was going to murder Kenny in order to keep him. It was late at night and they had both drunk great quantities of rum. Kenny was listening to the music through earphones. Nilsen came up behind him, wrapped the flex from the earphones around Kenny's neck and started to drag him, struggling, across the floor.

Bleep the dog was barking frantically in the kitchen. Kenny fought hard but Nilsen pulled harder on the flex. Once Kenny was dead Nilsen untangled the earphones, put them on, and listened to the records as he poured another drink. Later he stripped the corpse naked and hoisted it over his shoulder taking it to the bathroom to be cleaned and dried.

Then he placed it next to him in the bed and went to sleep. When he woke up the next morning, Nilsen stuffed the body into a cupboard and went off to work. That evening he took the body out again and sat it on a kitchen chair while he dressed it with clean socks, underpants and a vest. He took some photographs with a Polaroid camera, placing the body in various positions, then laid it down next to him on the bed and watched TV.

Over the next two weeks Nilsen would regularly sit in front of the television with Kenny's body in an armchair next to him. Then he would strip off the socks, vest and under pants, wrap the body in curtains and place it under the floorboards for the night. The disappearance of Kenny, the Canadian tourist, was big news for days in the media. Nilsen thought there must have been several people who had seen them together in the pub, at Trafalgar Square or at the off licence. He waited for the knock on the door, followed by questioning and probably arrest, but nothing happened.

After this, Nilsen's crimes became more and more frequent. Over the next twenty months that he was to remain a tenant of the ground floor flat at 195 Melrose Avenue, another ten men died. Sometimes he murdered two within the same month. Murder had become a habit, a pleasure, no longer tempered by inhibitions or resisted through fear of discovery.

Dennis Nilsen was eventually charged with six murders and three attempted murders and was committed for trial. As he was being led away to be taken to Brixton prison, one of the officers asked him why he had done it. Nilsen's reply was chilling: 'I'm hoping you would tell me that.'

The trial of Dennis Andrew Nilsen on six charges of murder and two charges of attempted murder opened at number one court in the Old Bailey on 24 October 1983. There was no dispute that Nilsen had killed. What was being questioned at the trial was Nilsen's state of mind during the murders. Was he sane or insane?

Even psychiatrists had difficulty explaining the actions of the normal, ordinary-looking man who stood in the dock. It took over 12 hours of deliberation before the jury were able to reach a verdict.

At 4.25pm on 4 November 1983, the jury returned unanimous verdicts of guilty on six counts of murder and guilty of two counts of attempted murder. The judge condemned Dennis Andrew Nilsen to life imprisonment with a recommendation that it should mean no less than 25 years. Nilsen was led away from the dock with the knowledge that it was unlikely that he would ever be free.

THE GRIM REAPER

Name: Thierry Paulin
Date of birth: 28 November 1963
Location: Forte de France, Martinique
Type of murderer: Sadistic psychopath
Body count: 20
Sentenced: Never brought to justice
Outcome: Died in prison of AIDS on 16 April 1989 while awaiting trial

'I love life, money, sex and power.'
THIERRY PAULIN

As the cold weather set in and the elderly ventured onto the chilly streets, a brutal killer hunted them down. In the space of five weeks, eight old women were murdered.

Paris is divided into 20 numbered districts called arrondissements. Like most districts in any major cities some are predominantly upmarket areas inhabited by the well off, while others are more working-class. The 18th arrondissement lies north of the Seine and stretches from the boulevard De Clichy up to the Peripherique motorway that circles the city. It is one of the most socially diverse districts of the city, with beautiful villas circling the Avenue Junot in Montmartre and dilapidated tenement buildings circled by seedy pornographic cinemas. The apartments are inhabited by artists, drug sellers, prostitutes and small-time crooks, but also by immigrant families, successful actors and singers, and retired people with modest incomes.

On 5 October 1984, an old lady of 91, Germaine Petitot was attacked in her home by two men. She was bound, gagged and beaten and all her savings stolen. When the old lady was found she was so blooded and distressed that she was unable to give the police any clear description of her two attackers. Nevertheless, the police took down the facts. Their files were already bursting at the seams of reports of attacks on pensioners in the area.

The very same day in the neighbouring 9th arrondissement, Anna Barbier-Ponthus was also attacked in her home, but she was not as fortunate as Germaine. Anna lived alone in a modest apartment.

At the end of the morning she returned home after doing her weekly shopping, as soon as she put her key in the front door, she was attacked, dragged inside, beaten and suffocated with a pillow. Her body was gagged and bound. Anna's life had cost the contents of her purse, 200–300 francs, less than £60.

Four days later, on 9 October, firefighters were called to a blaze on the Rue Nicolet in the 18th arrondissement. In the burned apartment, they discovered the body of Suzanne Foucault, aged 89. The old lady had been suffocated with a plastic bag. Her watch worth 300 francs and 500 francs of cash were missing.

For almost a month the brutal murders of elderly women stopped, but on Monday, 5 November, another body was found. Lona Seigaresco, a 71-year-old retired teacher had been beaten to death after being bound and gagged with a length of electrical flex. She'd been lying dead for two days in her apartment before her body was discovered. The violence of the killing was extraordinary. Her nose and jaw had been fractured, her ribs were shattered and a scarf had been used to strangle her. This time the crime had paid, the murderer had got away with 10,000 francs in treasury bonds.

Two days later, on 7 November, in the Rue Marcseguin, a fourth body was found, 84-year-old Alice Benaim was discovered by her son Andre. Just two hours after she had died. Andre had come, as he did every day, to have lunch with his mother. The old lady had been hit in the face, viciously beaten and tortured and had been made to swallow caustic soda, probably to make her tell where she had hidden her savings.

While her mouth and throat burned with acid, Alice's hands had been bound with an electric flex behind her back. She had been gagged with a dishcloth and thrown onto her bed. The cause of her death was strangulation.

The next day, just 20 metres from Alice's house, 80-year-old Marie Choy was murdered. She had been tortured, bound with wire and gagged with a dishcloth. Her skull had been fractured. The murderer had found no more than the meagre sum of 300 francs in the old woman's flat. The police had hardly discovered and identified one body, when yet another was found. The next day Maria Mico-Diaz, aged 75, met her death in a similar manner. Once again, the killer got away with no more than 300 francs.

Less than a week had gone by when another two bodies were found on the same day, one in the 18th arrondissement and another in the 17th. Jeanne Laurent aged 82, was found first, in her top-floor apartment. She had been bound with an electrical flex. The apartment had been devastated through shear vandalism, but nothing beside a small amount of cash had been stolen. Four hours later, 800 meters away, the second body of the day was discovered. Seventy-four-year-old Paule Victor was found dead with her head in a plastic bag under a pillow. She had been dead for about eight days.

Between 5 October and 9 November 1984, in little over a month, more than eight murders had taken place within the same area. Detectives had very little to go on apart from the similarity in the crimes. All the victims were old women living alone and several of them had been followed by the killer, or killers, at the end of the morning after doing their shopping.

In most cases, the women were attacked as they were going into their homes, which explained the absence of any kind of a break in. Almost all the victims were bound and gagged and the violence used against them was always extreme. Theft of cash seemed to be the only motives for the brutal crimes, but the amounts were so small that even the motive did not seem valid.

Elderly women of Paris were terrified. This killer did not rely on the cover of darkness, but struck when the city was bright and busy. The police were on call day and night to escort the weak and the frightened as they shopped on the streets of Paris. As the murders continued Paris residents protested against the incompetence of the police. Extra security measures had been introduced but they still failed to track down the killer.

The police were certain of one thing, the killer, or killers, were not after money. The shocking brutality of the attacks convinced them that the killer was, without doubt, on drugs or mentally ill.

On Wednesday, 14 November, a photofit picture of the killer appeared on the front page of the daily paper *La Parisien*. The picture had been constructed from the statements of an old lady who had survived an attack and police were convinced that the man who attacked her was the same man who had been terrorising the 18th arrondissement. That day the police took a man into custody. He was Jean-Luc R, and had been quietly drinking in a café when he was arrested. Jean-Luc bore a striking resemblance to the photo fit picture, and accompanied the police without any resistance.

At the police station it took the police almost four hours to realise that the man in custody had nothing whatsoever to do with the crimes. The pressure they had been under of trying to find the murderer had caused police to act hastily, purely basing their arrest on a likeness to the photofit picture.

The atmosphere on the streets was bordering on the hysterical and Prime Minister Laurent Fabius was brought in, in an effort to pacify the crowd. He gave out telephone numbers the public could call at any hour of the day or night with information on the killer. Heavily armed Police patrolled the streets, but despite their best efforts they were still no further with their enquiries.

While panic was taking hold in Paris, Thierry Paulin, the man police were frantically looking for and his companion, Jean-Thierry Mathurin were hundreds of miles away. The two friends had left the capital to go to Toulouse, where Paulin's family lived. Here they took up residency with Thierry's father, Gaby, and Thierry lost no time in making contact with his old friends in the area. In this provincial city far from the dangers of Paris, the future looked bright, and it was not long before the two young men began to enjoy the nightlife of Toulouse, flaunting themselves in the gay clubs.

A year had passed since the last old lady killing on 12 November 1984, and the Paris Police were beginning to feel that maybe the murder spree had come to an end. They were still no further in knowing who the killer was, but at least now, the murders had stopped.

Then, on 20 December 1985 in the 14th arrondissement, 91-year-old, Estelle Donjoux, was discovered strangled in her home. Shock waves went through the capital. The killer was back.

Less than two weeks later on January and also in the 14th arrondissement, Andree Ladam, aged 77, suffered the same fate. Five days later Yvonne Couronne, aged 83 was murdered at her home on the Rue Sarrette. All three of these crimes were committed in a radius of 400 yards around the church of d'Alesia. Each time, it was the same scenario, the victim was walking home to her apartment. As she unlocked the door, she was pushed into the building, attacked, suffocated or strangled. This routine was identical to the one that had been carried out in the murder of the old ladies in the 18th arrondissement the year before. However, the police were not convinced that this killer was necessarily the same person. In these more recent murders, the sadistic characteristics and the gratuitous violence of the first series of killings were missing. There were no signs of torture, in fact, these killings seemed to be the result of a quick, but brutal attack. It made no difference, the shadows of the killings of old ladies hung over the deaths and to the pensioners of Paris it was quite clear that the killer had simply changed areas.

In the course of a single day, 12 January 1986, the situation quickly deteriorated. Two more women were found dead in their homes. Marjem Jurblum, aged 81, from the Rue Pele in the 11th arrondissement and Francoise Vendome, a widow of 83 who lived on the Rue De Charenton, were both found strangled. Three days later, it was the turn of Yvonne Schaible, 77, who was discovered dead, this time it was in the 5th arrondissement.

Police questioned more than sixty suspects, most of them drug addicts, drug dealers, or people known to have mental problems, but each time they drew a blank.

At this low point of the investigation Police finally got their first real break. Fingerprints taken from the murder scenes in 1984 were found to be identical to many of the prints of the most recent murders. Now the police knew for certain that the same man was carrying out the killings.

On 31 January 1986 Virginie Labrette, aged 76, was found dead at her apartment in the 11th arrondissement. Again, the police deployed all their forces, and raids and checks on local nightclubs and bars were increased. The mayor of Paris suggested that all pensioners be accompanied on the streets and offered them free installation of security systems. Then, at the beginning of February, the crimes seemed to stop once again.

Throughout this period of murders, Thierry Paulin had been working as an office boy for a company called Frulatti which was involved in theatre and entertainment. Paulin had introduced himself to the company as a person with an impressive contact book and he was given the task of handling the contracts of the models, photographers and freelance illustrators on the books of the agency. He quickly became the office gopher, his boss even sending him to collect debts. Frulatti had been set up by a student from a Parisian business school and it was this connection to the school that persuaded the young entrepreneur to involve his agency in a project that would mark its downfall. In December 1985 Frulatti and three other students from the business school decided to promote the agency with a huge party, accompanied by a series of media coverage. Right from the start, the project proved difficult to organise. Thierry was given the task of selling the evening to various television channels.

He also found the venue, a hall at the cirque de Niver in the 11th arrondissement. The party was titled 'Un look d'Enfer' – roughly translated 'A glimpse of Hell'. The agency auditioned numerous singers, dancers and mime artists who would stage the entertainment.

On the night of 24 May 1986, the party, Un look d'Enfer, packed the hall. Four thousand people had turned up, but there were only 450 registered, paid entrants. Too many invitations had been sent out and the young entrepreneurs, victims of their own experience, found themselves with crushing debts. Frulatti went bankrupt, and Thierry Paulin disappeared into the night.

The summer of 1986 saw the murder of yet another elderly woman in Paris. On 14 June, again in the 16th arrondissement, Ludmilla Liberman, an American widow, was attacked and murdered when she entered her home. Sixteen murders had now been committed since 1984.

When two months passed without any more fatal attacks on old women, it did not occur to the police that the man they had been tracking for eighteen months might already be behind bars.

In August, 1986, unhappy that a wrap of cocaine didn't contain the right amount, Thierry went to the dealer's home in Alfortville and beat him up. The dealer was so badly beaten that he went to police. Thierry was arrested and sentenced to 16 months in prison, for theft with violence and for drug offences. But before his imprisonment, as a matter of course, a full set of his fingerprints were taken. Thierry was in prison, but the chances that the police would connect this small-time crook to the killer of old women were zero.

The computing systems available to the police at that time were limited. Comparison of fingerprints was still done by clerks and it was a long and laborious process. In the case of the old-lady killer, police had over 150,000 prints to compare. These prints were only taken from files of suspects who had been arrested in Paris. Thierry had been arrested and his prints taken in another town, a different district. Besides, Thierry had been charged with a crime that had nothing to do with attacks on old people. The police were as far from tracing the killer as ever.

Thierry Paulin had served just one year of his 16-month sentence when he was released in the summer of 1987. Free again, he picked up with his friends the nocturnal set of Paris and took up his old life where he had left off. Nothing in Thierry's upbringing had ever encouraged discipline or achievement. As a small child he had been ignored. His childhood had left him with no sense of belonging, nor had he experienced the affection of family life. Thierry was envious of those who seemed to attract attention. It was this longing for admiration that drew him to the theatrical world and led him to believe in the superficial appearance of things. He needed to be glamorous, have beautiful clothes and surround himself by people who admired him.

However, Thierry did not understand that the respect of others needed to be earned. He claimed that he wanted to have his own cabaret act, but he didn't train or rehearse for the stage, he just set about updating his address book. He started by frequenting the clubs and the bars of the Les Halles quarter, walking in with an even greater exuberance than before.

Thierry often visited Le Palace, a famous nightclub situated on the rue Montmartre. Always polite and charming, he spent money generously, the expensive drinks he ordered were always paid for with cash, and he left generous tips for waiters and barmen. He boasted to who was ever prepared to listen, that he was in the process of setting up a model agency. Thierry would not admit that he was unemployed and invented jobs that he believed were glamorous and theatrical. He also had to justify his ostentatious wealth. He was spending money like water, money that he had 'earned' from the stolen credit cards, thefts and drug dealing. Thierry was living a life without any routine or domestic attachments. The boy from far-away Martinique was now a sophisticated city person, street wise and fashionable. He rarely saw his mother or half sister. He called on his mother when he wanted money to undergo some cosmetic surgery on his face. When she refused to give him the money, Thierry threatened to kill her.

Beneath Thierry's seemingly cool worldly manner, the

young man was beset by dark anxieties and obsessions. He could not escape his feelings of inadequacies caused by the rejections and loneliness he had experienced in his childhood. Periodically, these hidden emotions broke the smooth urban surface of his life in Paris and manifested themselves in his killings of old women. Several months after the killing of Ludmilla Liberman, Thierry struck again.

On 25 November 1987, Rachel Cohen, aged 79, was killed in her home on the Rue de Chateau d'Eau. The same day, no more than 100 metres away, in the rue d'Alsace, Madame Finalteri, aged 87, was left for dead by her attacker who had tried to suffocate her with a mattress.

Two days later, Genevieve Germont, 73, was suffocated and strangled at 22 rue Cail.

The weekend following the murders Thierry celebrated his 24th birthday. That night, 28 November, he treated his friends to a sumptuous evening at Tourtour, an establishment in the Les Halles quarter, where he had worked in a waiter in 1985. The restaurant was reserved for over 50 revellers who had all received elegant invitations. It gave the young man particular pleasure to preside over this glittering event in the very place where he had worked as a lowly waiter. No detail had been overlooked. Thierry lorded it over his guests taking every opportunity to impress them. He had even invited his lawyer, Maitre Page to join the nocturnal crowd of cabaret artists, transvestites and drug dealers. The bill had even been settled in advance and the sophisticated menu was accompanied by champagne which flowed freely.

The following evening, Thierry invited 20 people to another restaurant. The night after, Monday, 30 November, he once again stepped out, this time to the New Copa, a big African nightclub frequented by black diplomats working in Paris.

As Thierry Paulin hosted his glittering parties, financed by his own secret and illicit means, he delighted his friends with his outrageously camp manners. Meanwhile the Parisian Police continued to scratch their heads over the files of the anonymous killer of old ladies. But now the police held a trump card. Madame Finalteri had survived. After she recovered she gave police an excellent description of her attacker. She described his as tall, mixed-race man with tinged blond hair and wearing an earring. A photofit picture was immediately distributed to all the police stations throughout Paris.

On Tuesday, 1 December, a police superintendent wandered the short distance from the Porte Saint-Denis police station to chat to some local shopkeepers. He had a copy of the photofit picture folded in his pocket. As he chatted his glance fell upon a young man, a half cast with an athletic build, walking along the street. Using instinct, as much as experience, the superintendent broke off his conversation to ask the young man for his identity papers. The young man was Thierry Paulin.

For 43 hours, Thierry Paulin was questioned without a break. He confessed to more than 20 murders, recounting in a jumbled manner his crimes, often mixing up the dates and the names of the victims. Throughout his interrogation, he showed no signs of remorse. He was quite incapable of understanding the terrible gravity of what he had done. The arresting officers were appalled that he had considered a human life to be totally worthless.

Thierry never gave any reason, excuse or apologies for his

actions. He was willing to explain to the police in detail, the way in which he operated, spotting an old woman on the street, following her home and chatting to her reassuring her that he was trustworthy. When he had gained her confidence, he would kill her.

He also told the police that he was not always alone on his killing sprees, but that his lover, Jean-Thierry Mathurin, was his accomplice. Cheerfully, he gave his boyfriend's address to the police. Mathurin was immediately arrested and admitted to his part in the first killings. The two men were remanded in custody, but justice, was far from being done. Thierry Paulin would once again slip through the net in a way that nobody would have foreseen.

After his arrest, Thierry Paulin was locked up in Fleury Merogis Prison. On his arrival he was put in isolation because the authorities feared that the other inmates would attack him. Thierry himself, seemed totally oblivious of his situation. His over riding concern, as it had always been, was that of his image. His earring was removed so that he would be unable to use it as a weapon and his hair was cut, but he continued to dress well. He managed to keep two bags of clothing containing, amongst other things, several pairs of trousers, a suit with a smoking jacket, white shirts and bow ties.

A few months after his arrest, Thierry Paulin began to lose some of his buoyancy and proud concern over his appearance. He showed signs of apathy and tiredness. Thierry Paulin was a homosexual and drug user and was now paying the price. Later that month Thierry Paulin was diagnosed with Aids and his condition deteriorated rapidly.

On 10 March 1989, Paulin was placed in an oxygen tent

and put on a drip. He soon fell into a coma in which he was conscious of his surroundings but unable to communicate with those around him. Paulin was transferred to the Claude Bernard de Paris Hospital, where he was given antibiotics for tuberculosis and meningitis, but his diminishing immune system could not fight and these were hopeless measures. As Thierry's immune system ceased to function his body disintegrated in the slow and tragic manner that is characteristic of an Aids sufferer.

In the last stages of his illness, Thierry Paulin, the man who had terrified Paris and achieved notoriety as the killer of old ladies, was taken to the hospital in Fresnes Prison, where he had expected to pass his prison sentence. He finally died on the night of 16 April 1989. He was 26 years old.

THE NIGHT STALKER

Name: Richard Ramirez
Date of birth: 28 February 1960
Location: El Paso, Texas, USA
Type of murderer: Satanic
Body count: 13
Sentence: Death
Outcome: Currently on Death Row in San Quentin

'I will be avenged. Lucifer dwells within us all.'
RICHARD RAMIREZ

The night of 5 August 1985 was stiflingly hot in the residential suburbs of Los Angeles. Windows had been left open to try to alleviate the heat, and as thousands of families were tucked up for the night, oblivious to any unseen dangers lurking in the darkness.

Christopher Petersen and his wife Virginia were asleep in their one story home, five miles from the Simi Valley freeway, when Virginia's sleep was interrupted by the sound of an intruder. Sitting up in bed she called out, 'Who are you? What do you want?'

Virginia froze in horror as she heard the intruder laugh and saw the gun that was pointing at her. There was a shot and she felt a searing hot pain in her face. The bullet had entered her cheek, just missing her left eye, and passed through the back of her head. As her husband Christopher, leapt to his wife's defence, a second shot rang out. The bullet from the intruder's gun exploded through his temple, lodging at the base of his brain.

Blood poured from Christopher Petersen's head, but he was a big strong man, and flew into a rage when he heard the intruder laughing. He dived out of bed and chased him from the bedroom. Suddenly, it was the assailant's turn to feel scared. In panic, he ran from the house, firing twice as he fled.

Four month's before the Petersens were attacked, an Italian-American couple Vincent and Maxine Zazzara, who lived in a single-storey ranch-style house half a mile from the San Gabriel freeway, had not been so lucky. Maxine who had just celebrated her 44th birthday was a successful lawyer. Her husband Vincent who was 20 years older, had retired to fulfil his dream of owning his own pizzeria.

The small but popular pizzeria served the 'best pepperoni pizza in town' and the couple was well liked by local people.

Early on the morning of 27 March 1985, their son Peter went round to visit his parents and let himself into the house. He was met with a scene straight out of a horror movie. Both his parents were dead. His father's clothed body was lying on the sofa in the study, and in the bedroom, lying on the bed, was the naked body of his mother. Both had been shot at point-blank range. The crime was sickening. What really disgusted the detectives called to the scene was the way Maxine's body and eyes had been mutilated after she had died. The killer had repeatedly stabbed her, leaving a large, ragged, T-shaped wound, and had gouged out her eyes. No trace of them was ever found. The killer had taken them with him.

The police were baffled. The killer behaved like a burglar, but deliberately chose houses where the occupants were at home. He seemed to concentrate on single-storey homes in middle-class suburbs in the San Gabriel and San Fernando Valleys, outside Los Angeles. For some reason, the intruder picked houses that were painted a pastel colour, usually a yellow or beige, and the houses were always close to a freeway, possibly to allow him to escape more easily.

The maniac soon embarked on another orgy of violence. This time the victims were two elderly ladies – Mabel Bell, aged 83, and her 80-year-old sister, Florence Lamb, an invalid. The sisters lived in a small two-bedroom house in the Los Angeles suburb of Monrovia. Mabel was a retired teacher and had lived there for 25 years, and had taken her sister in to live with her, rather than allow her to live in an old people's home.

Early in the morning of 1 June, Carlos Venezuela, the odd-job-man who did regular chores for the sisters, went round as usual to see them. Noticing that the house was silent, he let himself in. There he found Mabel, alive but barely conscious, lying in a pool of blood on her bedroom floor. In the second bedroom, her sister was lying on her bed in a coma, there was a puncture wound over one ear. A bloodstained hammer was lying on her dressing table.

As with the Zazzara killings, the victims' home had been ransacked, but the killer had also left a clue. There was a hammer and a half-eaten banana on the dining-room table. But there were other more sinister clues. The intruder had left an inverted pentagram – a Satanic symbol – that was found drawn in lipstick on Mabel Bell's thigh. A second pentagram was scrawled on her sister's wall. For two days after the attack, the sisters had lain helpless in their home before they were found. Even detective's who were used investigating crimes of violence in Los Angeles, were shocked by the cruelty shown by the killer. He had used a hammer to beat the two women, he had cut and tortured them and tried to rape Mabel the older sister. Two weeks after the attack, Mabel died. The younger sister Florence survived.

The citizens of Los Angeles first became aware that a new serial killer was in their midst in March 1985, around the time of the vicious Zazzara killings, but the Night Stalker as the press were calling him, had first struck nine months earlier on 28 June 1984. The victim was Jennie Vincow, who lived in the Los Angeles district of Eagle Rock. The 79-year-old woman lived alone in a one bedroom flat in Chapman Street.

Her mutilated body had been found spread-eagled on her bed. Her throat had been cut so deeply that she was nearly decapitated. She was covered in stab wounds and a post mortem revealed that she had also been raped. Her home had been ransacked. There was blood on the floors and walls of the bedroom and bathroom. Detectives were able to pick up five clear fingerprints from a window and a screen over it, which the intruder had removed in order to get into the flat.

For months, detectives believed that the first Night Stalker murder had been the shooting of Dayle Okazaki, a 34-year-old traffic manager from Hawaii, on 17 March 1985. This time though, there had been a survivor, Dayle's flatmate, Maria Hernandez. The attack took place just before midnight in the suburb of Rosemead. Maria had just returned home and driven into her garage. As she walked towards her flat, she heard a noise behind her, and turned. A man in black with a dark blue baseball cap was standing there brandishing a gun. Frozen with fear she raised her hands begging the intruder not to fire. He did, but miraculously, the keys she was holding deflected the bullet and saved her life. Maria fell to the ground and her assailant stepped over her, kicking her viciously as he entered her flat. Maria staggered to the front of the building hearing the sound of a gunshot behind her. Then she froze for a second time.

There in front of her was her attacker, who had just run out of her apartment, nearly knocking her over as he did so. Maria remained rooted to the spot and pleaded, 'Please don't shoot me again!' The gunman disappeared.

Inside the apartment, her flatmate Dayle was lying dead on the kitchen floor, shot through the head. The killer had claimed his second victim. He had also left a witness, Maria, and a clue – his baseball cap, bearing the logo of AC/DC, the name of a popular heavy metal band, which was found on the garage floor.

Incredibly, the stalker struck again that same night. Within the hour, he had dragged his next victim, 30 year-old Tsai Lian Yu, from her yellow Chevrolet, and killed her. Tsai was a law student from Tai Wan who lived in nearby Monterey Park. Her ambition was to become a top attorney. She was found lying next to her car, close to death. She had been shot several times. It was just before midnight when the young woman died, shortly before the ambulance arrived.

Two months later in the early hours of 14th May, the killer claimed two more victims. The attacks were carried out close to the scene Tsai Lian Yu killing in Monterey Park, and once again, the victims were Asian.

Sixty-six-year-old William Doi and his 63-year-old wife, Lilly. Lilly Doi was startled out of her sleep by gunfire. An intruder had shot her husband in the head. Lilly was repeatedly hit by the intruder as he demanded to know where she kept her valuables. Then he handcuffed her while he ransacked her home, looking for money and jewellery, before raping and killing her.

A fortnight later, on 30 May, Carol Kyle was woken from a deep sleep by a torch shining into her eyes, a gun pointing at her head, and a man's voice demanding that she get out of bed. The intruder frog marched her into her 12-year-old son's bedroom, threatening him with the gun. The man handcuffed the terrified boy and shoved him into a cupboard.

Carol gave him her diamond-and-gold necklace, then he savagely raped her. Bravely she told him, you must have had a very unhappy life to have done this to me, he snarled, 'I don't know why I'm letting you live. I've killed people before. You don't believe me, but I have.'

After ransacking her home, the intruder left. Carol Kyle was able to give a detailed description of her attacker, matching other descriptions already received by investigators. She said the intruder was Hispanic, had long dark hair and was skinny.

On 27 June, 32-year-old Patty Higgins was found dead in her home in Arcadia. Her throat was cut. Five days later, on

2 July, 75-year-old, Mary Cannon, also from Arcadia, was found dead at home, also with her throat slashed. Three days later, also in the same district, 16-year-old, Whitney Bennett was beaten with a crowbar in her home, although she survived, but two days later, on 7 July, police found the body of 61-year-old grandmother Joyce Nelson, who had been less lucky, beaten to death in her home in Monterey Park. The same night, a 63-year-old registered nurse, Sophie Dickman from the same neighbourhood was attacked in her home, raped and robbed.

A fortnight after this on the night of 20 July, the Night Stalker went on a rampage, unparalleled, even by his own standard. In one night, he shot to death an elderly couple Maxson Kneiding aged 66 and his 64-year-old wife Lela, in their Glendale home and murdered 32-year-old Chainarong Khovananth at his home in Sun Valley.

After gunning him down in his bed, the stalker raped and beat his 29-year-old wife, Sonkid, forcing her to swear to Satan that she would not scream for help. He then sodomised her eight-year-old son and stole $30,000 cash and jewellery from their home.

On the night of 8 August, the Stalker struck again shooting a 35-year-old East Asian man, Elyath Abowath to death, in his San Gabriel Valley home, and beating and raping his 28-year-old wife. Mercifully their two young children aged three years and three months were left unharmed, but not before the Stalker had tied up the three-year-old boy Armez. As before, the Stalker forced the young mother to swear in Satan's name, not to scream out for help.

By now Los Angeles was in uproar over the murders, rapes and violations. As residents read about the crimes and watched television reports, panic spread. Gun shops sold out of their stock, locksmiths did a roaring trade reinforcing people's homes and citizens formed their own neighbour-hood-watch groups.

So the Night Stalker turned his attention North to the San Francisco suburb of Lake Nerced. Here, on 17 August, he broke into the home of a 66-year-old Asian accountant, Peter Pan, and his 64-year-old wife, Barbara. He shot them both through the head. The Stalker left an inverted pentagram, and the message 'Jack the Knife' painted in lipstick on the bedroom wall. The small calibre bullets used to shoot the couple matched those take from two of the Los Angeles victims.

Twenty-nine-year-old computer engineer, William Carns and his fiancée Inez Ericson, also 29, were the Stalker's final victims. On 29 August, in their home 50 miles south of Los Angeles the Night Stalker shot William three times in the head and raped his fiancé twice. He taunted her saying, 'You don't know who I am, do you? I'm the one they're writing about in the newspapers and talking about on the TV.' He forced her to say the words ' I love Satan'. As he left the house she was able to make out the car he was driving, an old rusting orange Toyota. William Carns survived the attack, but suffered permanent brain damage. The couple never married.

A sharp-eyed local teenager, James Romero, saw a man drive past his home three times in an orange station wagon. He noted down the number and passed it on to the county sheriff's department. A couple of hours later, Donna Myers, was the first person from the general public to come forward with a positive identification. Mrs Myers, a 43-year-old grandmother, knew a man who had bought jewellery from the stalker in San Francisco, and put two and two together. She said the man they were looking for was in his twenties, had rotten teeth and was interested in Satan and Devil worship. She had known him for years and sometimes he would stay at her home in San Pablo, San Francisco. Mrs Myers knew him only as Rick.

Detectives staked out Donna Myers's home and the Stalker's other San Francisco haunts. They were also staking out a dental clinic in Los Angeles, where a man calling himself Richard Mena, had sought treatment for his decaying teeth. They believed rightly that he was the stalker.

At the same time, an all-points bulletin was put out to find the Toyota. Two days later the car was found abandoned in a parking lot in a rundown suburb of L.A. It was taken away to be examined for evidence. Finally, the breakthrough had happened. Using new and unconventional techniques, detectives managed to find fingerprints inside the car. Investigators swept the interior of the vehicle with a laser beam, which enhanced the marks left by any prints, even those the suspect had tried to wipe off. Eventually, a single print was found and a copy sent off to the NEC State computer in Sacramento. Within minutes, the computer came up with the Night Stalker's identity. The print belonged to a small-time thief from El Paso, 25-year-old Richard Ramirez. Soon his picture and description was splashed over the front page of every local and national newspaper in California.

Ramirez felt good as he stepped off the bus in Downtown Los Angeles. His thirst for blood satisfied by recent killings. He had killed at least 13 people in cold blood and was beginning to think he was invincible. Someone, down there, was on his side. He saw himself as Satan's servant, admired and protected by his master. But his run of good luck was about to run out.

At 8.15am on Saturday, 31 August, Ramirez got off a Greyhound bus at the main Los Angeles bus depot. As usual, he was wearing black, black trousers and a black T. shirt with a Jack Daniels whisky emblem on the front. On one shoulder hung a black backpack. Ramirez walked casually into the men's room. A couple of moment's later he walked passed several security guards, out of the station into the bronze smog of Los Angeles.

The bus station was opposite the LAPD's central division station, but nobody noticed the tall, emaciated Hispanic with the foul-smelling breath. He did not know it yet, but his picture was on the front page of every paper and on every major TV news bulletin. He had no idea he had been named as the stalker. After shooting Williams Carns and torturing his fiancée, Ramirez had gone to Phoenix to score some cocaine. When he arrived back in Los Angeles, he was feeling good listening to music on his Walkman. He sauntered to the corner of the street, boarded a local bus and travelled several miles south of Downtown Los Angeles.

At approximately 8.30am, he stepped inside Tito's liquor store, in Towne Avenue to pick up a can of Pepsi and a packet of doughnuts. He walked to the till to pay, and saw the front page of a local Spanish paper, *La Opinion*. There, splashed across the page was a picture of his face. Ramirez suddenly realised why other customers in the store were looking at him strangely and whispering behind his back. They knew he was the killer and panicked and fled from the store. Ramirez shot out of the door and ran for his life. He could hear people shouting 'It's him, the Night Stalker', and the sound of sirens were drawing closer and closer.

In nearby Percy Street, Bonnie Navarro was watching TV when she heard her gate open, and a man at her door shouting 'Help me! Help me!' When she opened the door she saw it was the Stalker, and slammed the door in his face. Ramirez ran into the street and tried to pull a woman out of her car but she fought him off. As bystanders rushed to her aid, Ramirez raced away, jumped over a fence and found himself in Luis Munoz's backyard. It was probably his last mistake.

Ramirez had stumbled into one area of Los Angeles, he could call his own, the Hispanic district. But the area's main drag, East Hubbard Street was a tough neighbourhood where family loyalties are strong and where a cowardly murderer like Ramirez is seen like a stain on the people's honour. He could expect no mercy or protection here.

Luis Munoz was cooking at his barbecue when Ramirez jumped over his fence. Shocked and angry by the intrusion, Munoz clumped him round the ear with his tongs. Ramirez begged for water, but Munoz said 'no', and hit him again. Ramirez fled. As he climbed back over the fence, Munoz clumped him again. Half-blinded by pain and exhaustion, the Night Stalker, now a frightened whimpering mess, looked up to see a 1966 red Mustang.

Its owner, 56-year-old Faustino Pinon, was working on the transmission. Faustino could scarcely believe his eyes, a man in his own backyard, trying to steal his car from under his nose. He dived at him and gripped him in a headlock – punching and kicking. As the two men struggled the car lurched forwards into the fence, Ramirez broke free and fled into the street. Ramirez was desperate to find a car to escape in, and there in front of him was a gold Ford Granada. A woman was getting into it. Angela de la Tores was about to drive to the neighbourhood shopping mall to buy her daughter candy for her birthday.

She looked up to see a 6ft 1in crazed and maniac careering towards her, demanding the keys and screaming at her, 'Te voya matar!' ('I'm going to kill you!') She screamed, shoving him with the car door, she leaped out of the car screaming for help.

Her husband, Manuel, picked up a steel rod from a chain link fence and ran towards her. On the other side of the street, 55-year-old José Vurgoin, a retired construction worker who had heard the shouts, phoned the police. Then he ran to the scene with his sons. Ramirez had stumbled into a neighbourhood of heroes.

Ramirez was surrounded. One of the men struck him in the back of the neck with a steel rod. Ramirez turned round and laughed and stuck his tongue out, halting them dead in their tracks. The baying mob didn't know what to make of Ramirez. They circled him. One of the men, hit him over the head, and Ramirez collapsed. Two boys, Julio and Jamie dropped onto him and pinned him to the ground. Within seconds, a police patrol car drew up and the deputy sheriff stepped out. The Stalker was on the floor screaming. He thought the men chasing him would kill him.

'Save me please!' he begged the officer. 'Thank God, you came, I am the one you want. Save me before they kill me!' Ramirez was handcuffed and bundled into the back of the police car.

Witnesses at the trial were at times reduced to tears by accounts of Richard Ramirez's orgy of violence. The killer himself reacted by smiling, grinning and making signs of the Devil to spectators. Once they had him behind bars, the authorities hoped to get Ramirez convicted and sentenced speedily. The case was cut and dried.

Witnesses who had survived his beatings had seen Ramirez gun down their husbands or boyfriends in front of them. But in the end, much to the disappointment of the media circus surrounding the case, Ramirez refused to testify in his own defence. In his closing argument, Ramirez's attorney tried desperately to throw doubt on the prosecution's evidence realising that the tiniest shred of doubt planted in the jury's mind would mean the difference between a life sentence and a gas chamber for his client.

When the jury finally retired to consider Ramirez's fate, they had a formidable task, and were plagued with problems. Not only did they have a daunting 8,000-page transcript to consider but, 13 days into their deliberations, they had to start again after a juror was dismissed for falling asleep, and two days later, tragedy struck. Juror, Phyllis Singletary was found murdered in her apartment. She had been beaten and shot several times. The next day, as detectives closed in on him, Phyllis's lover, 51-year-old James Cecil Melton, shot himself in the head, The death rocked other members of the jury. Phyllis was replaced with a new juror and the trial had to begin again. Ramirez, meanwhile was twice removed from the court for shouting obscenities at the judge. He said that he no longer wished to appear in court. After 22 days of deliberation, the jury of seven women and five men reached its verdict, guilty on almost all of the 63 charges. Ramirez was found guilty of 13 murders, 12 of them first degree, and 30 other offences including attempted murder, rape and robbery.

His attorney argued for Ramirez to be spared the death penalty, and suggested that Ramirez may have been possessed by the devil who made him do it, and that he was a helpless victim of his own sexuality which drove him to rape. Five days after being found guilty, the jury voted to sentence Ramirez to death.

Under Californian law, Judge Tylan could have disregarded the jury's recommendation of death, and sentenced Ramirez to life in prison without parole, but he chose not to. He asked Ramirez if he had anything to say, before sentence was passed. Ramirez stood up and replied, 'I have a lot to say, but now is not the time or the place. I don't know why I am wasting my breath, but what the hell.' He claimed that lies had been told about him in the past and would be again.

'I don't believe in the hypocritical, moralistic dogma of this so-called civilised society,' he ranted. 'You maggots make me sick, hypocrites one and all.'

With typical arrogance, he told Judge Tylan, 'You don't understand me. You're not expected to; you are not capable of me. I am beyond your experience. I am beyond good and evil.'

When Ramirez had finished his outburst, Judge Tylan calmly pronounced the death penalty 12 times over for each of the first-degree murders, together with a lengthy prison sentence for the second degree murder of 59 years and 4 months in prison.

Ramirez reaction to the death sentence was typical. As he was led away he screamed at reporters, 'Big deal! Death always went with the territory. I'll see you in Disneyland.'

On 16 November 1989, Ramirez was flown by helicopter from the central jail in Los Angeles to San Quentin Prison, where he joined 265 other men on Death Row.

MONSTER OF THE RIVER

Name: Arthur Shawcross
Date of birth: 5 June 1945
Location: Rochester, New York, USA
Type of murderer: Sex maniac
Body count: 2 previous murders plus 11 more recent killings
Sentence: 250 years
Outcome: Currently imprisoned at the Sullivan
Correctional Facility, Fallsburg, New York, USA

'She was giving me oral sex and she got carried away,
so I choked her.'
ARTHUR SHAWCROSS

When ten-year-old Jack Blake disappeared from his home in
Watertown, New York, on 7 May 1972, his mother, Mary,
suspected that a man named Art had had something to do
with it, but nobody would believe her.

Art liked to go fishing and had been known to take the
mischievous Jack and his younger brother with him. He had

told them scary stories about blood and guts and shown them pictures of naked women. Of course, boys being boys, they loved it. When their parents, Alan and Mary Blake, found out they ordered their sons to stay away from this 'Art', they didn't know his other name. So when Jack was late for dinner and one of his playmates remembered seeing him earlier in the day with Art, they were worried. Worry turned to alarm when Mrs Blake checked the garden shed and discovered that Jack's precious box of worms was missing. The boy must have gone fishing again with that weirdo, Art.

The night wore on and calls to all the homes of Jack's friends proved fruitless, so the Blakes decided to call the police. Unable to rest, Mary and her eldest daughter set out in the pouring rain for the Coverdale housing development where they'd heard that Art lived. It was 3.30 in the morning, when a squad car pulled up beside the distraught pair. The police had identified Art as Arthur Shawcross and had found out his address.

The lights in 233 Coverdale Apartments were out, but Shawcross appeared at the door fully dressed. He was a slim six-footer with long sideburns, prominent features and a deep cleft chin. His wife Penny was by his side wearing a dressing gown. Art Shawcross was understanding;

'Yes', he confirmed in a kindly soft voice, he had seen little Jack playing with his friend called Jimmy. He was sorry, but that was all he knew. The Blakes were driven home too weary to think any more.

In the morning, Art knocked on the door and offered to help look for Jack. 'We don't need your kind of help,' Alan Blake angrily told him.

The Blakes had traced the friend Jimmy Knight, and Jimmy

told them that he had overheard Jack offer to supply the worms if Art would take him fishing. Jimmy had not seen Jack after that.

The next day Art changed his story. He told the police he had taken Jack as far as the local school swimming pool, then gone fishing on his own. This brought the Blakes to his doorstep once more.

'I want to know where my Jack is right now!' Mary Blake shouted.

Art lost some of his coolness, 'I dropped your fucking son off at Starbuck School!' he yelled at her.

On the day he disappeared, Jack Blake had been wearing a green jacket and his favourite T-shirt. Among the dozens of phone tips, the police received one from a caller who claimed to have seen a boy in a grey T-shirt being led into the woods by a man in his twenties. Shawcross was 27. Mary Blake felt certain Shawcross was the man. The police decided otherwise. Art Shawcross was known for being kind to kids, ready to buy them an ice cream or offer to take them fishing. Besides, he had recently married. Three days after the boy's disappearance the police declared that Mrs Blake's suspicions were unfounded.

'We have questioned the man, and there is nothing to his story', remarked the police chief.

The police turned their suspicion instead on to the Blakes themselves. They were a big, poor, boisterous family who had been in scrapes with the law. After searching the Blakes' home on Water Street from attic to cellar, detectives privately concluded that the boy was a runaway. But the Blakes didn't believe this suggestion and thanks in part to an emotional phone call from Mary Blake to the commander of the near by

Fort Drum military base, State police and the army were called in to help search for the boy. Soldiers joined boy scouts and scores of volunteers including a group organised over the citizens' band radio to scour the area. A human chain made a dragnet of the woods, creek, railway tracks and abandoned buildings along the banks of the Black River. When this failed, the Blakes appealed for help from a clairvoyant and issued a 'Jack Come Home' appeal, just in case the police were right.

Jack Blake had been gone eleven days when Art Shawcross found himself in trouble over another young boy when Coverdale residents saw him stuff grass cuttings down the shirt and shorts of a six-year-old boy, then put the boy down on the ground and spank him. Somebody reported the incident and Shawcross was given a $10 fine and a reprimand from the city court.

Four months later on a beautiful Saturday afternoon, another child went missing, eight-year-old Karen Ann Hill. Karen had been playing on the front lawn of Pearl Street, not far from Coverdale Apartments. One moment she was there and the next she was gone, her mother Helen told the police. The response this time was immediate, with city, county and state police launching a full scale search. A description of Karen was broadcast on the radio and television.

By 9pm, the police had found a witness who had seen a blond child with an adult male wheeling a bicycle near Pearl Street steel bridge. This was an industrial area normally deserted at the weekend. The teenage witness could not name the man, but said he knew him by sight.

An hour later, the beam of a police torch searching the water beneath the bridge caught a flash of gold from a mop of hair. A search party clambered down and shifted stones, slabs and debris to reveal the child's crumpled body. The small corpse lay face down and was naked below the waist. Dirt was stuffed into her mouth and nostrils. Karen Ann Hill had been raped and strangled.

On Water Street Jack Blake's sisters cried out when they heard the television broadcaster describe the bicycle the man had been wheeling, it was white with brown mud guards. They knew that Art Shawcross had recently bought a bicycle and wasted no time in reminding the police of Shawcross's address. Next morning bloodhounds were brought to the crime scene, pausing only occasionally to sniff a patch of grass, pavement or fence. The first dog sniffed the area hard and then trotted across the bridge up Pearl Street to Starbuck Avenue and directly to 233 Coverdale Apartments.

Art Shawcross was brought to the police headquarters and four girls picked him out in an identification parade as the man they had seen clambering over a fence by the bridge on the afternoon of the killing. After hours of interrogation, Art Shawcross told detectives that he could have killed Karen Ann, and eventually admitted, 'I must have done it, but I don't actually recall doing it. I must have blacked out,' he suggested.

Three days later after an intense search of dense woods two miles from the Blakes' home, police found the skeleton of a boy. The suggestion of where to look had come from Shawcross while he was being interrogated over Karen Ann. The next day, the boy's blue dungarees were found with the pants still inside, almost lost in the thick bed of damp and blackened leaves, was a tooth.

On 17 October 1972, Arthur Shawcross pleaded guilty to and was found guilty of first-degree manslaughter. The judge imposed a long prison term, the maximum of a 25-year sentence, telling Shawcross, 'I trust that you will get some assistance in your difficulties during that period.'

Shawcross showed no reaction and was hustled off to the notorious Attica State Prison in Albany, New York shackled to a beefy deputy with eight other lawmen forming a protective shield from vengeance-seekers.

Art was a model prisoner. He stayed out of trouble, gained his high-school certificate, and qualified in woodworking. He was transferred from Attica prison to Stormville, on the edge of the rugged Catskill Mountains, about 50 miles north of New York City. He even became a recreational councillor in the mental unit at Stormville.

From his very first year in Stormville prison, Art had been applying for parole. He applied eight times in all. After fourteen and a half years, it was granted. He emerged, aged almost 42, grey haired, fat and sweaty. It was 30 April 1987.

Arthur Shawcross went to live with his penpal, Rose, in a retreat in the Catskill mountains, but the local police chief objected, as did some of Rose's relatives. After four weeks, the pair was evicted. Much the same happened when they moved into an even more remote community. Art thought about dying his hair and changing his name, but his parole officer encouraged him to move to Rochester, New York, a major urban city, where he was more likely to vanish in the crowd. He found a job preparing vegetables for a produce store in a suburban market. Rose took a job nursing invalids. She worried about Art mainly when he talked with his mother on the phone. Afterwards he would fly into a rage and storm out of the door.

Art had been free for just under a year when young

Rochester women began to disappear. Their bodies would turn up sometime later in out of the way places, usually near fishing spots. Dorothy 'Dotsie' Blackburn, was the first to go. The 27-year-old vanished after lunching with her sisters at Roncone's Grill, in the city. Nine days later she was found floating, face down in Salmon Creek, a stream that meanders its way through woods and farmlands on Rochester's eastern fringe. Dotsie had been strangled.

Police stopped Art the very next day for a traffic offence. He had a small child with him which was a violation of his parole conditions, but that fact was somehow over looked. All he received was a $25 fine for failing to have proper restraining seats for the child. He was also ticked off for not possessing a valid driving licence.

Six months later, a man searching the Genesee Gorge for discarded bottles and cans, checked what looked like a bundle of refuse and found bones with a pair of jeans on them.

The badly decomposed body of a young woman, Anna Marie Steffen, was lying on its left side. She was crouched in a semi-foetal position with her jeans down around her right ankle and her left hand clutching a T-shirt. As in the case of Dotsie, police had no suspect and could discover no leads.

Art and Rose were making the best of city life. They had a scruffy apartment in an old building near the heart of the city. It was close to Genesee Hospital where many of Rose's clients received treatment and an easy bike ride to good fishing in the river Gorge. Art now rode a metallic brown bike, a woman's model with three baskets, one in the front and two straddling the rear wheel, in which he would stow his fishing gear.

The Shawcross apartment at 241 Alexandra Street was on the ground floor next to the foyer, which was how Art liked it. He liked to know everybody's business and he made some curious friends. He particularly charmed Clara Neal, a nursing home cook he met through Rose. Clara was 58 and had ten children and 17 grandchildren. She became Art's mistress and through her he had a choice of cars to borrow: a grey Chevy or a blue Dodge Omni. Trusting Rose assumed that they were just good friends. Clara's large family assumed likewise.

In September 1989, Art proposed to Rose and she accepted. The relationship with Clara continued as before. The following month, a fisherman found the fully clothed skeleton of a woman under some shrubbery on an island in the gorge. As a macabre touch, police found a brown wig tied in a ponytail, but no skull. The only other clues were a blue handy-wipe towel and a pair of white socks rolled up together.

A week later, children hunting a lost ball saw a foot sticking out from a heap of cardboard under a large maple tree near the eastern lip of the river gorge. When police removed the cardboard, they found the body of Patty Ives, a young prostitute.

About this time Art Shawcross was wearing a plaster cast. He told neighbours he had hurt himself in a fall along the river.

A week after the discovery of Patty Ives, a pretty brunette named Maria Welch was reported missing by her boyfriend and that same week the gorge gave up yet another body.

It was a cool, drizzly Saturday afternoon when anglers Michael Bassford and Charles Hare spotted what they took to be a dress-shop mannequin with the buttocks sticking out from the undergrowth about 50ft below them. Bassford scrambled down the slope, curious but half-fearful.

'Oh no!' he gasped, as the dummy proved to be real. The female body was naked with blonde hair tumbling over its shoulders. On one buttock there was a tattoo. 'Kiss it off', it said. Police assumed that this was Maria Welch, who was known to have a tattoo, but the fingerprints did not match. By now, the Rochester Police Department was having to face up to the fact that they were dealing with a serial killer. The blonde was identified as 22-year-old Frances Brown who had been chatting to her neighbour only hours before her death.   Art Shawcross was taking a big interest in the killings. He took to dropping into Dunkin' Donuts, an all-night pastry shop around the corner from his apartment, for a snack and a gossip with the local police who also went to the place.

A man walking his dog was the next person to find a body, this time much further along the gorge amongst some reeds and rusted river barges. Mark Stetzel noticed a piece of ice-covered carpet lying in a clump of tall catstail reeds. Stetzel glanced underneath and ran for the hills.

'I didn't feel like losing my stomach,' he told the police, who were able to identify the badly decomposed body as the remains of June Stott, Shawcross's mentally disturbed friend. A few feet away hanging from a 4ft-long catstail stalk was another handy-wipe cloth, this time bloodstained.

Four days later, one-time beauty queen Elizabeth Gibson was found by a deer hunter in woods ten miles to the east of Rochester. She had been suffocated. Police found tyre impressions and blue paint chips where a vehicle had scraped a tree.

When Art Shawcross turned up for work with a large bruise on his head and several scratches on his face, his colleagues took the piss out of him when he explained that he had been hurt trying to break up a violent argument between one of his hunting buddies and the buddy's mother-in-law. He had been punctual in seeing his parole officer twice a month and never missed his weekly group counselling sessions at the mental health centre. He was, the authorities felt, coming along nicely.

On the last day of November 1989, the police department admitted publicly that a serial killer was at work, preying upon women whose lifestyles exposed them to danger. On Alexander Street Art Shawcross was caught up in the spirit of Christmas, fussing over presents to give his lady friends, a coffee maker, a set of steak knives and candies.

On 17 December, one of Rochester's most hardened and streetwise prostitutes went missing. June Cisero was known to police as a wild cat. If June had fallen prey to the killer no one was safe. On 23 December Darlene Trippy disappeared without trace. She was a petite brunette, just the sort the killer seemed to like most. On 31 December, a pair of boots and black jeans were found by a roadside, not far from Salmon Creek. A social-security identification card was in the pocket. It belonged to Felicia Stephens, a prostitute like the others, but this suspected murder was out of pattern for Felicia was black. Police chiefs feared that the killer might be entering a new, even more frenzied phase.

That night, a crowd of 25,000 people braved the freezing weather to link hands and see in the 1990s with a riverside firework display that lit up central Rochester, and one of Rose's patients threw a party for the Shawcrosses. Art arrived slightly dishevelled, confiding to a fellow guest that he'd run a friend's car into a ditch on a country road.

State and city police had given up their New Year's celebrations to search the woods, fields and swamps looking for Felicia. By Wednesday, 3 January, eight square miles had been systematically searched without results, but as the sun broke through and the blanket of snow began to melt hopes were raised. Later that morning a state police helicopter flying along Salmon Creek at tree top level spotted a body lying face down amongst the ice. It was nearly two miles from where Felicia's pants had been found and half a mile from where Dorothy Blackburn had been discovered in 1988.

A grey Chevy was parked on a bridge overlooking the spot, the passenger door was open and a man was leaning out, apparently taking a pee.

The officer trained his binoculars on the odd spectacle and radioed word to the ground. State troopers trailed the Chevy for six miles to the Wedgewood nursing home in Spencerport, where they questioned the man. It was Art Shawcross. He explained that he had stopped for lunch by the creek while on his way to pick up his girlfriend at the nursing home. Clara Neal was due off at 1 pm. One trooper chatted amiably with Shawcross in the nursing-home car park while the other ran a routine identity check. All hell broke loose when the information revealed the record of the man standing in front of them.

Art Shawcross had an explanation for every single murder. It was all there in his 47-page signed confession. Take Frances Brown, the blond with the saucy tattoo on her bottom. She incurred a death sentence because her foot got caught in the gear lever while doing her $30 'trick'.

'I got pissed off and just kept hitting her in the throat,' Shawcross told investigators. Frances Brown had nothing on but her socks when she died. Shawcross took those off too and dumped all her clothing into a nearby skip. With her naked body propped up by his side in the passenger seat, he drove around Rochester in the blue Dodge Omni and eventually parked by the river gorge near one of his favourite fishing spots. There he sat with the body for an hour listening to country and western music on the radio. He then opened the car door and rolled Frances body over the cliff side.

Another victim, Anna Marie Steffen, surprised Shawcross with a display of joyous abandon down by the river on a hot summer's night. She took off all her clothes and started swimming in the river.

Art joined her and they began fooling around. They were on the riverbank when Steffen made the fatal mistake of playfully shoving Shawcross back into the water. He clambered out and retaliated with a shove that knocked her to the ground, hurting her. She begged him to be more careful as she was pregnant. As this his rage exploded, 'Why the hell did you come down here, fooling around?' he hollered. Steffen threatened to call the police, so Art strangled her.

Dorothy Keeler was next. He suspected her of stealing during visits to his apartment and when he complained she threatened to tell his wife that they were having an affair. He took her on a fishing trip down to the gorge. 'We didn't get any fishing done,' he recalled, 'I picked up a log and hit her hard. I think I broke her neck.'

Patty Ives died because she was being too noisy during sex and Art panicked at the thought that some children playing near by might hear them together. 'I put my hand over her mouth and held her nose. When she continued to struggle, I used my forearm on her neck and she shut up. Afterwards, I went for a walk.'

June Stott was killed for insisting that she was a virgin. They had gone for a drive, Shawcross said, and were sitting on the grass by the river when she told him that she had never had sex and she would appreciate some instruction. Shawcross told the police that he obliged, but became suspicious. 'You ain't no virgin,' he said. Stott started screaming so he suffocated her.

Art kept June Stott's pocket-knife and three days later returned and cut open the body from throat to crutch. He told the police that he did not know why had done that, but later said that he had done it to hasten decomposition.

It was a trick he had learned from 'Uncle Sam', he told them, in a reference to his war service in Vietnam. Asked why he simply did not drop the body in the river, he answered that he had rather liked June.

Art suspected Maria Welch of stealing money from his wallet, 'So when I got done, I grabbed her and choked her.'

Elisabeth Gibson also fell foul of his wallet story. She put up a fight, grabbing at his eyes and digging her nails in. He put his hands around her throat and she just quit breathing. For some reason he felt concerned this time. 'I tried to revive her, and then I gave her mouth to mouth, but that didn't work.' He told the detectives that he wept a little and then dumped her body in near by woods. He then drove back to the city pausing for a while at a scenic spot on Lake Ontario.

Darlene Trippy, another prostitute, died because she called Shawcross 'hopeless' after an unsuccessful sex session. He got mad, he said, and crushed her face against the car door until she was dead. Shawcross became bold enough to kill Anne Marie Steffen a block and a half from the police headquarters after she'd stuck her head through the car passenger window and propositioned him. He trapped her by the neck by activating the automatic window then reached over and choked her before hauling her into the car. Felicia Steffen was the only black woman he admitted to killing and he did so reluctantly.

'I don't do black girls. Never even talk to them', he insisted, denying that he had murdered her, but after hours of interrogation and being confronted by forensic evidence, he admitted to making an exception in Steffen's case, but he still denied having sex with her.

When police asked him why her body was found naked, his explanation was that he just wanted to look at her.

Shawcross had gained three and a half stone while waiting trial. He sat expressionless at the defence table, hands clasped on top of his fat belly, seemingly oblivious of the events unfolding around him. He was quite alone, his family had disowned him and neither his wife Rose, nor his mistress Clara Neal attended the trial. While on the stand, Arthur Shawcross claimed that as a child he had engaged in oral sex with his mother, two sisters, a cousin, two neighbours and one of his kindergarten teachers. He also maintained that during his adult life he was raped by five men in prison. He told the jury he had had sexual activities with a chicken, a cow, a dog and a horse. He said that, yes, he 'did it' with a chicken, and the chicken died.

As the case came to a close, the final argument began. The lawyer for the prosecution told the jury to look into Shawcross's mind. It was a wicked, sick and perverted mind, he said. He asked the courtroom to remain silent for thirty seconds, ticking the time off on his wristwatch. The jury and packed courtroom held its collective breath. When the half minute was over, the lawyer made his point. It took thirty seconds to strangle a person to death. In other words, it was something that took strong effort. The lawyer pointed his finger at Arthur Shawcross and urged the jury to brand him a murderer, cold, calculating and remorseless, for whom killing was not an emotional disturbance but simply business as usual.

The jury deliberated for six and a half hours. Friends and family of the victims sat quietly, some tearful, some holding hands till the jury returned. At 10.57am on Thursday, 13 December 1990, they delivered their verdict.

Shawcross was found guilty of murder, ten times over. Later he pleaded guilty to an eleventh murder, that of Elizabeth Gibson.

On 8 May 1991, Arthur Shawcross was sentenced to 250 years in prison.

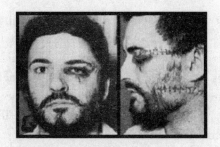

THE YORKSHIRE RIPPER

Name: Peter Sutcliffe
Date of birth: 2 June 1946
Location: Yorkshire, England
Type of murderer: Pathological maniac
Body count: 13 murders, 7 attempted murders
Sentence: Recommended 30 years
Outcome: Sent to Broadmoor Hospital for the Criminally
Insane, Berkshire, UK

'The women I killed were filthy bastard prostitutes who were
littering the streets. I was just cleaning the place up a bit.'
PETER SUTCLIFFE

It was a freezing-cold Yorkshire morning. In the northern
suburb of Leeds, a milkman shivered on his rounds, in the icy
fog of an October dawn. As he peered through the freezing
mist to see his way past the bleak recreation ground just off
Harrogate Road, he noticed a bundle huddled on the frosted
wintry grass. It was probably only a Guy Fawkes dummy;

bonfire night was only a week away, but something made him go over and have a look. A girl's body was sprawled, face up on the grass, her hair matted with blood and her body exposed. Her jacket and blouse were open and her bra pulled up. Her trousers were pulled down below the knees, although her knickers were still in position. Her chest and stomach were lacerated with fourteen stab wounds.

Wilma McCann had thumbed a lift home after a night out on the town. She had died horribly only some 100 yards from her council house in Scott Hall Avenue. She was a good time girl and had drunk 12 to 14 measures of spirits on the night of her death, 30 October 1975. On that fateful night, Wilma wore her favourite outfit – pink frilly blouse, white flares, dark blue bolero jacket. At seven-thirty, she left the house telling her oldest daughter, Sonje, to keep the three younger children in bed and the front door locked. Sonje followed these orders faithfully until five o'clock the next morning, when one by one the tearful youngsters clambered down the stairs. The bleary-eyed and anxious girl took the young children, and went for help. They were discovered shivering at the local bus stop, hugging each other for warmth and reassurance.

The first victim was just 28 years-old. There seemed to be no sexual motive for her murder, her purse with a clasp bearing the words 'Mummy', inscribed by Sonje, was missing.

Wilma McCann's murder was to be the first in a long line of vicious killings which was to strike fear into the hearts of women in the North, particularly those who had lived and worked in the area of Chapeltown. This was a red light district of Leeds, it still is, but is a sadder place these days. Then, it had barely changed for years. Not all the women who worked there were professional prostitutes, some were housewives who sold themselves for a little extra 'pin' money. Some were women who were bored with their home lives and some few were just sex-mad amateurs who did it just for fun.

One such good-time girl was 42-year-old, Emily Jackson, who lived with her husband and three children in the respectable Leeds suburb of Churwell, five miles west of Chapeltown. On 20 January 1976, Emily and her husband arrived at the Gaiety Pub on the Roundhay Road, a watering hole for the Chapeltown regulars and their would-be clients. Within minutes of their arrival, Emily left her husband in the main lounge and went looking for business. Less than an hour later she was spotted climbing into a Land Rover in the car park. That was the last time she was seen alive. At closing time Mr Jackson, still alone, drank up and took a taxi home, assuming that his wife had found a punter for the night.

It was still dark the next morning when a worker on an early shift noticed a huddled, bulky shape on the ground covered with a coat. Underneath lay Emily Jackson's body. Like Wilma McCann, she was sprawled on her back, her breasts exposed but her knickers left on. Like Wilma McCann, she had had two massive blows to the head with a heavy hammer. Her neck, breasts and stomach had been lacerated with stab wounds. But, in Emily's case, her killer had stabbed her body over 50 times, gouging her back with a Philips screw driver.

Once again, there seemed to be no motive and the police admitted the killings were linked and they were looking for a double murderer. The police also admitted they were dealing with a clever killer who had so far only left one clue - he took a size-seven shoe.

Over a year went by before the murderer struck again. By now the horrific deaths of McCann and Jackson were fading memories amongst the good-time girls of the Chapeltown area. Like Emily Jackson, Irene Richardson was a part-time amateur who worked on the street corners to make ends meet and led a sad, existence in a squalid bedsit in Chapeltown's Cowper Street. Just before midnight on 15 February 1977, Irene Richardson left her tawdry bedsit to go dancing. Next morning, an early-morning runner was jogging across Soldier's Field, a public playing field just a short car ride from Chapeltown. He saw a body slumped on the ground behind the pavilion and stopped to investigate. It was all sickeningly familiar. She lay face down, three massive hammer blows had shattered her skull. Her skirt and tights were torn off, her coat had been draped over her buttocks.

Underneath her coat, her calf-length boots had been removed from her feet and laid neatly by her tights. Her neck and torso had been savaged with a knife. She was 28 years old.

There could be no denying that a serial killer was on the lose. As details of Irene Richardson's death came to light, the Yorkshire Police were not slow in drawing parallels with another woman killer who still stalked police files and the public's imagination – Jack the Ripper, the Victorian murderer who specialised in killing, mutilating and disembowelling prostitutes in the foggy back streets of London's East End. The unknown murderer of Wilma McCann, Emily Jackson and Irene Richardson now had the name of the Yorkshire Ripper.

It was too much for many of the red-light girls who moved away in their droves to safer areas such as Manchester, London and Glasgow. Those who could not, or would not, leave their homes shifted their operations to near by Bradford, where there was a thriving red-light district.

Tina Atkinson was a Bradford girl who lived just around the corner from Oak Lane. She counted herself lucky that she did not have to ply the dangerous car trade. Her marriage to an Asian had produced three daughters in quick succession, but the marriage had not survived the cultural differences. In 1976, Tina lived alone entertaining a string of regular punters. She was attractive, slim and dark haired, and there was no shortage of admirers. The memory of the Leeds' murders simmered under the surface of most women's minds, but two months had gone since Irene Richardson's body had been found.

It was a bright April evening and Tina got ready to go to her local pub, the Carlisle. Dressed in her favourite black leather jacket, blue jeans and a blue shirt, she had a good drinking session with her friends, and reeled out of the pub, just before closing time, absolutely drunk as a skunk. She was not seen all the next day and people assumed, she was sleeping it off. The following evening, friends dropped round to her house and found her door unlocked. When they went in, they found a lumpy bundle on her bed, shrouded in blankets. Tina had been attacked as she came to her flat, four hammer blows smashing the back of her head. Then she had been flung on to the bed, her clothes pulled off, a knife plunged into her stomach seven times, and her body was slashed to ribbons. Any doubt of the killer's identity, or fear that this was a copycat murder, was dispelled by one discovery: a size-seven Wellington boot print found on the bottom bed sheet. It was the same as the footprint found on Emily Jackson's thigh.

On the evening of Saturday, 25 June 1977, Peter Sutcliffe dropped his wife Sonia off at the Sherrington nurses' home, where she worked the occasional night shift. He then went for a drink with his next-door neighbours and regular drinking buddies, Ronnie and Peter Barker. The trio spent the evening in three Bradford pubs, finishing off at The Dog in the Pound, where the highlight was an ex-sailor behind the bar who dressed in drag. At closing time, they went for fish and chips before heading home. Although it was well past midnight when Peter dropped the Barker brothers off at their front door, he drove on and rejoined the traffic on the main road.

At around two in the morning, he spotted a lone girl wearing a gingham mini-skirt emerging into the streetlight in Chapeltown Road, Leeds. He watched her transfixed as she passed the Hayfield pub turning left down Reginald Terrace, one of the side streets running off the main road. Parking his white Ford Corsair, he got out and began to follow her. The body of Jane MacDonald was found by a small wall at 9.45 that morning, when the first group of giggling children made their way to the adventure playground in Reginald Terrace. She had been struck on the back of the head, dragged 20 yards from the pavement and hit twice more. She was then stabbed in the back and repeatedly through the chest. Immediately, the police knew who they were dealing with. The trade marks were unmistakable. Yet, there was one alarming difference. Jane MacDonald was only 16, she had just left school, and worked in the shoe department of a local supermarket. On the night of her death, she had been with friends in Leeds and the attack took place on the way back to her parents' home, just a few hundred yards from where the body was found. The MacDonalds were typical of the other side of life in Chapeltown, a happy, hardworking family unit who outnumbered the prostitutes, that survived on their ill-gotten gains. Jane MacDonald was not a prostitute, not a good-time girl. Her only connection with the red-light district, was that she lived in the same area.

When it became clear that the Yorkshire Ripper was now killing teenage girls, barely out of school, the affect on the investigation was electric.

By the time Jane's inquest got under way in September, the police had interviewed almost 700 residents in 21 streets in the immediate vicinity of Reginald Terrace and taken around 3,500 statements, many of them from prostitutes.

The pressure on the police to come up with results was mounting. Two weeks after the killing of Jane MacDonald, the Ripper savagely attacked Maureen Long, on some waste ground near her home in Bradford. By some miracle, she survived, but her description of her assailant did nothing to help the enquiry. In fact, she got it completely wrong. Over six foot tall, aged 36 to 37, with collar-length fair hair.

Had the police known the type of man they were looking for, it would have helped but they would never have guessed. He was to be found in an immaculately kept home in a middle class suburb of Bradford. Peter and Sonya Sutcliffe had moved into 6 Garden Lane, their new home in Heaton on August 1977, living on their own for the first time. At the age of 31, Peter was a polite and mild-mannered neighbour, a hard working and trusted employee. A good son and loyal husband. He was the sort of man who tinkered happily with his car at weekends. There was not a great deal about him to cause raised eyebrows, and certainly not enough to cast him in the role of mass murderer.

On Saturday, 1 October 1977, Jean Jordan was climbing into Sutcliffe's new red Ford Corsair. Close to her home of Moss Side in Manchester she accepted five pounds in advance and directed him to some land two miles away between an allotment and the Southern Cemetery used by prostitutes.

A few yards from the car, Sutcliffe brought the full force of a hammer down on to Jean Jordan's skull. He stuck her again and again, eleven times in all. After pulling her body into some bushes, he was startled by the arrival of another car and made a rapid getaway.

As he drove back to Bradford that night he was concerned that he had left clues by the body, the £5 note he had given her was brand new, taken straight from his wage packet, which he'd collected only two days before. For eight long days, Sutcliffe waited and, when the body was still not discovered, he decided to risk returning to Manchester to find the note. Despite a frantic search he could not find Jean Jordan's handbag and in an act of frustration began to attack the body with a broken pane of glass. He even tried to cut off the head, thinking that this would remove his telltale hammer-blow signature. In the end, he gave up, kicking the body several times before driving home.

One day later, an allotment owner found Jean Jordan's naked body and rang the police. Her head was unrecognisable and there was no identifying evidence among her scattered clothing. She was eventually identified through fingerprints on a lemonade bottle she had handled before leaving home for the last time. Jean Jordan was 21 and had been cautioned twice for prostitution. She lived with a man she had met in

Manchester on her arrival from Scotland five years earlier, and they had two sons. When Jean Jordan failed to return to their council house that weekend, her boyfriend thought little of it. As a result her name did not appear on the missing-persons file for ten days.

The discovery of the £5 note near her body meant the tempo of the investigation was raised dramatically, but three month's later there was an air of dismay at its complete lack of success. One of the 5,000 men they had talked to was Peter Sutcliffe. Helpful and courteous, he had failed to arouse any suspicions. After leaving Sutcliffe's spacious detached house, the detectives filed a five-paragraph report which left Sutcliffe in the clear.

Sutcliffe's was the sort of house that Helen Rytka, a striking 18-year-old girl had always dreamed of owning. By 31 January 1978, she was sharing a miserable room next to a motorway flyover in Huddersfield, with her twin sister, Rita. The sisters tended to work as a pair, concentrating on the red-light district in and around the depressed and derelict Great Northern Street area. The railway arches under the Leeds to Manchester line formed brothels but Helen and Rita were a step above that. They liked to work the car trade. Because of the Yorkshire Ripper murders they had worked out a system whereby they picked up separately outside public loos, each giving the client precisely 20 minutes, and returning to the toilets at a set time. They even took a car number of each other's clients when they set off.

It all went terribly wrong, on the freezing cold snowy night of Tuesday, 31 January 1978. Helen arrived back at the rendezvous, five minutes early at 9.25 in the evening. The bearded man in the red Ford Corsair offered her the chance of another quick fiver, possibly even before Rita returned. The sisters never saw each other again.

Helen took the stranger to nearby Garrard's Timber Yard, a regular haunt for down-and-outs and prostitutes.

Unusually for him, Sutcliffe had sexual intercourse with Helen, mainly because of the presence of two men in the yard delayed his hammer attack. He struck when the girl stepped out from the back seat to return to the front of the car, anxious, no doubt, to return to her twin. His first blow missed hitting the door of the car, the second attempt bashed her head in. Then he hit her another five times. The attack was a couple of feet from the foreman's shed in the wood yard, and the wall was splattered with her blood. Helen's body was dragged to a woodpile, where it was hidden. Her clothes scattered over a wide area, her bra and black polo neck sweater were found in the same position above her breasts and her socks left on. Her black lace knickers had been found earlier by a lorry driver on the site and pinned to a shed door. She had been horribly mutilated with three stab wounds to the chest and marks of repeated stabbings through the same wound. There were also scratch marks on her chest.

Back at the public loo, Rita was desperately worried about her sister. But Rita's fear of the police was so bad that it stopped her from going to them straight away. It was three days before a police dog found the hidden body. The police were hopeful. The Ripper's latest victim had vanished in the early evening from a busy street. More than a hundred passers-by were traced and all but three cars and one stocky fair haired man, eliminated.

A couple of weeks later on 26 March 1978, a passer-by spotted an arm sticking out from under an overturned sofa on wasteland in Lumb Lane, part of Bradford's red-light district. The putrid smell from what he had thought was a tailor's dummy sent him rushing to the telephone.

By any standards, 22-year-old Yvonne Pearson was a seasoned, professional prostitute, having worked the streets in most of the big cities. Although a Leeds girl, her diary contained address of clients all over the country. She had been killed two months earlier, ten days before Helen Rytka, by a large blunt instrument blow to the head, and her chest had been jumped on repeatedly. Her bra and jumper were pulled above her breasts, while her black flared slacks had been tugged down. Horsehair from the sofa was stuffed into her mouth. It seemed as if the killer had even returned to the scene to make her body more visible, as he was thought to have done with Jean Jordan in Manchester four month's previously, by placing a copy of the Daily Mirror newspaper dated four weeks after her death, under one of her arms.

Yvonne Pearson knew only too well the dangers that her business held and had told a neighbour and a friend about her fear of the Yorkshire Ripper. On the night of her death, she had left her two young daughters, Collette and Lorraine, with a 16-year-old neighbour and had set off for the Flying Dutchman pub. She left there at nine thirty that night and within minutes was climbing into a car driven by a bearded man with black piercing eyes. They parked on wasteland on nearby Arthington Street. He killed her with club hammer, dragged her by the collar to the abandoned sofa and jumped on her till her ribs cracked.

Two months after Yvonne Pearson's body was found, Vera Millwood —frail, ill, and looking at least 15 years older than her 41 years — died in a well-lit part of the grounds at

Manchester Royal Infirmary. The Ripper had hit her three times on the head with a hammer and then slashed her across the stomach. Spanish-born mother of seven children, Vera Millwood had arrived in England after World War II as a domestic help. She later lived with a Jamaican and soon resorted to prostitution in Manchester's Moss Side district to support her family. On the night of Tuesday, 16 May 1978, her boyfriend thought she was going out from their flat in Greenham Avenue, Hulme, to buy cigarettes and get painkilling drugs from the hospital to ease her chronic stomach pains.

When a guard discovered her body at 8.10am the following morning on a rubbish pile in the corner of the car park, he thought at first that she was some sort of doll. Vera Millwood was lying on her right side, face down, her arms folded beneath her body and legs straight. Her shoes were placed beside the body and rested against the fence. She was partly covered by a grey-coloured coat and a piece of paper was placed over her badly disfigured head.

By the end of 1978, in a little over 12 months, detectives had been face to face with the ripper four times. Twice they had visited him in connection with the £5 note clue. The third, because his car registration number had cropped up during special checks in Leeds and Bradford. The fourth occasion, Sutcliffe was questioned about the tyres on his car. As usual, Sutcliffe was accommodating and unruffled, betraying absolutely nothing. The officers were never asked to check Sutcliffe for blood groups, rare, or shoe size, which was unusually small for a man – at least two of the firm facts known about the killer.

Between June 1977 and May 1978, Peter Sutcliffe attacked

seven women, leaving five dead and two horrifically injured. But, just as soon as his killing spree accelerated, it abruptly stopped. For the next 11 months, the Yorkshire Ripper simply went out of circulation. Theories started to spread about what had happened to him. One possibility was that he had committed suicide. If he had taken his identity with him to the grave, then the eerie similarity to his Victorian counterpart would have been complete.

On the night of Wednesday, 4 April 1979, Sutcliffe drove from Bingley to Halifax. Just before midnight he got out of his car, and followed 29-year-old Josephine Whittaker as she walked across Savile Park playing fields. He spoke to her briefly and then as she moved away from the streetlamps smashed the back of her head with a hammer and dragged her into the shadows. Josephine's body was found early the next morning. Like Jane MacDonald, she had been a respectable girl who lived at home with her family and worked as a clerk at the headquarters of the Halifax Building Society. With her murder, the Ripper was telling women that he had not mistaken Jane MacDonald for a prostitute, he would attack any woman who had the nerve to walk the streets after dark. Overnight, all women in the North of England lost their liberty.

All this time, Peter Sutcliffe had been keeping up an astonishing game of bluff with his family and friends. He would make a point of picking up Sonya to 'protect' her from the Ripper, and confided in one colleague that whoever was doing these murders had a lot to answer for. On one occasion his fellow drivers at Clarks Depot, even made a bet that Sutcliffe was the Ripper, but Sutcliffe just laughed and said nothing.

Sutcliffe's rampage had lasted four years. Ten women

were dead and the police were no nearer to finding the sadistic killer.

Another Christmas, another Easter came and went and still no progress was made. As the summer of 1980 faded, the public had pushed the Ripper to the back of their collective mind. Still at Garden Lane, Peter and Sonya Sutcliffe maintained the same unobtrusive lifestyle as before, seldom entertaining and preferring to keep themselves to themselves. Peter still went out to the pub with his mates and brother in the evening, and the combination of this and his travels at work meant that it was always going to be difficult for the police to pin down his movements.

On Thursday, 18 August 1980, Sutcliffe went to Farsley, Leeds and killed for the twelfth time. Marguerite Walls was a 47-year-old civil servant, working at the Department of Education and Science. She had worked late to tidy up loose ends before going on a ten-day holiday. She left the office at 10pm to walk the mile or so home. Two days later, her body was found buried under a pile of grass clippings in the wooded grounds of the magistrate's house. Marguerite had been bludgeoned and strangled but her body had not been mutilated.

Only three months later, Jacqueline Hill, a language student at the University of Leeds got off a bus in Otley Road opposite the local Kentucky Fried Chicken restaurant. She was in sight of Lupton flats, a hall of residents, when Peter Sutcliffe, his fingers still greasy from his Kentucky Fried supper, brutally struck her down. He dragged her body to wasteland behind the shopping parade and attacked her.

The Ripper had stuck Jacqueline so suddenly that one of her eyes remained open. Sutcliffe stabbed repeatedly at the sightless eye.

It was the second day of the New Year 1981, when Sgt Bob Ring and PC Robert Hydes started their evening shift; they were cruising along Melbourne Avenue in Sheffield, a haunt of prostitutes and their customers when they saw a girl climbing into a car. It was a toss of a coin whether they would bother to investigate but they decided to stroll over. The driver identified himself as Peter Williams and said that the car was his own – the short bearded man wanted no trouble. He scrambled out of the car asking immediately if he could go for a pee behind some bushes. Bob Ring was cheesed off, another day, another prostitute; exasperated, he nodded and the little man shuffled over to the bushes. Under the cover of darkness he removed a hammer and sharpened knife from a special pocket of his car coat. Olivia Reivers – the prostitute – was arguing with the policemen; she had no idea that she was abusing the men who had saved her life. By the time the man strode back to his car the police had established the number plate on it, and the prostitute and client were taken to the police station for further questioning. The man's name was Peter William Sutcliffe.

At the police station, Sutcliffe's main worry was that the police would tell his wife that he had been picked up with a prostitute. Otherwise, he was calm and obliging and helpful. After he had been to the toilet, and hidden a second knife in the cistern, he readily admitted that he had stolen the number plates from a scrap yard in West Yorkshire. Peter Sutcliffe was locked up for the night and the next morning he was taken, still unprotesting, to Dewsbury Police Station.

Sutcliffe was a chatty, eager interviewee. He told the police that he was a long-distance lorry driver, travelling regularly to the Northeast. Almost in passing he told them that he had been interviewed by the Ripper squad about the £5 note and of his regular visits to Bradford's red-light district.

Within an hour of Sutcliffe's arriving at their station, the Dewsbury Police had notified the Ripper squad at Millgarth, Leeds, of his apprehension. Soon after this, they discovered that Sutcliffe's name had come up several times since in their enquiries. Meanwhile, Peter Sutcliffe slept soundly through a night in his cell that saw frantic activity at police headquarters. Later, Sonia Sutcliffe was brought in for questioning and her neat suburban house in Garden Lane was searched.

While Peter Sutcliffe was being interviewed, the police discussed almost everything apart from the Ripper murders with him. Then, early on Sunday afternoon, he stopped talking about nonsensical things such as bonfire night and mentioned the hammer and knife found in Sheffield. Sutcliffe fell silent. The officer probed gently, 'I think you're in trouble, serious trouble.'

Sutcliffe finally spoke: 'I think you're leading up to the Yorkshire Ripper.'

The officer stayed calm, containing his mounting excitement, 'Well, what about the Yorkshire Ripper?'

'Well,' said Peter Sutcliffe, 'that's me.'

Eventually, Sutcliffe admitted to killing eleven women. The officers could not believe their ears. At last, the Ripper inquiry was over. This seemed to be as much as a relief for Sutcliffe as it was for his captors. 'Just thinking about them all reminds me of what a monster I am,' he said.

He did not want a solicitor present as he recalled, unprompted, the long list of dead, nor at this stage did he mention the voice of God. Over the following day and a half, the detectives took down Sutcliffe's confession, which took almost 17 hours to complete. Asked why he did what he did, Sutcliffe said that he began killing after a Bradford prostitute cheated him out of ten pounds in 1969.

Sixteen weeks later, Peter Sutcliffe stood trial at the Old Bailey's Number One Court. The jury listened to evidence to decide on behalf of the British public whether Peter Sutcliffe was a madman or a murderer. Pleading guilty to manslaughter, Sutcliffe was calm and assured, and in his high-pitched Bradford voice, hardly faltered as his defence counsel accompanied him through his recital of death. Sutcliffe's defence team had tried to dissuade him from giving evidence under oath, but he refused.

Departing from the police statement, Sutcliffe claimed that he had been following instructions from God. He admitted that in 1969, two years after he had first heard the voice of God, he had been planning on killing a prostitute in Bradford. On his first attempt at 'street cleaning', as he referred to it, he was arrested and charged with being in possession of a housebreaking implement, his hammer. For the jury it was a straightforward decision: was Sutcliffe mentally ill, as the defence maintained, or a sexual sadist, as the prosecution were now treating him?

In the late afternoon of 22 May 1981, Peter Sutcliffe rose to his feet to hear the jury's verdict. They found him guilty of 13 murders and seven attempted murders. Peter Sutcliffe was sentenced to life imprisonment with a recommendation that he should serve at least 30 years.

Later he was transferred to Broadmoor Hospital for the Criminally Insane.